# LOUISA MAY ALCOTT

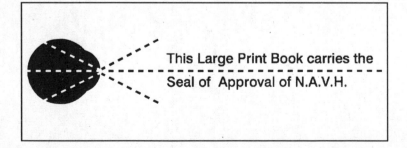

This Large Print Book carries the
Seal of Approval of N.A.V.H.

# LOUISA MAY ALCOTT

## A PERSONAL BIOGRAPHY

## SUSAN CHEEVER

**THORNDIKE PRESS**

*A part of Gale, Cengage Learning*

Detroit • New York • San Francisco • New Haven, Conn • Waterville, Maine • London

**GALE**
CENGAGE Learning

Thorndike Press, a part of Gale, Cengage Learning.

**LIBRARY OF CONGRESS CATALOGING-IN-PUBLICATION DATA**

Cheever, Susan.
   Louisa May Alcott / by Susan Cheever.
     p. cm. — (Thorndike Press large print biography)
   Includes bibliographical references.
   ISBN-13: 978-1-4104-3552-1 (hardcover)
   ISBN-10: 1-4104-3552-0 (hardcover)
   1. Alcott, Louisa May, 1832–1888. 2. Authors,
American—19th century—Biography. 3. Large type books. I.
Title.
   PS1018.C47 2011b
   813'.4—dc22
   [B]               2010047945

Published in 2011 by arrangement with Simon & Schuster, Inc.

*For my daughter, Sarah.*

# CONTENTS

# PREFACE: A TRIP TO CONCORD

For more than a century, the portrait of *Little Women*'s Jo March, a young woman who is as rebellious as she is talented, has offered readers a kind of sympathy and guidance that didn't seem to be available anywhere else. I was twelve when my mother handed me *Little Women,* and the book electrified me. It was as if this woman from long ago was living inside my head. Here was a story about girls doing the things I did; a story about being obsessed with how a dress might look, or trying hard to be a good girl and then finding that, somehow, one's actions were those of a bad girl. Jo got so angry at her pesky little sister Amy, who had thrown Jo's manuscript into the fire, that she almost let Amy drown.

The younger, prettier Amy is the voice of conventional wisdom in *Little Women.* "I detest rude, unladylike girls," she sniffs at Jo who retorts, "I hate *niminy piminy chits.*"[1]

Like Jo, I was uncomfortable with the pink trappings of conventional girls, the lipstick and the curlers that my classmates wielded with mysterious teenage panache. Like Jo, I disdained the efforts by *niminy piminy chits* to look feminine and elegant; at the same time I yearned to look feminine and elegant anyway.

Jo lived with women who delighted in food (the popovers) and clothes (the soiled gloves and turned dresses) and determinedly navigated all the familiar scrapes and potential shipwrecks in the treacherous world of flirtations and true love. At home with my parents, I also lived in a world where women cooked and cleaned and tried to look pretty. The sexual stereotypes of the 1950s were our family standard. Any divergence from those stereotypes — my brother wearing an apron, my appearance in black pants and flats — was a cause for trouble. In *Little Women,* I discovered the same kind of rigid world with petticoats and gloves in place of the curlers and garter belts my mother bought for me. In Jo March I found the antidote to that world.

I went on to read *Little Men* and the rest of Alcott's novels (or what I thought were the rest of her novels), but I came back to *Little Women,* rereading it so many times that I needed a new copy. I even persuaded my father to take me to Concord, Massachusetts, to see Orchard House, where the fictional Jo March had lived and where Louisa May Alcott had written *Little Women* in one spring and summer back in 1868.

Orchard House, when we finally got there, seemed smaller than the house in my imagination. The actual rooms where *Little Women* had taken place were somehow less inviting than the warm, lively household of my dreams where a wild, rebellious girl named Jo was loved just as much as if she had been ladylike and obedient. Not for the first or last time, I was confronted with the differences between fiction and life.

Still, I was thrilled to be in the presence of the real thing, the place where the writing of *Little Women* actually occurred. While the tour guide was distracted by a literary question of my father's about Ralph Waldo Emerson, I secretly stroked the little desk where *Little Women* had been born, as if some alchemy in the wood might pass into my own restless spirit. I couldn't wait to get home to the book.

As a naughty, rebellious girl in the throes of puberty, I needed help, and it seemed to come from the pages of *Little Women*. What did it mean to be a woman, anyway? Should

I do as my parents suggested and aim at being pretty and popular and having my pick of desirable men? Should I become a woman whose identity was a wife and mother as my mother had; should I be some man's Little Woman? Or should I strike out like Jo March and have great adventures and live alone in a house I paid for and risk being lonely?

With the character of Jo March, Louisa May Alcott gave words to the dialogue between woman as sexual, domestic creature and woman as successful professional. How can a woman avoid the trap of dependence and still have family satisfactions? How can she enjoy the rich satisfactions of good work and earning money without missing out on a domestic life? *Little Women* seemed like a guide through this morass of feminine questions, many of which I could not articulate in those days.

Last summer, decades after my first trip to Orchard House, after a life that has only imperfectly answered the questions I had as a girl, I sat and watched as crowds of young girls walked up the path to the pretty brown house where Alcott wrote her masterpiece. Now lovingly restored and under the directorship of Jan Turnquist, a woman so in tune with Louisa May Alcott that she sometimes portrays Louisa by dressing in the clothes Louisa would have worn, Orchard House is backed by a stand of trees and sits near the Lexington Road about a mile away from the center of Concord. Walden Pond, where the Alcotts' friend and teacher Henry David Thoreau built his famous hut, is another mile on through the trees. The white house where their friend Ralph Waldo Emerson lived with his family and ran a brilliant rotating literary salon is down the road in the other direction.

The thousands of women who visit Orchard House each year seem to be looking for guidance. Many of them have read *Little Women;* some of them have only seen one of the excellent movies made of the book that star, in chronological order, Katharine Hepburn, June Allyson, and Winona Ryder, but they are there for the same reasons. The house gets as many as 100,000 visitors a year. They patiently listen as local guides begin in the Alcotts' dark kitchen, with its soapstone sink and woodstove, where Abba Alcott and her daughters did the cooking and washing with water from the well. They troop into the small dining room with a cupboard filled with Abba's green and white May family china. Fiction and fact are overlaid in this small room where the Alcotts ate their vegetarian meals and the fictional Marches also ate meals. The March meals were spare but conventional. There was no meat because they were poor. The Alcott meals often consisted of graham meal and apples. Meat was not just expensive; it was one of Bronson Alcott's many personal devils.

Although Louisa May Alcott set her story in Orchard House, and the rooms coincide with the scenes in *Little Women,* the actual events of her teenage years occurred in a different house, a yellow clapboard place called the Wayside a hundred yards down the road, where the Alcott family lived when the sisters were growing up. That house, in which the young Louisa experienced her actual adolescence, is more rarely visited than Orchard House. It is run by the National Park Service and is frequently closed. By the time the Alcotts moved into Orchard House in 1858, Louisa was a young woman, her beloved sister Lizzie was dead, and her older sister Anna was engaged to John Pratt.

The merging of real and fictional during the Orchard House tour heightens the sense that it is a kind of spiritual journey. Visitors aren't there to see the real place where the Alcott sisters came of age. If they were, they would walk down the street to the Wayside.

They are there to visit the fictional sisters who lived and thrived and laughed and cried in Louisa May Alcott's imagined Orchard House. They chuckle when the guide points out Jo's "mood pillow," a horsehair rectangle which was horizontal when the fictional Jo felt like talking and vertical when she was best left alone. The tour guide usually explains that the March family hung a curtain between the parlor and the living room for Jo's theatrical productions. The audience sat in the front parlor; the actors and actresses — the March sisters — could use the back stairs for costume changes. The Alcott sisters never used the Orchard House parlor for their theatrical performances; the March sisters did.

The visiting young women and their parents, classmates, and friends climb the narrow staircase and crowd into the upper bedroom where Louisa May Alcott slept and worked. They learn that May Alcott, a talented artist, was allowed to draw anywhere she pleased, and the upstairs walls are adorned with her flowers. Lilies twine up the wall next to Louisa's desk. In her own room, May decorated every inch of wall space with portraits and landscapes. Across the landing, the master bedroom is the nicest, sunniest room in the house. The Alcotts lived in a world where parents were adored and respected just for being parents. Bronson and Abba Alcott were far from the perfect, loving guides Louisa wrote about in *Little Women,* but it didn't matter. Everyone stops to read Bronson Alcott's "Order of In-door Duties," posted on the wall. In it the Alcott children are urged to do their chores with "prompt, cheerful, unquestioning obedience." In the 1850s, as in the 1950s, parents were obeyed, and children were not invited to question their authority. As I watch mothers and daughters shuffle through the Alcotts' world, I wonder if they are also yearning for this old order. A reproduction of the "Order of In-door Duties" is a bestseller in the Orchard House gift shop.

Many tourists these days come to Concord for Orchard House, but the town is the place where American literature was written in the 1850s, the home of a cluster of genius writers who were Louisa May Alcott's friends and neighbors and mentors. She was taught by Henry David Thoreau, who later wrote *Walden* after living there, and she discussed writing with the great essayist and lecturer Ralph Waldo Emerson, who was Concord's elder statesman and who helped the Alcotts financially at every turn. Nathaniel Hawthorne and his family lived next door at the Wayside. Herman Melville and Henry James came to visit.

The 1840s and 1850s were a time of liberation when the colonial settlers' great adversaries — the Native Americans, the brutal force of nature in New England, the aggressive British and French colonial powers — had been tamed or eliminated. Suddenly nature was a beautiful friend, and European and English literature inspiring and fascinating. It was a time like the 1960s, when the rules seemed to be changing fast and everything from the past was questioned. "Why should we grope among the dry bones of the past?" asked the young Ralph Waldo Emerson in his first essay, *Nature.* "The sun shines today also. There is more wool and flax in the fields. There are new lands, new men, and new thoughts. Let us demand our own works and laws and worship." Louisa May Alcott's father would step up to be one of Emerson's new men, but it was Louisa herself who would change the way we think about young women.

Written twenty years after the first women's rights conference at Seneca Falls in 1848, *Little Women* also provides a spirited alternative to conventional marriage ambitions — the pretty girl in search of a wealthy husband. A lot has changed since the nineteenth century, but not everything. At a party recently, I asked a friend what she was looking for in a man. Her reply? "A reliable income stream."

Alcott never married: "Liberty is a better husband than love,"[2] she wrote. Jo March's rejection of a marriage proposal from the adoring Laurie, with his very reliable income stream, inspired generations of women to look for something more than resources in a marriage. Alcott, pressured by readers and editors to have Jo end up with Laurie after all, refused. "Girls write to ask who the little women marry, as if that were the only end and aim of a woman's life," she wrote indignantly in her November journal while working on the second half of *Little Women.* "I won't marry Jo to Laurie to please anyone."[3] In *Little Women,* it is Amy with her feminine airs and ambitions who ends up marrying Laurie.

# 1
# TRAILING CLOUDS OF GLORY.
## 1832–1839

She had gone back to Concord to write, but instead she wasted time. Louisa May Alcott arrived at Orchard House to join her parents in February of 1868 while there was still snow on the ground; now she noticed crocuses and daffodils. The elms in Monument Square were spring green; the lilacs were about to explode into blossom. She had left her steady job as a children's magazine editor in Boston to write, but she wasn't writing.

Many mornings Louisa settled her aging mother happily downstairs in the parlor. "She sits at rest in her sunny room and that is better than any amount of fame to me," the thirty-five-year-old wrote in her journal.[1] Then she found a hundred excuses to avoid her own desk upstairs. There was so much to do besides writing! She had to visit the Emersons down the road to borrow the latest Dickens novel; she had to gossip with

Mr. Emerson about Dickens's disappointing reading in London and his farewell reading in Boston, and play blind-man's buff with the Emerson children. She had to deliver a gift of her father's Sweeting apples to Mrs. Thoreau in town. She had to get some lamp oil. Her father's blue shirt had to be mended.

Some days she still felt too sick to work. The dizziness was mostly gone, but the effects of what had happened four years earlier when she was a Civil War nurse at the Union Hotel Hospital in Washington, D.C., were still with her. Her right hand hurt so much when she wrote in her journal that she had to switch to her left for a few sentences. She wanted to write. She was a writer. She put it off. The truth was that she didn't want to write the book that her editor and publisher Thomas Niles had first suggested almost a year ago. She had pretended she didn't really hear him. "Niles, partner of Roberts, asked me to write a girls' book," she wrote in her journal. "Said I'd try."[2]

Still, she hadn't tried, even when her father had brought it up more than once. She did not want to write a girls' book. After everything she had been through — the war, her illness, the death of her sister, the decades of gritty poverty, the dozens of melodramatic stories written to make money, the serious novel, *Moods,* and then *Hospital Sketches* about her nursing experience, the magazine jobs and advice columns — hadn't she earned the right to choose her own project? After being published in the *Atlantic Monthly* and reviewed by young Henry James she wasn't about to happily churn out some kind of simple book for young ladies. Would they ask Emerson to write a girls' book? Or Dickens?

Thomas Niles hadn't given up. He kept asking about the book she didn't want to write, and he even got her father to pressure her by offering to publish Bronson's book *Tablets* if Louisa wrote the book for young women. Her father had been thrilled, and he happily told Niles that she was hard at work on the book and would be done by September. Not true. Writing the kind of story Niles had in mind, a story about a family like her own and their domestic trials and tribulations, was the last thing she wanted to do. She didn't think the "Pathetic Family," as she called the Alcotts, were a good subject for stories. She had asked everyone's permission, hoping they would say no. They all said yes.

It was the middle of May already! Time

was wearing down her resistance. She had run every errand she could think of. Her mother, Abba, was comfortable, and sometimes she could hear her father chopping wood in the distance. The family of owls in the elm outside her bedroom window had built a nest, and perhaps there would be owlets soon.

Finally, just to see how it would feel, she sat down at the little half-moon desk between the windows. From there she could see between the elms over the road toward the meadows where Walden Pond sat like a watery jewel in the landscape. There she had spent afternoons idling with her friend Henry David Thoreau in his little boat on that pond. He had played the flute; she had gazed at the sky. But Thoreau had been dead for six years. She still thought of him every time she took a walk toward Walden. Walks became a way of avoiding the book she was supposed to write. She had enough paper; the quill and ink were next to her. Maybe she could write just one scene before lunch.

She reached for the happiest times she could remember, the childhood times of visiting Thoreau in his hut on Walden Pond, the times of haunting Mr. Emerson's library, the times when her father called his four girls the golden band of sisters. A reluctant invalid sitting at the cramped desk, she remembered Christmas in Concord when the family was young and bursting out of their ramshackle house — a house that, coincidentally, was next door to the house where she sat writing twenty years later. " 'Christmas won't be Christmas without any presents,' grumbled Jo,"[3] she wrote. Jo March would be the leader of the golden band, the smart sister with the plain face who was always in trouble. Meg would be the ladylike one. Amy would be the prissy artist. Sweet, lost Beth would be the one who was always happy with what she had.

Outside her windows, apple blossoms came and went, but for Louisa it was a cold Christmas Eve a long time ago, a Christmas when their mother, Abba, was still vigorous enough to organize the sisters to visit a poor family, bringing their own Christmas breakfast. Still, she resisted. The sisters' experiences together seemed so ordinary compared to the drama and passion, the howling winds and demonic men and desperate love affairs of the melodramas, written under the pseudonym A. M. Barnard, with which she had helped support her family for many years. "I plod away though I don't enjoy this sort of thing," she wrote in her journal.

"Never liked girls or knew many except my sisters, but our queer plays and experiences may prove interesting, though I doubt it."[4]

Books often seem to have a life of their own. Scratching away at her little desk, Louisa was taken over by the story she was writing and did not want to write. The scenes of family life seemed to her to be dull and ordinary, but they fell into place one after the other. Even Jo March had something to say about writing: "She did not think herself a genius by any means; but when the writing fit came on, she gave herself up to it with entire abandon, and led a blissful life, unconscious of want, care, or bad weather, while she sat safe and happy in an imaginary world, full of friends almost as real and dear to her as any in the flesh."[5] Soon, Louisa was at her desk every morning, and the lives of her sisters, partly remembered, partly as she yearned for them to have been, became more vivid than the Concord summer with its abundant wildflowers and heady birdsong. Deftly transposing the events of the three years the Alcott family had spent in the house next door to the house where she now sat writing, Louisa May Alcott found the pages quickly piling up next to her. Within six weeks, she had sent off 400 pages to Niles. Like Alcott, Niles thought the material was dull, but he said he would publish it anyway. They would have to see about a sequel. At least she agreed that he had suggested a good title: *Little Women.*

In *Little Women,* the story of four sisters growing up in a house like Orchard House, the father has barely a cameo. Mr. March is away during the bulk of the action, and the girls' growing fits and starts are handled by their beloved mother, Marmee, and by each other. Because of the intimate voice of the writing — it's written in close third person so that all the girls' deepest thoughts and feelings are revealed — the book sounds like a memoir. In some ways, with its emphasis on domestic drama and personal search and salvation, *Little Women* is the mother of the modern memoir.

At the same time, *Little Women* is definitely fiction. Most strikingly, Louisa May Alcott is not Jo March. Jo is a rebel who is nevertheless beloved. Louisa was a rebel who often seemed genuinely disappointing to her parents and who found scant love from them or their friends.

Furthermore, Louisa May Alcott was so dominated by her father that it is hard to unravel their lives from each other. As an infant, Louisa was subject to her father's experiments. All through her life, Louisa's father was prodding and bullying, commanding and occasionally rescuing, letting Louisa know what was wrong with her and telling her what to do. In every big decision she made, from going to Washington to be a Civil War nurse, to the commitment to her family that kept her from marrying and starting a new family, to the writing of *Little Women,* her father hovers in the background. His hold on her was incalculable. She loved him and fought with him. He called her a "fiend."

Yet Louisa had a stubborn soul and sometimes a sympathetic mother and sisters. She was born in 1832 in Germantown, Pennsylvania, because her father had won the job of running a school there, but she came to consciousness when she was three years old, at the apex of her father's success as a Boston celebrity. Our earliest memories and our experiences as babies, before we can remember, are arguably powerful factors in the formation of our personalities. This "dance of the giant figures," as the psychiatrists call it, can have lifelong effects that are especially resistant to change because the memories can't be retrieved and understood. In Louisa's earliest memories, and in the years before she started remembering, her father was a hero. During the winter of 1835, as she approached her third birthday, Bronson Alcott was one of the most respected and sought-after men in Boston.

That winter the temperature in the city hit record lows.[6] Shouting schoolboys had epic snowball fights on the Boston Common; and icicles covered the pediment of the new courthouse. Boston Harbor froze over from Hingham to Nahant. In a schoolroom on Temple Place with a single inadequate stove, schoolmaster Bronson Alcott was undisturbed. "I will kindle a fire for the mind,"[7] he told his students. Even in the record cold, his fire spread quickly.

Bronson Alcott's new Temple School, his fourth academic venture, was more than just the talk of the town. Visitors from as far away as London came to sit on the schoolroom's green velvet couch and watch the charismatic schoolmaster hold forth in his sunlit kingdom at the top of the building that featured high arched windows and busts of Plato, Shakespeare, Jesus, and Sir Walter Scott. There, the sons and daughters of progressive, aristocratic Boston were educated and enchanted by this dramatic character with wild blue eyes and a broad-brimmed hat.

Most nineteenth-century education was

memorization and punishment, and most educators thought of children as evil savages in need of civilization. Not Bronson Alcott. Seated in cunning desks, each with its own private bookshelf, the little Tuckermans, Shaws, Jacksons, and Quincys — the grandson of former President John Quincy Adams was the school's youngest student — were entranced by this mysterious Pied Piper of a schoolmaster. The schoolroom at the Temple School was filled with progressive delights that had previously been emphatically excluded from education. Dozens of books invited exploration, a pitcher of water was always filled for the thirsty, the room sparkled with wonders: alarm clocks, decks of cards, an hourglass, blocks, and paintings. The students, boys in stovepipe trousers and wide-collared shirts and girls in dresses and pantalettes, were encouraged to sing and clap during frequent breaks from lessons. Instead of raising hands, students were asked to stand up at their desks. Twice a day a twenty-minute recess allowed them to run and play.

The basis of Alcott's pedagogy was the Romantic and revolutionary idea that children were holy innocents, able to teach adults important moral lessons instead of the other way around. Alcott believed that children were born perfect, as the English Romantic poet William Wordsworth had written in his already famous *Intimations of Immortality* less than thirty years earlier in 1807. Children, Wordsworth wrote, in an image that would help to change the world, were born "trailing clouds of glory . . . from God, who is our home."[8]

From the first, Louisa seemed to trail clouds of mischief rather than clouds of glory. As an infant, Louisa had suffered plenty of hitting and scratching from her jealous and obedient older sister, Anna, who was very good at escaping punishment. By the time the family moved to Boston and into a boardinghouse at 1 Bedford Place, the tables had turned. Louisa had become the aggressor in fights with her older sister; she suffered from "a deep-seated obstinacy of temper," her father wrote; "she seems practicing on the law of might — the stronger and colder has the mastery over the weaker and more timid. She is still the undisciplined subject of her instincts."[9] In another world, what might have been called the "terrible twos" was diagnosed as a severe character flaw by the attentive Alcott.

What could be the source of this two-year-old's inability to act like the civilized visitor from God her father knew her to be? Perhaps, Bronson speculated, it was that her mother persisted in feeding her meat. Perhaps it was her coloring — Bronson believed that dark eyes and dark hair, unlike his own vivid blue-eyed blondness, was a sign of inferior morality. Subscribing to a repulsive, popular pseudoscience of the day, Bronson theorized that blond, blue-eyed people like himself were angelic and god-like, while dark-haired, dark-eyed people like his wife and Louisa were less elevated and further from heaven. Their dark coloring and olive skin was, as Emerson paraphrased it, "a reminder of brutish nature." Or perhaps Louisa's bond with her overly indulgent mother was ruining Bronson's attempts to bring out the angel in Louisa.

That angel was often obscured by Louisa's hot temper, a trait she seemed to have inherited from her mother. Even as an adorable toddler, Louisa had the power to drive her father a little crazy. In the nursery, Louisa was the villain. He believed, of course, that spanking was a "brutal" and "barbarous" method, an animalistic and even impious method of punishment. Yet he spanked Louisa often, sometimes repeatedly. Although this sometimes worked temporarily, she became more and more rebellious.[10] She was always the freer of the two sisters and adored her father's game of letting the two little girls run around naked before getting dressed for bed. "I always thought I must have been a deer or a horse in some former state, because it was such a joy to run. No boy could be my friend till I had beaten him in a race, and no girl if she refused to climb trees, leap fences and be a tomboy,"[11] she wrote.

Bronson Alcott was an aristocrat of nothing but the schoolroom. He was born Amos Alcox to a poor farming family in Spindle Hill, Connecticut. His fire for educational reform was stoked at the dreadful local school he went to with his brother William. Bronson always loved books, but at the schoolhouse he and William were shut up indoors for the best hours of the day, lined up with all the other pupils on backless benches in fetid air. An automaton of a teacher dragged his charges forward by rote and punishment toward the goal of a basic literacy that most of them would never use. The brothers both quit after elementary school and went to work as laborers.

The Alcox family had few resources, but distinguished connections. Although the boys' mother wrote haltingly, her brother Tillotson Bronson was a distinguished scholar who had gone to Yale and was the principal of Cheshire Academy. Her father, Amos Bronson, was a country patriarch who had turned against the prevailing Calvinism of that part of Connecticut and joined the Episcopal Church. Bronson's father's father was also a distinguished man who had fought in the American Revolution, had seen General Washington, and had received his commission from Jonathan Trumbull.

All this distinction wasn't of much use to a farm boy whose principal tasks were herding sheep, planting crops, mending stone walls, husking corn, milking cows, collecting eggs, fetching water, and picking beans or whatever was in season. William nevertheless ended up at Yale and later went to medical school; he suggested many of the physical changes that Bronson employed in his schoolrooms. "It is certain at any rate," writes Alcott biographer Odell Shepard, "that as time went by, the two earnest youths became equally convinced that there was something deeply wrong with primary education, and that they must do their best to change it. In the planting of this conviction, the little gray schoolhouse at the crossroads must have played some part — as a horrible example."[12]

By the 1820s, Bronson had left the family farm and become an itinerant Yankee peddler of women's notions, going door-to-door up and down the Atlantic seaboard, drinking too much and building up substantial debts. A reinvention was in order. He changed his name from Amos Alcox to A. Bronson Alcott and turned his energies to education. As a peddler, he had seen the way the wealthy live — their airy sunlit rooms, their books and beautiful objects, their choices when it came to food. Teaching was his way to achieve that kind of life for himself and for his students. He embraced Wordsworth's ideas and rebelled against the predominant idea of children promulgated by the great preacher Jonathan Edwards, who had written that children "are young vipers, and infinitely more hateful than vipers."[13]

By 1825, Bronson's career as an educator was off to a promising start. Although he had only an elementary school education, he was widely read and brilliantly self-taught. He established himself as the head of a small school in Cheshire, Connecticut, where he began to put his ideas into practice. This was almost ten years before he opened the Temple School, but his pedagogical methods were already in place: a physically comfortable schoolroom, a respectful attitude toward the children, an absence of corporal punishment, and a rule by example and affection. He even had a jury of schoolmates to decide punishments for their peers when discipline was necessary.

Abigail May, called Abby or Abba, Louisa's mother, came from an entirely different sort of background. She was the youngest daughter of the distinguished Colonel Joseph May, who had won his rank in the War of Independence, and Dorothy Sewall May, a cousin of the Quincys and the Hancocks. At twenty-six, she was officially an old maid when she met Bronson Alcott. Abigail had been brought up in a distinguished Boston house named Federal Court. Although her father's once-great fortune was diminished, he was still a respected citizen, a Revolutionary War veteran who wore the "small clothes" of the eighteenth century — breeches and buckled boots — and went by the title of Colonel because of his rank in the revered Revolutionary militia.

All this changed when Abigail's mother died, and her father quickly remarried and turned Federal Court over to a new wife. In what seemed like a moment, Abigail May was transformed from the beloved daughter of a respected household to an unwelcome, aging spinster. Abigail, distraught, moved out of her family home in Boston to Brooklyn, Connecticut, to keep house for her brother Samuel May. In the meantime, the aristocratic, educated, and generous Sam May, interested in reforms of all kinds, had heard about a local educational progressive named Bronson Alcott. May had written Alcott inviting him to Brooklyn for what would turn out to be a fateful visit.

Looking back, it seems as if Louisa May Alcott's parents, Abigail May and Bronson Alcott, were made for each other. Their marriage and their passionate regard for each other were as sturdy and handsome as a Connecticut oak. At first this was far from evident. They met while Abba was at her brother's house, escaping from the fraught atmosphere created by the new marriage at Federal Court. She was in flight from the strictures and customs of aristocracy; he was flying toward the same strictures and customs. She was a Brahmin princess; he was a self-made man acting his way into a role he had dreamed for himself. He was brittle; she was easily offended. She would inherit family money; he was an unemployed idealist. Still, both were odd, eccentric, and devoted to the idea of service. Both were committed to progressive education. It took two years from their first meeting for them to get up the nerve for a kiss.

Bronson and Abba had many serious discussions about the state of education during that first visit at the May house in Brooklyn. Bronson, with Sam May's help, landed another position as a schoolmaster in a Bristol, Connecticut, school. Again, he instituted the changes that had become his educational trademark. In what would become a pattern for Bronson Alcott's teaching career, the parents and the community of the school were at first thrilled to have him as a schoolmaster, then nervous about his methods, and finally condemnatory. He was always asked to leave.

During the ten months between their first two meetings, Abigail and Bronson exchanged increasingly intimate letters. In person, however, their social and emotional awkwardness took over. When they met at Sam May's house, they managed to offend each other. "I went into Mr. May's study to see a friend," Abigail wrote in her diary. "He proved merely an acquaintance, whose reserve chilled me into silence."[14]

By 1828, Abigail had returned to Federal Court. Bronson was also in Boston. Once again Sam May helped him land on his feet, and he was offered the job of headmaster of Boston's first infant school, on Salem Street. School for children younger than five was a revolutionary idea that Bronson Alcott embraced. Again he immersed himself in theories of education and traveled to New York and Philadelphia to visit other progressive infant schools, which he found disappointing. "The source was pure, but one tasted the lead pipe,"[15] writes Odell Shepard of Bronson's reaction to the new schools' lack of originality. The schools he visited incorporated the principles of the Swiss educator Johann Pestalozzi and other educational progressives, but he felt this was done in a spirit of repression and regimentation. Bronson believed that teaching must be an act of love; teaching was a higher form of preaching. Oh how Abigail May agreed! She applied for the job of his assistant at the Salem Street School. He asked her to withdraw her application because, he said, he wanted to work with her at a larger, better school he was already planning.

By September, when Bronson visited Abigail in Brooklyn, where she had gone for the summer, these two dedicated idealists finally managed to connect with each other. On or around the first of September, Bronson proposed to Abigail May and was accepted. "I do love this good woman, and I love her because she is good. I love her because she loves me,"[16] he wrote in his journal. In October he opened yet another school in Boston, an elementary school for boys.

Although Abba and Bronson were now officially engaged, Bronson was no more in a hurry to get married than he had been in a hurry to propose. For one thing, his new school was attracting a lot of attention. On some days, there were so many interested visitors to the classroom that Bronson felt it interfered with his teaching. One of his favorite visitors was Frances Wright, a Scottish-born reformer who believed in free love and who was a follower of another education reformer, Robert Owen. Fanny Wright was impressed with Bronson and thought his teaching talents deserved a wider audience. She was instrumental in offering Bronson a better job at the head of a school teaching according to Owen's principles. Bronson turned it down in spite of his friendship with Wright and in spite of the offered salary that was double what he was making. When he was asked to choose between financial advantage and his personal principles, Bronson Alcott always chose principles. He could not teach another man's philosophy.

Finally, on Sunday, May 23, 1830, Bronson Alcott at the advanced age of thirty was married to Miss Abigail May at King's Chapel on Tremont Street by the Reverend Francis Greenwood. Their honeymoon was the walk from the chapel back to Newall's boardinghouse on Franklin Street, where Abigail moved in with her impecunious dreamer of a husband. In January, as was his habit, Bronson had made a list of his hopes for the New Year. There were seven: meeting men with great minds, influencing public opinion, self-improvement, writing a book, running the school, and the last two — a good marriage and enough money. A year later, the Alcotts' first child, Anna, was born, and Louisa May Alcott — named after one of the distinguished May aunts — was born the following November.

By the time the Alcotts returned to Boston after the failure of the Germantown school in 1835, the economy was growing, land speculation was feverish, and the city, formally incorporated in 1822, expanded around the new Court House, a Greek Revival building with wide steps and impressive Ionic columns. This symbol of civic pride joined the dome of the impressive

Charles Bullfinch Statehouse at the top of the Boston Common. The Common was the city's center, where cows grazed, children played, and great men took morning walks. Once a year during the general election in May, vendors set themselves up in rows by products, with the alcoholic beverages closest to the polls.

In the spring of 1835, with Bronson Alcott's new Temple School — his fourth school in five years — triumphantly opening, the family moved into a spacious boardinghouse owned by a Mrs. Beach at 3 Somerset Court. Their loyal friend Elizabeth Peabody, who was Alcott's assistant at the school, left the house where she had been staying and moved in with them rent-free in lieu of her postponed Temple School wages. Peabody was one of three daughters of a Salem, Massachusetts, doctor, sisters whose history would be twined around the history of nineteenth-century literature and ideas: her older sister, Mary, eventually married educator Horace Mann, and her younger sister, Sophia, married Nathaniel Hawthorne. Elizabeth, who never married but ran a bookstore and taught, became a kind of favorite maiden aunt for many of the century's literary lights.

One of her first projects was the Alcotts.

She got along well with Abigail Alcott, and sometimes babysat for Louisa and Anna. On June 24, after a difficult pregnancy, so difficult that the naughty little Louisa was sent away to live with her cranky old grandfather at Federal Court for the final weeks, Abigail Alcott gave birth to her third daughter. The baby was named Elizabeth Peabody Alcott after the family friend and her father's greatest admirer.

Living at the Alcotts', Peabody began work on a book about the growing Temple School titled *Record of a School.* Peabody worked directly from her schoolroom notes, and both she and Alcott were thrilled by the emerging portrait. The book's publication in September brought more success. It was reviewed in a New York magazine, the *Knickerbocker.* The bestselling book, infused with Elizabeth Peabody's literary enthusiasm and her passion for the subject, became the instruction manual for a new era in American thought. As Peabody biographer Megan Marshall has suggested, *Record of a School* was a nineteenth-century version of educator A. S. Neill's *Summerhill,* a 1960 book that was read for its revolutionary attitude toward children and education.[17]

Buoyed by the Temple School's success, Bronson Alcott optimistically expanded the

41

enterprise rather than paying off old debts. The Alcott family moved into a big house on Front Street, and again Elizabeth Peabody moved with them, into a large upstairs room with a view through the trees toward Dorchester. Reading in her perfectly arranged room with its rugs and a bookcase borrowed from the Alcotts, Peabody began some dreaming of her own. The review of *Record of a School* in the *Knickerbocker* had called her a woman of genius, and she began to imagine starting a school herself and doing more of her own writing.

The first sign of trouble for the Temple School came from close to home. Slowly, and perhaps inexorably, the Alcotts and Elizabeth Peabody began to get on each other's nerves. To some extent, they had always disagreed. Bronson's aim was to bring his students into a harmonious society, the perfect community that remained his transcendent vision. Community would always be his goal, his religion, and his finest creation. Elizabeth was more interested in bringing each student to maximum individual intellectual and spiritual consummation.

Increasingly, Elizabeth was bothered by one of Bronson's imaginative punishments. He would invite students to disobey, suggesting, for instance, that they would rather go sledding on the Common in the winter than go to school. When they said they *would* like to go sledding, he exiled them to the hallway — denying them for a time the stimulation and fun in the schoolroom.

Many of the New England Transcendentalist writers — Emerson, Thoreau, Longfellow, Oliver Wendell Holmes, and William Ellery Channing — were educated at Harvard. Most of them believed that holiness would be achieved through the cultivation of the individual in communion with nature or with other men. "Know thyself," was one of the Transcendentalist commandments. Writers like Thoreau imagined man at his best alone in a natural landscape. Alcott, perhaps because he had no formal education, came at the world from a different direction — he believed in community. To him man was at his best working with other men.

Living with the Alcotts, Elizabeth Peabody discovered, made admiration for the family patriarch harder to sustain. Alcott, a tall slender man in his thirties with his graying blond hair worn long, was brilliant with children and sometimes less than brilliant with adults. He didn't like being disagreed with, especially at his own dinner table. One evening, Elizabeth felt she had to argue with Alcott's preaching of the principles of the faddish Sylvester Graham. Graham, a Connecticut zealot, would soon cause riots in Boston as the town's butchers and bakers protested his recommended diet of crumbly brown graham flour — his own concoction — and fruits and vegetables. This was the diet served by Abba Alcott at the dinner table, although Abba occasionally provided chicken or meat for her daughters on the sly.

Alcott had heard Graham lecture in February at the Swedenborg Chapel in Cambridge, and he asked Peabody what people thought of Graham in Salem, her hometown. She responded that Graham's claims of two-century life spans for those who followed the Graham diet didn't sound inviting. Alcott called her desire to die before the age of two hundred suicidal. Peabody, whose father was a doctor, angrily shot back that Alcott was against doctors in general. Alcott, she reminded him, had once said that doctors were like vampires feeding on society. Then Peabody retired to her room in distress.

Added to the complications in the Alcott household was Abba Alcott's famous temper. This temper and its results in a household of young women became a character in *Little Women* and one of the things Louisa refused to sentimentalize. "Jo's hot temper mastered her, and she shook Amy until her teeth chattered in her head; crying, in a passion of grief and anger — You wicked, wicked girl! I can never write again and I'll never forgive you as long as I live!"[18] Jo March gets so angry with her sister Amy that she leads her into danger on the frozen Concord River, and Amy almost drowns. When Jo weeps with remorse, Marmee, the sisters' loving mother, tells Jo that she too had a ferocious temper that she has learned to control with the help of their father. But the real Bronson Alcott didn't have the calming effect on his wife that Father has on Marmee. There were times when Abba's irrational temper had an uncanny resemblance to her formerly three-year-old daughter's tantrums.

Elizabeth Peabody described all this in letters to her sister Mary, and Mary began urging Elizabeth to sever ties with the Alcotts, even offering to take her place at the school and in the house. Mary Peabody was no fan of either of the Alcotts, and both she and Elizabeth were also writing passionate letters to another educator, Horace Mann, who had mixed feelings about Bronson Alcott's revolutionary ideas. Alcott lacked modesty, Mary wrote to Elizabeth, and she was certainly right about that. It was time for Elizabeth to stop "sacrificing your own comfort for his convenience,"[19] she wrote.

Elizabeth Peabody seemed to agree in her letters to Mary, but she wasn't ready to act. In the meantime, she was shoulder-to-the-wheel taking notes for a sequel to her great success, and trying desperately, since her name was on the book, to rein in Bronson's wilder, more narcissistic tendencies. Mary was too busy with her own school in Salem to intervene, so instead, in the spring of 1836, she sent their younger sister Sophia to Boston as an ally against the Alcotts — a move which was to backfire in a painful way for the beleaguered Elizabeth.

This electric knot of connections and disconnections, men and women struggling to find their place in the world, sisters, great men arguing with each other, civic ferment, debt and wealth, and passionate personal relations, was the rich atmosphere in which Louisa May Alcott began life in the 1830s. Louisa wrote in a short memoir that one of her earliest memories was playing with her father's books, building towers and bridges, and scribbling on blank pages when she could find a pen or pencil.

Another early memory was the day before her fourth birthday, the Saturday she and her father celebrated in the sunny upper rooms of his triumphant new Temple School. Louisa and her father were both born on November 29, under the sign of Sagittarius the horse-man. According to astrologers, Sagittarians are steady, hardworking, are good at bearing burdens, and make great friends. The end of November in New England is a gray time following the vivid show of red and gold when the leaves change color in the early autumn. The air smells like apples. Crowds of geese vee their way south; squirrels and rabbits disappear; there are days that foreshadow the bitter winter freeze of the coming months.

The day of the celebration, a day early because the birthday was on a Sunday, the Alcotts left the boardinghouse and headed down Bowdoin Street toward Temple Place. The young Louisa was shown the school's delightful playthings, the globes and blocks, books and hourglass. Then the students gathered to crown their teacher and his daughter with laurel wreaths. Bronson Alcott held the students spellbound while he told them the story of his own education, his upbringing in Wolcott, Connecticut, his marriage to Abigail May, and the birth of his three daughters. Everything about him seemed to fascinate his audience, and the birthday girl listened too as if nothing could be more gratifying than hearing her father's story.

Carried away by his own eloquence, her father told the happy story of his visit to Concord to walk and talk with the great Ralph Waldo Emerson and the unhappy story of his recent visit to see the noble William Lloyd Garrison in Boston's Leverett Street Jail. Garrison, the editor of an abolitionist paper, the *Liberator,* had been incarcerated after being pursued by a mob outraged at his antislavery beliefs. The morning ended with refreshments and a recitation by one of the girls in honor of the double birthday: *with hearts of happy mirth; we've sallied forth from home to celebrate a birth.*[20]

It was during the serving of the refreshments — small cakes — that Louisa was taught another complicated lesson about sharing to add to the already implicit lesson of the day: that her biggest gift on her own birthday was to celebrate her father's birthday. The toddler had been given the important job of passing out the cakes to the children who marched past her. As the last child approached, Louisa saw that there was only one cake left. Should she give it to Lucia, a guest, or keep it? It was her own birthday! But with a reminder from her mother that "it is always better to give away than to keep the nice things," Louisa, famous in her family for her aggression, her tantrums, and her temper, quietly handed over the "dear plummy cake"[21] and got a kiss from her mother instead.

This test of conscience — had the wrong number of cakes been engineered by Bronson Alcott? — was one of many small tests conducted on Louisa and her sisters by their father in his scientific approach to the human soul. Alcott questioned his students and experimented on some of them, but his daughters were his prime laboratory rats and pigeons, his double-blind clinical trials.

In one experiment, Bronson produced an apple just before dinnertime, when his subjects were especially hungry, and asked Anna pointedly if little girls should take things that did not belong to them without asking. No, Anna responded obediently, they should not. Then he asked both Anna and Louisa if they would ever do such a thing as take an apple without asking for it. They both agreed that they would not.

Yet when Bronson returned to the room after dinner, the apple had been reduced to a core next to Louisa's place at the dinner table. Bronson asked what it was. "Apple," admitted the honest Louisa. Anna, always the pleasing child, blurted out the whole story, a story in which she and Louisa had both tried to get the apple, but Louisa had gotten there first. Then Louisa had eaten some of it. Anna had grabbed it and thrown it into the grate, but Louisa had fished it out and eaten some more. Louisa as usual was the villain of the piece. Bronson always believed Anna. Louisa confessed that she had eaten the apple "because I wanted it." Then, sensing that she had somehow failed, she added, "I was naughty."[22]

In another apple experiment, Bronson left an apple on the wardrobe alone with Louisa, who put up a valiant struggle as her father and mother secretly listened and took notes. During the course of the morning, Louisa's mother reported that she several times took the apple in her hands and caressed it wistfully. "No — no — father's — me not take father's apple — naughty — naughty," said the toddler. Then she succumbed and ate the apple. When confronted by her mother, she explained, "Me could not help it. Me *must* have it."[23]

Although the apples were eaten, Bronson was delighted at his children's show of conscience. They had struggled against their desires, evidence that children are born with a well-developed moral sense. Bronson tried similar experiments with apples as well as, especially in Louisa's case, different kinds of punishments. Once when she pinched him, he pinched her back. That didn't seem to calm her down. At other times, he spoke sternly to her. He took her bodily from the dinner table to her room, undressed her and coldly put her to bed, exiling her from the family.

With her parents distracted by the success of the Temple School, Louisa's curiosity grew as supervision shrank. She began to spend more and more time outdoors, first rolling her hoop on the Boston Common and then wandering away from home, where no one seemed to notice if she was gone. "Running away was one of the delights of my childhood," she wrote later. It doesn't *sound* delightful for a five- or six-year-old child to be running loose on the dirt streets of Boston in the 1830s, picking up urchins and sharing their food and getting lost before returning home. Still, Louisa describes it in holiday language. "Many a social lunch have I shared with hospitable Irish beggar children, as we ate our crusts, cold potatoes and salt fish on voyages of discovery among the ash heaps of the waste land that then lay where the Albany station still stands."[24]

Louisa, who had once been one of her father's principal objects of study, could now be gone for hours and travel miles on her little girl's legs before anyone went after her. One day she headed for the wharves and got seriously lost. Comforted by a large, ownerless dog, she was eventually found and brought home by the Boston town crier. After that her mother tied her to the sofa to keep her from leaving the house.[25]

Thrilled by the success of Elizabeth Peabody's *Record of a School,* Bronson Alcott began another more complicated and spiritual record of his teaching, and again he pressed Peabody into the hard service of amanuensis and assistant. In the new book, *Conversations with Children on the Gospels,* Alcott decided to get the children talking about higher subjects — religion and the nature of man and, of course, the heavenly place they had come from before landing on earth and coming to the Temple School. He told his class that they had something to teach him and the rest of the world. "I have often been taught by what very small children have said; and astonished at their answers . . . all wisdom is not in grown up people."[26]

This time, the children would be named and get credit for their ideas, he decided. This decision made Elizabeth Peabody nervous. She was steeped in the Bostonian culture of privacy and priggishness in a way that Alcott failed to understand. She was a direct descendant of the Puritans; he was a New England farm boy who had created his own culture. Peabody worried that, in the service of discovering and teaching, Bronson was sacrificing something private. "The instinctive delicacy with which children veil their deepest thoughts . . . should not be violated . . . in order to gain knowledge,"[27] she had written in *Record of a School.*

First, Alcott gave a series of lectures for adults on the subject of the Gospels, held at the Temple School in the evening. Alcott, like Emerson and the other men and women who would call themselves Transcendentalists, believed that Jesus was an extraordinary man but that there was God in every man. This was the doctrine that would get his friend Emerson banned from Harvard after his controversial Divinity School speech in 1838. The Boston elders and their Harvard educators were horrified by the idea that God could be everywhere, not just in the churches they had built for Him.

Alcott decided that his investigations into the nature of Jesus Christ were too good to save for the adults — his beloved students must also be asked these questions, questions that also brought up the subject of childbirth and, by indirection, sex. Almost as soon as he began asking the students questions like that — "How do you think a Mother would feel when she knew she was to have a child?" and "What does love make?" — Elizabeth Peabody began to balk. She sensed that Bostonians weren't ready to have their children discuss childbirth.

At home, the personal connection between the great teacher and his loyal assistant began to degenerate even further. Peabody's sister Sophia had arrived to help at the school, but this made the situation worse instead of better. Sophia had become a slavish fan of the adult Alcotts at the same time that Bronson's connection to Elizabeth was beginning to fray. Even as her sister Mary was writing letters urging Elizabeth to leave the Alcott house, even offering to pay her board somewhere else, Sophia was more and more enchanted by the family.

Then one evening after dinner, Bronson walked upstairs and knocked on Elizabeth's door. Standing in the doorway, he began to berate her about her educational views and the views of her sister Mary. He scolded her in words that sounded eerily familiar. Slowly, Elizabeth realized that the information he was using could only have come from private letters from her sister Mary that she kept in her desk drawer in her room.

Incredulous, she began to realize what must have happened while she was out during the day. The Alcotts had been snooping around her room and going through her private drawers and reading her letters — it was the only way that Bronson could have known the things he was talking about. When she tentatively asked Bronson if it was possible that the Alcotts had read her private correspondence, he baldly admitted to the whole thing.

Yes, the Alcotts had read the letters that they had found while going through her room. What was the problem? Privacy in the Alcott family was equated with secrecy and furtiveness. Although all the Alcott daughters kept journals in which they were urged to confide their innermost thoughts, for instance, their parents routinely read the journals and commented on them in the margins. Elizabeth Peabody did not have this tolerance for sharing. For her, privacy meant, well, privacy. She was furious. The Alcotts, who had found in the private letters a great deal of criticism of Bronson Alcott and even one letter from Mary Peabody urging her sister Elizabeth to distance herself from Bronson's "mistaken views," were equally furious. Both Peabody and Alcott felt betrayed.

"Don't you think Mrs. Alcott came into my room & looked over my letters from you & found your last letter to me and the one to Sophia and carried it to Mr. Alcott — & they have read them,"[28] Elizabeth howled in a letter to her sister Mary. Far from apologizing for rifling through Elizabeth's room, Abba Alcott turned on her with the force of her famous temper, saying that Elizabeth was condemned to eternal damnation and had committed the greatest crime she had ever heard of — the crime of doubting Bronson Alcott. What made the situation even more painful for Elizabeth was that her own sister Sophia continued to worship the Alcotts and to take their side in the argument. Sophia claimed that her sister Elizabeth had often gone through other people's private mail. Furthermore, she was sure it had only happened once. Now betrayed by her sister as well as her friend and employer, Elizabeth hid many feelings when she reassured Mary about Sophia: "She will be protected by heaven — in her purity and innocence of intention."[29]

Angry and worried about Alcott's definition of privacy, a definition which also seemed to be ruling his questioning of the students at school, Elizabeth Peabody abruptly moved out of the Alcott house in August 1836 and, in spite of an invitation from the Emersons to visit Concord, decamped for Salem. The Alcotts promptly renamed their third child. She was no longer Elizabeth Peabody; from now on she was Elizabeth Sewall, and she was named after Judge Samuel Sewall. Sewall, a distinguished ancestor of Abba's, was famous for presiding at the Salem Witch Trials and later regretting his actions and apologizing to the survivors of the nineteen executed so-called witches. Elizabeth Peabody turned the Temple School job over to the pliant Sophia, who was less seasoned in assessing public opinion. Sophia also took over the job of transcribing the new book. "Sophia is compensated for any pain of thinking ill of me — by being able to keep up her adoration of Mr. Alcott," Elizabeth wrote to Mary.[30]

Elizabeth Peabody's angry departure may have been the beginning of the end for the

Temple School. Peabody was an honorable woman, and she did not publicly tell the whole story of her friendship with the Alcotts. Nevertheless, children began to be drawn out of the school. Peabody also wrote Alcott asking him to remove her name from the new book. Boston too had changed. Boom had been followed by bust. The angry conflicts over race that would eventually blow up the relatively new country in a civil war were beginning to gather steam. For all their progressive ideals in prosperous times, Bostonians were still at heart religious conservatives, not too far from the Calvinism of their forebears. This was the Boston where anti-Catholic mobs roamed the streets and yet an anti-Catholic man named Abner Kneeland would later be thrown in jail for ridiculing the concept of a virgin birth as manifest in the Immaculate Conception.

"Power corrupts," wrote Lord John Acton years after the founding of Bronson Alcott's school. "Absolute power corrupts absolutely. Great men are almost always bad men."[31] The story of the mighty and their falls is such a cliché that it's hard to believe it happened to a mind as informed and original as Bronson Alcott's. Did his inability to see what was happening around him start when he began calling his students "disciples"? Was it the way he conducted discussions around the family dinner table, which often included a few students and Elizabeth Peabody, so that no one was allowed to contradict him? Or did his humility vanish when the great Emerson begged him to visit in Concord? Was the turning point the visit of the English reformer Harriet Martineau on a journalist's tour of the United States? Was he a profligate narcissist unable to deal with adversity, or was he a prophet without honor in his own country? Was he an innocent pawn of a changing economy, or was it that Bronson Alcott was a man ahead of his time, as his daughter Louisa believed?

"My father's school was the only one I ever went to," Louisa May Alcott wrote fifty years later, "and when this was broken up because he introduced methods now all the fashion, our lessons went on at home, for he was always sure of four little pupils who firmly believed in their teacher, though they have not done him all the credit he deserved."[32]

The publication of what was to be the second triumphant book from Alcott's great Temple School, *Conversations with Children on the Gospels,* happened in a different world from that of the earlier publication. Bronson Alcott was a man who didn't care what anyone thought — that was one of the things about him that fascinated Emerson. But a teacher serves his community as well as his students.

When it was published in December of 1836, *Conversations with Children on the Gospels* was received by the Boston community with horror. The *Boston Daily Advertiser,* the *Boston Courier,* and the *Christian Register* all took off after Alcott, calling the book "radically false," "indecent and obscene," and its author "half-witted or insane" and "an ignorant and presuming charlatan."[33] Alcott had some prominent defenders, including the principled Elizabeth Peabody, who put aside her personal anger; the glamorous intellectual Margaret Fuller, who had also taught at the Temple School, and Bronson's new friend Ralph Waldo Emerson. Emerson wrote Alcott: "I hate to have all the little dogs barking at you, for you have something better to do than to attend to them."[34] But the community had made up its mind. This book was just too much for them. What was this man doing with their children? What disgusting question had Alcott asked innocent little Josiah Quincy that caused the boy to answer about the "naughtinesses of other people" putting "together a body for the child"?[35] Almost immediately the thriving Temple School began to die. Enrollment dropped from forty to ten.

By April of 1837, when Louisa was four, Bronson was forced to auction off many of the wonderful things that he had bought for the school on credit in happier and more prosperous times. The national economy was in a slide and even the auction was a disappointment. The three hundred books, the busts of Plato and Socrates, the perfect little desks and chairs, were all on the block. Some things didn't sell. The total netted less than $200, a drop in the school's $6,000 bucket of debt. Whatever her ambivalence, Louisa adored her larger-than-life father. In Van Wyck Brooks's *The Flowering of New England,* the author tells the story of Louisa lashing out at the sheriff who had come to collect the schoolroom's furnishings. "Go away bad man," the little girl yelled with an obstinacy and passion which, in happier times, might have been the subject of a new experiment. "You are making my father unhappy."[36]

In a world before birth control, when women could not vote or own property,

61

when it was illegal for a woman to speak in public for money, marriage was often more like prison than liberation. The ubiquitous *Godey's Lady's Book,* a nineteenth-century compendium of social rules and observations that was used in child-raising as well as for adults, urged married men to "Be to her faults a little blind; Be to her virtues very kind; Let all her ways be unconfined, and place your padlock on her mind."

American marriage had incorporated all the moral and intellectual repression of English marriage and added more. Although Abigail May had waited to marry for love at the age of twenty-nine, she was no rebel when it came to this institution. She was luckier than most in her choice of husband. "It is a glorious thing," she wrote in her journal, "after moments of misunderstanding, even of reciprocal transgression, to rest again heart to heart and to feel, to deeply feel that there is a certainty in the world, in spite of all the power of Hell, a certainty which is heaven on earth — that they love each other, that they belong to each other, that nothing, nothing in the world shall separate them who have found each other again in true in perfect love."[37] Although there was plenty of hell in her marriage to Bronson Alcott, she continued to love him passionately in spite of their problems.

At least a dozen books have been written about the Alcotts since Louisa May Alcott's death at the end of the nineteenth century. Biographers disagree sharply over the true nature of Bronson Alcott. To some he is the Platonic ideal sketched by Emerson, a man too innocent to navigate the modern world. To others he is the self-regarding so-called genius whose refusal to compromise and whose inability to make money drove his daughters, especially Louisa, into domestic slavery as teachers and governesses and paid companions.

In his own journal, Bronson admitted that one of the reasons for his dismissal from an earlier school in Cheshire, Connecticut, had been the parents' disapproval over his "caressing the students — especially the females."[38] By modern standards, this is a damning admission with far-reaching implications, yet this information appears in Bronson's own journal. Did Bronson Alcott let himself handle his students and his daughters in sexual ways? Did he take advantage of nineteenth-century children's helplessness and powerlessness? We know now that being molested can create permanent psychic and sexual scars — scars of defensiveness, self-doubt, and an inability to connect with others that might easily be applied to the character of the adult Louisa May Alcott. Can we apply a twenty-first-century context for a few scraps of nineteenth-century journal?

Bronson was an intensely physical and sexual man whose journals are sprinkled with his own struggles to be an ascetic and to define his desires — struggles not unlike his little daughter's struggles with the apple. "Mettle is the Godhead proceeding into the matrix of nature to organize man. Behold the creative jet,"[39] he wrote in his journal in as close a description of sex as anyone tried in the nineteenth century.

Where posterity is concerned, Bronson's greatest failing may be the dreadful quality of most of his writing. Teaching and conversations are ephemeral and, from the opinions of people like Emerson, we can assume that Alcott's were something special. Books last forever. Emerson, urging Alcott to morph from a teacher to a writer after the failure of the Temple School, was taken aback by the manuscript his protégé presented. Reading Alcott's writing, one critic aptly said, "was like watching fifteen boxcars go by with only one passenger in them." The clever James Russell Lowell even wrote a poem about the difference between Alcott's spoken and written words:

> While he talks he is great, but goes out
> like a taper
> If you shut him up closely with pen, ink
> and paper;
> Yet his fingers itch for 'em from morning
> till night,
> And he thinks he does wrong if he don't
> always write;
> In this as in all things a lamb among men,
> He goes to sure death when he goes to
> his pen.[40]

It wasn't his writing that brought about the death of the Temple School and the end of Alcott's teaching career. It was his belief in the inherent wisdom of the children he taught, and his inability to gauge the mood of the people around him. Read today, *Conversations with Children on the Gospels* includes nothing that suggests impropriety. The use of the children's first names does not seem intrusive; instead it enables readers to come away with an idea of who each one is from the talkative Charles to the adorable six-year-old Josiah. Each conversation ranges from two to ten pages and begins with a reading from the New Testament Gospels. Then, the conversation of the children with Mr. Alcott is written as dialogue. Occasionally a third voice, the voice of the Recorder (Elizabeth or Sophia Peabody) chimes in to add an interesting fact or even to correct Mr. Alcott.

The conversation that set off a landslide of negative opinion begins with Bronson reading from Matthew 1:18. This is a problematic passage for anyone. Joseph and Mary are about to be married, when as the reading explains without comment, *she found she was with child of the Holy Ghost.* The passage describes Joseph's surprise and distress; he and Mary had not yet slept together. Then an angel appears telling Joseph that the situation was not what he assumed. *Behold a virgin shall be with child.*

After reading the passage, Bronson asked the children what interested them. Josiah said he thought it was about Jesus being born. When Bronson asked what being born was, the innocent Josiah responded, "It is to take up the body from the earth. The spirit comes from Heaven, and takes up the naughtiness out of other people, which makes other people better."[41] The true import of the passage from Matthew — the fears of a man presented with a pregnant fiancée — were neatly sidestepped by Bronson, who led the conversation into a sweet discussion of the differences between the spirit and the body.

"What is birth?" he asked the children, and Charles responded that birth is when the spirit is put into the body. Finally, Alcott told the children what he thought — but only after they had a chance to explore the question. His theory was that the spirit made the body even as a rose created rose leaves. After most of the children had their say, a student named George added a comment that may have caused more trouble than all the talk about sex and childbirth. He said that he thought Joseph and Mary were probably poor because poor people were generally happier.

This line of questioning may have been even more offensive to the burghers of the new Boston than any sexual investigation. To be honest about sex is tricky; to be honest about money is taboo. It's not the sex that shocks in these conversations; it's the openness of Bronson to question everything and anything, even the authority of his students' parents. "I want each of you to ask yourselves this," he says, "are my father and mother spiritual persons — are they devoted to the culture of their own and other people's spirits, as much as they should be, or do they care more than I wish about outward things."[42] This invitation from a teacher to students to question the wisdom and circumstances of their own families is pedagogical dynamite. Of course, a teacher's first responsibility is to the truth and to the development of student hearts and minds. Still, at the Temple School, Bronson Alcott seems to have been oblivious to the fact that he was biting the hand that fed him. A teacher is responsible to parents, who pay the bills, as well as to students.

Although the powers that controlled Boston may have been offended by Bronson's challenge to their authority, they fastened on the sexual element of *Conversations with Children on the Gospels* and mounted their attack. Worse, they withdrew their children from the school. By the spring of 1837, the Temple School as it had once been, with its high hopes and optimistic beliefs about the nature of children, was gone. Bronson Alcott moved from the airy rooms at the top of the Temple to a dark basement room where he taught his dwindling class.

Bronson had been a teacher for years, but this would be the last formal classroom teaching of his life. His great dream — to change the way children were taught — was over. Within a few months, the school was forced to move out of the Temple entirely, and Bronson continued to teach a few students — his three daughters and a few others — in the parlor of the less elegant house to which the family had moved on Cottage Street.

In the fall of 1839, Bronson enrolled an African-American student in his dying school, a girl named Susan Robinson. It made perfect sense. Bronson was an early abolitionist, a friend of William Lloyd Garrison's, and one of the first members of the Anti-Slavery League. He knew the South from his peddling days, and he had seen the injustices of slavery at first hand. Bronson had mounting debt, angrily frayed friendships, an impeached reputation, and only a few increasingly hysterical defenders, but he never let go of his principles. The enrollment of Susan Robinson was too much even for the Alcott diehards, and by the winter of 1839, Bronson Alcott had only his own daughters as students. His daughters were entirely loyal to their father, but the young Louisa May was forming her own secret opinions and thoughts. Her journals are entirely loyal to her father. As a daughter, she never spoke a word against her father, against his irresponsibility or his bullying or his prejudice against her. As a writer, she expressed her feelings in a far more effective and literary way. She left him out of her masterpiece.

# 2
# Concord. Louisa in Exile.
## 1840–1843

In the winter of 1840, as life in Boston became less and less affordable for the Alcotts, Emerson redoubled his efforts to get them to move to Concord. He located a small run-down cottage in Concord near the slow-flowing Concord River on the estate of Edmund Hosmer, secured it for a rent of $52 a month, and offered it to the Alcott family for nothing.

"It was a tiny house, with a little garden behind, and a lawn about as big as a pocket handkerchief in front," Louisa May Alcott wrote years later in describing the Hosmer Cottage, where she installed the fictional Meg March and John Brooke as newlyweds in *Little Women.* "The shrubbery consisted of several young larches, who looked undecided whether to live or die. . . . The hall was so narrow it was fortunate they had no piano . . . the dining room was so small, that six people were a tight fit, and the kitchen stairs seemed built for the express purpose of precipitating both servants and china pell-mell into the coal bin."[1]

As humble as the cottage may have seemed, it was not enough for Alcott to move into a situation that looked like charity; always a teacher, even when he had failed at teaching, he had to spin some ideas around this new offer. At each stage of his life, he provided a new metaphor for himself and his growing family. As long as he could produce a sympathetic story, his optimism was undimmed. "You may ask what I am about now," he wrote his mother that year; "I reply, still at my old trade *hoping,* which thus far has given food, shelter, raiment, and a few warm friends."[2]

Not for the first or the last time, it was the Alcotts' friend Emerson who provided. Emerson was the financial father of the Alcott family while Bronson took care of the mythmaking. In fact, during the first decade of their friendship, Emerson often seemed to have been put on earth partly to bail out his friend Bronson Alcott and his family. For Emerson, Alcott represented the brilliance of the unschooled. He admired Alcott's confidence and optimism. Emerson was also amazed by Alcott's ability to spout cascades of language while he, Emerson, often agonized over a sentence or two until he got it right.

Emerson was in his thirties, but he had already lived a lifetime of exhilaration and sorrow. Growing up in Boston in a large family raised by a single mother, he had known the discomforts and fears of real poverty, although the Emerson family had deep roots in colonial New England. Emerson's step-grandfather Ezra Ripley was a respected minister in Concord who lived at the Old Manse, a house above the Concord River, and welcomed his sisters' children whenever they chose to visit. Emerson had managed to go to Harvard with help from his energetic Aunt Mary Moody and a series of scholarships, and he had become a minister in the Congregational Church.

At the age of twenty-five, he fell in love with a seventeen-year-old Concord, New Hampshire, girl, Ellen Tucker, and the two planned out their life together, a plan that depended on Ellen's money and her desire to write poetry and Emerson's talent and ministry. Her death from tuberculosis two years later devastated Emerson. He obsessively visited the cemetery in Roxbury, and in March, fourteen months after her death, actually opened her coffin in an attempt to understand his own devastation.[3] He quit the ministry and fled to Europe. On his return, he sued the Tucker family for Ellen's portion of her fortune; her brother had argued that since she was still underage her money could not be inherited. Emerson took the family to court in 1836, and won.

With the Tucker money and a second wife, Lydia Jackson, whom he had met while giving a lecture at Plymouth, Emerson moved to Concord, the small town inland from Boston where he had spent happy childhood summers. In Concord, a long stagecoach ride from Boston, Emerson and his new wife, Lidian — one of the conditions of his proposal was that she change her first name as well as her last name — bought a large white house on the Cambridge Turnpike. With Lidian's help, for she was a competent partner more than a passionately beloved new wife, Emerson determined to create a lively intellectual community that would rival anything he could have had in Boston or Cambridge.

The Alcotts were not the only recipients of Emerson's largesse. The genius cluster that sprang up in Concord in the 1840s, and which essentially created American literature as we know it, was largely assembled through Emerson's judicious use of money, power, and personal persuasion.

The Alcotts moved in, and soon enough Henry David Thoreau, a Concord native, had moved into the Emersons' house too; Emerson then recruited Thoreau to plant a garden for Nathaniel Hawthorne and his new wife, the former Sophia Peabody. The couple had taken Emerson up on his offer of a low rent for the empty Ripley House — the Old Manse. Margaret Fuller sometimes stayed with the Hawthornes and sometimes with the Emersons.

When he couldn't entice people to live in Concord, Emerson brought them for visits at his new house, and his study sometimes resounded with the voices of Henry Longfellow from Cambridge and Thomas Wentworth Higginson, Henry James the elder and his son Henry James from New York. Emerson also corresponded with those he couldn't host like Thomas Carlyle in London and Walt Whitman in Brooklyn. Later, Herman Melville came to Concord to visit the Hawthornes. Sophia Peabody's sister Mary visited with her husband, Horace Mann. (In the competition for Mann with Elizabeth, she had won.) Choosing Concord, a relatively remote outpost where he felt very much at home, Emerson assembled the most extraordinary literary community ever gathered in a small town. He was the force behind the first community of professional writers in the New World, a community whose work and ideas underlie almost everything we write and think even today.

Alcott justified his family's move to Concord with a hare-brained decision to be a simple farmer. He would live his ideas instead of writing and teaching them. "My garden shall be my poem," he wrote. "My spade and hoe the instruments of my wit and skill."[4] He would abandon intellect, he decided, and make his living from the land. Armed with his own knowledge of planting and his strong arms and back, he would create a garden that would feed his family. "I have now abrogated all claims to moral and spiritual teaching," he wrote to his brother-in-law Sam May. "I place myself in peaceful relations to the soil — as a husbandman intent on aiding its increase — and seem no longer hostile to things as they are the powers that be."[5]

So on March 31, 1840, the Alcott family boarded the stagecoach in Boston at Hanover Square for the bumpy ride the sixteen miles to Concord, where they spent their first night. "A long soaking rain, the drops trickling down the stubble," wrote Henry David Thoreau the day before the Alcotts left Boston. "I lay drenched on last year's bed of wild oats, by the side of some bare hill, ruminating. These things are of the moment."[6]

April 1 was Town Meeting Day, so the arrival of the strangers didn't cause much notice. Concord still takes its town meetings very seriously; crowds turn out to debate and vote on everything from local offices to stop lights. The Hosmer Cottage, a good walk from the town center, was small but thrilling for the Alcott family, especially Louisa, an active eight-year-old who was extremely fond of running and all forms of movement. The neighbors near the Hosmer Cottage agreed. "Louisa was always the leader in the fun," wrote Lydia Hosmer, who lived in a larger house nearby. "It seems to me that she was always romping and racing down the street, usually with a hoople higher than her head. . . . She was continually shocking people . . . by her tomboyish, natural and independent ways."[7]

"It pleases both housewife and little ones," Bronson wrote of the modest new house, "and the neighborhood enjoys the highest reputation."[8] The Alcotts named the wreck "Dovecote Cottage" and proceeded to make themselves at home.

In a few weeks, Bronson had repaired

leaks in the roof, fixed the drains, white-washed the fences, transplanted trees, and trellised the entire house. Always an energetic and imaginative landscape gardener, Bronson also ploughed a fresh garden and planted a new crop of fruits and vegetables. In the spirit of living his ideas, Bronson ran an eccentric household. No meat was eaten and animals were not used for work — they were to be regarded as partners rather than slaves and could not be slaughtered or exploited. Oxen could not be yoked for ploughing; horses could not be harnessed for transportation.

Alcott had remained an admirer of Sylvester Graham, and he believed that animal flesh was not a natural food for human beings. Some of Alcott's dietary rules were moot because of the Alcotts' poverty. Bronson's income was nonexistent, and his debts from the Temple School had not been repaid. All clothing was made from flax because cotton was picked by slaves. The family also gave up everything that may have used international slave labor in its manufacture or transportation — spices, sugar, and coffee, for instance. Abba went around singing as she cleaned out rooms and made curtains; she too loved a move. The Alcott family was very good at getting a fresh start. They knew how to do this well. The move to Concord was the fifth move in their decade of marriage, and the family would move twenty-nine times before they came to a rest back in Concord on the other side of town almost twenty years later.

Concord in 1840 was much more than an escape for the Alcotts. It was a community of men and women who understood them. The Thoreau brothers, Henry and John, had created a private school — Concord Academy — and were running it with progressive methods that Bronson Alcott immediately found familiar. Anna was soon enrolled. Other students at the school often boarded with John and Henry's mother, Cynthia Thoreau, who ran a pleasant boardinghouse in the old Parkman house across the street. At school, John taught writing and arithmetic and Henry classics, Greek, and higher mathematics. But the brothers taught much more than the required curriculum, and Henry often took his delighted pupils on field trips, giving them lessons in the names and attributes of plants and animals and in the history of the Indians and the way they were driven out of Massachusetts. He took them fishing on the river and showed them how land was surveyed.

It was also an election year — and Concord takes politics seriously. William Henry Harrison, a sixty-seven-year-old soldier from the Indian Wars, had been the hero of the Battle of Tippecanoe. He and John Tyler were running against the incumbent, Martin Van Buren. Although there were some in Concord who didn't believe that the Indian Wars yielded heroes, on the Fourth of July the whole town turned out to campaign for the Whigs, the log cabin party, against the aristocratic Van Buren.

Louisa and her sisters watched by the roadside as hundreds poured into town for the celebration. Dozens of pigs were roasted for those less vegetarian than the Alcotts, and hogsheads of cider prepared. By dawn the three roads into town began to be jammed with people, the fife and drum corps, and a giant log cabin drawn by twenty-three horses; delegates from Boston formed a two-mile-long line as they began their march through town. The Tippecanoe Club of Cambridge rolled their famous red, white, and blue campaign ball. The speakers' stand at the edge of the river was under a tent for 6,000 people, who crowded in to hear Daniel Webster and other party luminaries.

The Alcotts thrived as Bronson spaded the earth for his acre of garden. The girls, especially Louisa, began understanding the beauties and consolations of the natural world. "I remember running over the hills just at dawn one summer morning, and pausing to rest in the silent woods, saw, through an arch of trees, the sun rise over river, hill, and wide green meadows as I never saw it before," Louisa wrote years later in the closest she ever came to a conversion experience. "Something born of the lovely hour, a happy mood, and the unfolding aspirations of a child's soul seemed to bring me very near to God."[9] The summer of 1840 was a tumultuous time in American politics, and the excitement of the log cabin parade to an observant, receptive eight-year-old was just the beginning of Louisa May Alcott's political involvement. As the Alcotts and the town of Concord were caught up in intense political forces beyond their control, one of the most fascinating and dreadful times in our history began to unfold.

Old Tippecanoe was elected in a landslide carrying Massachusetts, but on the day of his inauguration a few months later, he caught a cold that became full-blown pneumonia and killed him within months of his ascension to power. The man the country got as president was Vice President John Tyler, the afterthought who was principally known as being the Tyler in Harrison's campaign slogan: "Tippecanoe and Tyler Too." Tyler was an unknown whose bungling of the delicate issue of states' rights during the four years of his presidency may have laid the ground for disagreements that led to the Civil War.

Concord would be torn apart by the issue of slavery even before the war. Concord people were furiously law-abiding, yet they were also deeply invested in individual rights. Every Concord resident knew the glorious part Concord had played in the American Revolution, after all. Three years before the Alcotts arrived in Concord, the town had proudly erected a battle monument, an obelisk at the Old North Bridge to commemorate Concord men's part in the first exchange of shots in the Revolutionary War.

Emerson had been chosen to write a "Concord Hymn," as if the town itself were a kind of religion. The hymn would commemorate the events of April 19, 1775 when British militia marching across the river had encountered the farmers and drovers and citizens who had blocked their way. In his "Concord Hymn," Emerson wrote, "By the rude bridge that arched the flood;/Their flag to April's breeze unfurled;/Here once the embattled farmers stood;/And fired the shot heard round the world." The hymn is partially engraved on another battle monument — a Daniel Chester French statue of a Revolutionary minuteman placed at the bridge in 1875.

When the Alcotts arrived in Concord in 1840, the family was regarded with some suspicion, especially when the local farmers and householders heard from Bronson Alcott that he was a philosopher who intended to till the soil. Concord is a close-knit community. Strangers are not immediately welcomed; neighbors are treated like family. A good example of the way the community of Concord worked together in the nineteenth century is the story of Franklin Sanborn and the federal agents.

Sanborn, a schoolteacher who had come to Concord at Emerson's invitation, had been one of the principal supporters of the rebellious John Brown, the abolitionist who had been captured at Harpers Ferry and executed. Late one night in 1859, a pair of federal agents with a warrant for Sanborn's arrest pulled up to the Sanborn house in a horse and carriage. Sanborn answered the door of his house, realized what was happening, and began to struggle. His sister rushed down the street and rang the church bells that summoned a crowd of sympathetic townspeople, including Ralph Waldo Emerson. As Sanborn was dragged toward the waiting carriage, a writ of habeas corpus was produced and waved at the federal agents. Before the agents could stuff their quarry through the carriage door, the crowd had closed in, threatening to unhitch their horses or begin throwing stones. The agents released Sanborn and took off with all deliberate speed.

The townspeople of Concord responded to outsiders and disasters by working together with uncommon efficiency. Years later, the Emersons' house on the Cambridge Turnpike was seriously burned. A collection was taken, and Emerson and his daughter Ellen were sent abroad on a monthlong trip. While they were away, the town got together to rebuild the house. On his return, the whole town turned out to welcome him. His possessions and books had been moved back in and it was as if the fire had never happened.

Yet Concord, for all its support of its own

residents, also had a guilty secret when it came to the Native Americans who had originally settled this lovely piece of landscape along the Concord and Assabet rivers. Even though Concord men and women revered the idea of individual freedom and respect for the land, they had engaged in a bloody war against the individuals who were there when they arrived. In King Philip's War at the end of the seventeenth century, and later in the 1700s, Concord men went musket to musket and atrocity to atrocity with the Indians — the Abenaki and the Pawtuckets — who were, at least at first, just trying to protect the life they had peacefully led for generations. Concord's Captain Richard Lovewell was a famous "Indian fighter," as was President Harrison, a man who hunted down the Indians and decapitated them or scalped them for bounty.

The dark side of community spirit can be intolerance, and Concord's history when it comes to those who don't belong or those who are disenfranchised is definitely mixed. During the Indian Wars of the eighteenth century, although the town of Concord was never the subject of an Indian raid, no one seemed inclined to ask if the Indians had rights or if there was anything wrong with decimating their villages and slaughtering their braves.

The arrival of Emerson in Concord, a man who came from one of Concord's original families but who also had been educated and raised in Boston, was part of a change in the mood of the town. When the United States government drove the Cherokees off their land, Emerson himself wrote a letter of protest to President Van Buren. Later, Concord seemed to reverse itself again by becoming a center of passionate abolitionism and a stop on the Underground Railroad.

Politics, at least passionate politics, often comes from personal experience. In Concord, abolition became a personal matter in 1850 when the United States Congress, with Daniel Webster's support, put teeth in an old eighteenth-century fugitive slave law. At that point, it became illegal for anyone to help a slave on the run. Slaves had to be returned under the law no matter where they were found. As a result, anyone involved in the Underground Railroad or any other means of escape for slaves became a criminal.

The summer the Alcotts arrived in Concord, the town was already debating the slavery question; a question fired up by the wild William Lloyd Garrison and the brilliant young lawyer Wendell Phillips and others like him. At one point, another group tried to keep Phillips from speaking at the local Lyceum. The Lyceum was for educational purposes, it was argued. Many were abolitionists, but they deplored controversy. By planting himself in the audience with the help of Emerson and his friend Henry David Thoreau, who was a Lyceum curator, Phillips managed to speak anyway during the question-and-answer session.

For Louisa, the exhilaration of the country was as brief as it was thrilling. Her pregnant mother, for all her happiness at the new situation, found that her most difficult daughter was just too difficult to have around during the final months of her pregnancy and delivery. Abba had miscarried a baby boy in 1838 as the Temple School disintegrated, and she didn't want to risk having that happen again.

In early July, just a few months after the family moved to Concord, Louisa was on the stagecoach, banished from her newly beloved country home back to urban Boston. Staying at Federal Court with her distinguished grandfather Colonel May, an old man in his eighteenth-century clothes, was no fun at all for an active, questioning little girl. At Federal Court there were no open fields for romping in or kittens for playing with or even any sisters. "We all miss the noisy little girl who used to make house and garden, barn and field ring with her footsteps," her father wrote her from Concord. The letter, with unintentional cruelty, describes all the wonderful things Louisa is missing — the birth of six chicks, dolls, hoops and other things "you would have enjoyed very much." The letter ends with the warning Louisa must have been sick of hearing. She should be kind and gentle and speak softly and step lightly. "Grandpa loves quiet."[10] A postscript reminds her how much her own cat misses her.

Six weeks later when the baby was born and safely healthy, Louisa was finally readmitted to her family. She took the stage back to Concord, the one place in the world where she was allowed to run free. No wonder she refused to have anything to do with the golden-haired, blue-eyed baby girl who had brought on her exile. Once again, Louisa was required to suppress her natural feelings of jealousy about her sisters and her natural feelings of anger at her parents. She lived a life in which such feelings were not allowed. No wonder her early work is studded with passionate storms, murders, and melodramas.

In his inspired community-building that year, Emerson had also put together a new magazine, one of the first intellectual magazines in America; Alcott had christened it *The Dial*. Margaret Fuller was the editor. The plan was to have George Ripley and Elizabeth Peabody, as well as Alcott, Thoreau, and Emerson, work together to produce something that would be the voice of their romantic new way of seeing the world. Their critics dubbed this view Transcendentalism — the belief, in short, that intuition could trump reason or what Perry Miller has defined as "the first outcry of the heart against the materialistic pleasures of a business civilization." Bronson Alcott began work on a long piece for *The Dial* titled "Orphic Sayings." They were mocked in the Boston press as "Gastric Sayings," and Emerson's brother William called them "Alcott's unintelligibles." Fuller didn't like Alcott's work, and she didn't want to print Henry David Thoreau's work either. Thoreau kept submitting poems and essays to *The Dial*. Fuller rejected them or edited them heavily. When Thoreau complained to Emerson, Emerson took Fuller's side. *The Dial* lasted for four years, with Fuller as its editor for two of them. Emerson, who had planned to spend time helping Fuller with the new magazine, was distracted by his own work. In the spring of 1841 he published his own *Essays, First Series.*

By the autumn of the Alcotts' first year in Concord, it was clear that Bronson's plan to become a farmer and support the family through manual labor was not going to work. The family would have food but nothing else. Abba Alcott, as always, was the family member who raised the alarm when it came to financial problems. Fuel and many other things needed to be paid for with money. She asked her father and brother for help, but they were tired of Bronson's needs. Emerson was distressed at the plight of the family, and when he visited, he often left some money behind, hidden in the sofa cushions or under a candlestick. Abba Alcott dismissed her laundress and began to look for a paying job for herself. Anna and Louisa both became expert seamstresses and the family took in sewing.

Emerson came up with what he hoped would be a solution, again. The Alcotts would move in with his family — his wife, Lidian, and their two young boys. The two women would manage the household, and Bronson would work the land. Abba was desperate, but even in her desperation she knew this would not work. Then in February Abba's wealthy father sickened and died, leaving a will that left his daughter as poor as ever and feeling hurt and rejected. Colonel May had divided his fortune strictly according to person rather than according to need. Even the small sum he had left to Abigail, his will spelled out, was not to come under the "control of her husband or the liability of his debts."[11] Worse, the paltry $2,000 she would inherit was to be held in escrow for an indefinite length of time because of her husband's debts. That Thanksgiving the Alcott family gathered around a plate of apple pudding.

Yet the three years that the Alcott family spent living in the Hosmer Cottage that Emerson had rented for them by the river were, in retrospect, idyllic. "Those Concord Days were the happiest of my life, for we had charming playmates in the little Emersons, Channings, Hawthornes and Goodwins with the illustrious parents and their friends to enjoy our pranks and share our excursions,"[12] Louisa wrote later. In spite of everything, Louisa met Thoreau and Emerson, two men who would be lodestones in her intellectual development. These were two men she fell in love with in her own preadolescent way, men for whose thoughts and eccentricities she was as hungry as only a family black sheep can be.

It is hard to know how much Louisa saw of Emerson in those early years at the Hosmer Cottage, but it is certain that he opened his library to her as soon as she was old enough to use it. As her father's patron, Emerson was often a visitor at the Hosmer Cottage and Louisa also frequently played with the Emerson children and wrote poems for Emerson's daughter. Louisa May Alcott's first published book, *Flower Fables,* in 1854, was a collection of stories she had told Ellen when they were girls. "Emerson remained my beloved 'Master' while he lived," she wrote, "doing more for me, as he did for many another young soul, than he ever knew, by the simple beauty of his life, the truth and wisdom of his books, the example of good."[13]

Bronson Alcott was hard to idolize, but Waldo Emerson was an easy man to worship. Louisa would walk across town and leave anonymous bunches of wildflowers on his door when she had time in the morning. Sometimes, from the trees she would see him smoking the cigar that his wife did not allow in the house, then putting it out and stashing it in a hollow rail in the fence.

Her connection to Henry David Thoreau was more passionate, and in many ways

Thoreau is the model — as Martha Saxton has suggested in her biography *Louisa May Alcott: A Modern Biography* — for the mischievous boy next door in *Little Women,* Laurie Lawrence. Also, in her novel *Moods,* a young woman is caught in a love triangle with two men: an Emerson-like intellectual and a Thoreauvian naturalist named Adam Warwick who had a "massive head, covered with waves of ruddy brown hair, grey eyes that seemed to pierce through all disguises, and an eminent nose."[14] In the novel as in real life, Warwick/Thoreau's ungainly appearance hid a man in tune with the world and nature, a great heart and a powerful yet innocent intellect.

Many readers and writers have speculated on the real-life models for Louisa May Alcott's characters. Readers of *Little Women,* especially, often talk as if Louisa May Alcott were Jo March, although even basic research shows that this is far from true. Was Laurie really based on Henry David Thoreau or was he based on Louisa's friend Alf Whitman, as she once wrote, or was he perhaps modeled on the Polish pianist with whom she had a whirlwind romance on her first trip to Europe and who followed her to Paris for a heady two weeks when she was thirty-four years old?

What is the connection of fictional characters to the writer and to the people in the world around the writer? My father was a fiction writer who always insisted that the characters in his novels and stories had no connection to the real characters in our lives. He insisted on this even though there were many striking similarities, and even though he sometimes seemed to be reporting as much as he was imagining. My father believed — and many critics agreed with him — that literature had to be read as if it were a self-contained dream. To begin to deconstruct it into the elements of the writer's life was to destroy its power and reduce it to gossip. Of course, most fiction writers use the nuts and bolts of their own experience to build their imaginative mansions, but by taking a character like Laurie apart detail by detail and trying to match him up with what we know about the life of Louisa May Alcott, we certainly violate his delicious, rosy-cheeked, heartbroken, and ultimately redeemed character.

Yet this conflation of art and life is now thought to be an important aspect of studying any work of fiction. Was Dickens a child molester? Was Scott Fitzgerald mean to Zelda? These questions are part of the study of literature as it is taught today. Have we gone too far in trying to bring great works of the imagination down to the detective work we have done on the lives of great writers? Are we robbing ourselves of the knockout experience of reading a great work of literature as if it were a given and not the creation of just another struggling human being?

Reading Louisa May Alcott's papers at the Houghton Library at Harvard, the scholar comes upon repeated requests to destroy the letters one is about to read. Yet there are the letters in question, sorted into neat folders for convenient perusal. The fly-leaf of Abigail May Alcott's journals is sternly inscribed with a similar warning. "Do not loan this book or allow any use of it for publication. Keep in the family *always* or *destroy*. Such were the wishes of Mrs. Alcott, & L. M. Alcott to whom the diaries were given by her mother." Yet I calmly pull the folder over to my laptop and type in the best passages from the journals. Am I bringing the past to life with diligent research? Or am I violating the most intimate wishes of those I revere?

The Hosmer Cottage where the Alcotts

lived for three years is still there next to the railroad bridge built in 1844, a year after the Alcotts left the west side of Concord and went farther west to Harvard, Massachusetts. It's near the Concord River and the docks where canoes can be rented, and the little house has been thoroughly renovated with asphalt shingles and a gleaming yellow façade. Once an outbuilding on a larger farm, it has become a house among houses. Between it and the river there are a dozen new houses, many only a few years old, most built in a kind of inflated architectural version of the clapboard and shutters of nineteenth-century New England. The road going by, which was once a dirt track, is heavily traveled asphalt now; the Hosmer Cottage has security signs on its small front yard although no one seems to be home. Because of the traffic, there is no possibility of stopping even for a minute to gaze at the house where the Alcotts lived in those slower years before the car and the train and electricity and the telephone, in a world we can hardly imagine.

As it became clear that the experiment of living off the land wouldn't work, and as they realized that moving in with the Emersons was also impractical, the Alcotts began to search for another alternative. Alcott began giving the occasional "Conversation," a kind of interactive community talk that would ultimately be his most reliable source of income. Conversations were the movies and dinner theater of New England in the nineteenth century. Many scholarly men traveled around, often stopping at a local Athenaeum, the kind of educational assembly hall in which New England men and women imagined themselves descended from Greek orators and their listeners, or at the house of a town worthy to give their Conversations, which were usually paid by subscription.

Even Margaret Fuller, breaking the mold of masculine supremacy in all things intellectual, gave Conversations, often traveling from city to city on successive nights throughout New England and in New York. A typical Conversation was announced to be on a specific topic: Civil Disobedience, or Socrates, or A Definition of Man. Sometimes the visiting lecturer would stay in town for successive nights and give a series of Conversations.

On the night of a Conversation, at about seven in the evening after an early supper, the town thinkers would gather in a parlor or in a local meeting hall to hear the visiting speaker opine on the announced subject.

They sat in pews or in Hitchcock and Windsor chairs around a table with an oil lamp. Sometimes local sages served as questioners to elicit more thinking from the visitor, or sometimes the audience asked the questions. Alcott with his combination of Connecticut Yankee bearing and the southern manners he had picked up as a peddler on the Virginia plantations was a slightly exotic and wholly confident lecturer. Apparently, onstage he sometimes had a brilliance and immediacy absent in his writing style. "He is very noble in his carriage to all men," wrote Emerson, "of a serene and lofty aspect and deportment."[15]

Alcott's "Conversations" were modeled on his classroom. He took for himself the kind of absolute authority that he had as a schoolmaster. He hoped to encourage the audience to speak for themselves on his subject rather than to harass them with prefabricated ideas, but it was often a sleepy, preoccupied audience. As he spoke, sometimes in vague abstractions, a strange kind of hypnosis sometimes seemed to hang in the air over the listeners. It wasn't that any of what he said made perfect sense, but somehow the whole of the evening — the high-ceilinged room, the uncomfortable chairs, and the drone of his voice — seemed to make sense.

When this magic didn't quite work, when an upstart heckled or questioned him, Alcott sometimes responded with a haughty, wounded silence. During lectures at Emerson's house in Concord, he was sharply questioned by both Henry James and the abolitionist William Lloyd Garrison. Thomas Wentworth Higginson was not a fan. Neither was Theodore Parker, who questioned him sharply on a different occasion. "Parker wound himself around Alcott like an anaconda," Emerson wrote later. "You could hear poor Alcott's bones crunch."[16] Nevertheless, Alcott's "Conversations" continued to draw audiences in and around Boston for decades.

For a while, Bronson flirted with the idea of joining Brook Farm, a commune in nearby Roxbury that was just starting up and had already enlisted Nathaniel Hawthorne. But Brook Farm's founder, George Ripley, required a down payment that the Alcotts didn't have. Bronson had some talks with Emerson about starting a university in Concord, but that idea didn't pan out either. Another small Utopian community in Providence, Rhode Island, invited the Alcotts to join. Led by Christopher Greene, a young man who did not believe in private property, this community had taken Bronson Alcott as one of their figureheads. Bronson visited, but he declined their offer. In the meantime, the family grew hungrier and poorer with every day. In December, Abba's Aunt Hannah came to visit and was shocked by the destitution in which the Alcotts lived. There was no money for necessities and little to eat but sugar, bread, potatoes, apples, and squash.

If Bronson Alcott was always living on a bet, the odds dictated that he occasionally win. This time help came from England, where his books about the Temple School had started an education movement that had been prospering even as he and his family had been starving. Harriet Martineau, one of the sharp-tongued critics of the Temple School back in 1837, had taken *Record of a School* and the fateful *Conversations with Children on the Gospels* home to England with her, where they had been met with excitement and investment.

James Pierrepont Greaves, a former merchant who had studied under Pestalozzi — the same Swiss educational reformer who had been Bronson Alcott's inspiration — had started a school in Ham Common, Surrey. When he read Alcott's two books, he knew he had found someone who agreed with him. Eventually he wrote Alcott an admiring thirty-page letter about his educational principles, and soon he renamed his school Alcott House. Alcott House became a thriving success. In his letters to Concord, Greaves urged Alcott to visit the school that bore his name and carried out his ideas and to meet its headmaster, Henry Gardiner Wright. How could he resist? Alcott's desperation and Greaves's and Wright's admiration obscured their many differences. The Englishmen were businessmen, merchants, and financiers whose money was certainly thrilling for Alcott. They were not overly concerned with philosophy and had far more practical ends than Bronson could ever accept. Even in the matter of the essential nature of children, there were sharp disagreements. Men of Alcott House clung to a belief in the dark side of human nature, and they believed that children were born with the shadow of some kind of original sin. This, of course, was the opposite of the real Alcott's beliefs about children, with their Wordsworthian clouds of glory.

There were other disagreements beneath the surface admiration the Alcott House men felt for Alcott. The school had recently almost been disbanded after a scandal caused by a former parlor maid who ended up as the pregnant wife of Henry Wright. Two of the founders had many problems with women; one, Charles Lane, was in divorce court for three years and currently had custody of his nine-year-old son, William. Their solution to the problem of sex was celibacy. For the men of Alcott House, women were nothing more than temptation, and family was regarded as a myth propagated by those who would distract them from the business of reform and education. Bronson, of course, equated family with God, and his marriage and sex life were sometimes close to a religion for him. But in the heat of the moment, all differences seemed small. As the winter set in, Alcott began planning a trip to England and figuring out how to raise the $500 he would need for the trip.

Emerson, asked for help by Bronson for the umpteenth time, balked. In the 1830s he had been enchanted by Alcott's teaching and Alcott's freedom. Now Alcott was a neighbor, a pensioner, and a needy friend. Alcott, he had come to think, was only truly interested in Alcott. The examples Alcott used to illustrate his ideas always came from his own life, and he seemed ready to abandon everything, even his wife and children, in order to pursue some new idea that was based on nothing more than some high-flown language. "This noble genius discredits genius to me,"[17] Emerson wrote.

Then in January of 1842, Emerson's life changed again forever, shattered by more losses than he could have imagined. The first tragedy struck the Thoreau family at a time when Henry was living happily at the Emersons'. A few days after the New Year, John Thoreau, Henry's beloved older brother, cut his finger with his straight razor while shaving. He thought it was nothing. By the time Concord's doctor looked at the swollen hand a few days later, it was too late to do anything about the tetanus that had taken over John's body. Henry left the Emersons to nurse his brother, who was raving and in terrible pain. He died in Henry's arms. Thoreau, after burying his only brother, seemed to have some kind of breakdown. He also thought he was suffering from tetanus. Slowly he recovered.

Then later in January, Emerson once again was faced with an unthinkable loss when his five-year-old son Waldo contracted scarlet fever. Three days later, the boy was dead, and Emerson grieved fiercely. "All his wonderful beauty could not save him," he wrote to his beloved Aunt Mary Moody Emerson. "My boy, my boy is gone. Fled out of my arms like a dream."[18] That morning the young Louisa dropped by the Emerson house to see if Waldo was feeling better. She never forgot the broken man who answered the door. Gaunt and grey, Emerson was almost unrecognizable when he told Louisa that his son was dead.

After two dreadful deaths and two wrenching funerals, Alcott's needs seemed less burdensome to Emerson. The Alcotts too had lost a son a few years earlier, a boy who had only lived a few minutes but whose birthday was a memorial to him for the rest of Abba Alcott's life. Bronson had been given the sad job of taking the baby's body to the May family plot at the Granary Burying Ground in Boston, near the Temple School. Now, Alcott himself seemed to be in deep trouble. By 1840, he had four girls, a wife whose father had practically disowned her, at least as far as the present was concerned, and who had recently suffered a miscarriage. As always, in spite of her own hard life, Abba Alcott was worried about her brilliant husband. "If his body don't fail, his mind will," she wrote to her brother.

In Concord, as the awful winter wore on, Emerson's old friend Alcott the Hoper seemed less burdensome and cranky. So amid all this grief, only two weeks after the death of his beloved son, Emerson offered Alcott the $500 he needed for a summer at Alcott House in England. He added a letter of introduction to Thomas Carlyle in London, a man whom Emerson had met and also revered. Alcott was thrilled. Once again his hoping had been proved to be correct. "My passage is paid," he exulted in a letter to his wife back in Concord the night before he sailed from Boston to Southampton on the small ship the *Rosalind* on May 7, 1842. "The ten sovereigns are in my red pocketbook, with the bill of exchange for twenty pounds on Baring Brothers & Co."[19] With many letters of introduction and his charm set to stun, Bronson Alcott descended on a London where the reform movement was at its height. Here was a Connecticut Yankee with money in his pocket, letters from the smartest men in America, and a way of listening enraptured by the speaker's ideas. Back in Concord, Bronson's brother Junius moved into the Hosmer Cottage to help with the family.

Bronson would be away for six months of the three years the Alcott family spent in the Hosmer Cottage, and these were months — four of them summer months — which Louisa enjoyed to the fullest. They were months of taking walks with Thoreau, who told her that the cobwebby way the dew formed on the Concord grass in the morning was really handkerchiefs left by fairies, and months of going for long lazy rides in Thoreau's hand-built boat. As they swished down the shallow river, the landscape seemed to come alive when Thoreau pointed out the way the scarlet tanagers lit up the scene, or a great horned owl perched on a log in a way that made it look just like a branch, or a heron stood on one impossibly thin leg in the middle of a sandbar waiting for fish. Louisa was ten years old going on eleven. She was a girl who had experienced some of the most severe deprivation imaginable and plenty of what we now might call abuse, but she was also being schooled in one of the most beautiful places on earth by some of the greatest minds of the century.

Bronson was delighted by London, where he met Carlyle and was feted by the growing leaders of the reform movement. He was even more enchanted by the school at Ham Common named after him. "A week's stay in this abode of divine purposes and loveliest charities, has quite restored me to a good degree of health and vivacity,"[20] Bronson wrote home. Everyone he met pleased him. Visiting the school seemed like a "return home"; it was like being back at the Temple

School, he wrote. Unfortunately his principal admirer, James Greaves, had died in the interim, but there were many other admirers to take his place. The men Bronson met — Henry Gardiner Wright, the headmaster of Alcott House, and Charles Lane, one of its backers — seemed to understand him as he had never before been understood.

Transformed from an obscure, small-town failure, a debtor, and an object of mockery in Concord to a progressive hero in London, Bronson Alcott could hardly believe his luck. "Providentially I was directed hither," he wrote home. Then he referred to a new plan that may have caused sharp ambivalence in his wife and daughters. "Next week we have a meeting of those who are waiting for a new order of things, and this new plantation in America is the topic among others for discourse."[21] Bronson, who had perhaps wisely turned down the possibility of living in other men's Utopias, was now sufficiently confident to imagine that he might start his own. How he could have thought that the problematic Henry Wright and Charles Lane and his son could blend in with his own boisterous family in a tiny cottage in a remote Massachusetts village is hard to imagine. But Bronson, as always, hoped for the best.

So on September 28, 1842, Alcott; Wright, who left his wife and baby behind because of the difficulty of the voyage; and Charles Lane, his son, and his life savings, all set sail on the ship *Leland.* They were headed for Boston with the intention of founding a New Eden, Bronson Alcott's personal Utopia, which he now called the Consociate Society.

At first the great adventure of a personal Utopia created with someone else's money, the third such great adventure of her father's in Louisa's ten years, seemed to go well. Soon enough the little Hosmer Cottage was far too small for the fan club Bronson brought with him. Loyal Emerson had faithfully called at the Hosmer Cottage and invited Wright and Lane to stay in his larger house. They moved into Emerson's house, but they were back within a week. Lane apparently needed to be the man in charge. The Alcotts allowed him to control them; Emerson did not. Emerson slowly came to dislike the two Englishmen, calling them the "two cockerels." Lane and Alcott's plans were a subtle undermining of the community Emerson had imagined he was building in Concord.

As the days grew colder and night came sooner and sooner — and New England winters are brutal — the Hosmer Cottage seemed to shrink. The despotic Lane had become a power in the household, usurping the Alcott parents. Lane was the only one of them who had any money, and this may have contributed to the way Abba and Bronson turned their children over to a regimen of cold baths at 6 A.M., enforced music lessons, study under Mr. Lane, and very little time for running free and indulging in play.

"Circumstances most cruelly drive me from the enjoyment of my domestic life," Abba Alcott wrote in her journal in November after a few months under the rule of Charles Lane. "I am almost suffocated in this atmosphere of restriction and gloom . . . perhaps I feel it more after five months of liberty."[22] If these men were to establish a Utopia, they were off to a bad start. Lane and Alcott began looking for a place in which they might begin a new world order.

Henry Wright was the first defector. At first he had seemed to be missing the wife and baby he had left behind in England, but at a reform meeting he went to with Lane and Alcott, he met a woman named Mary Gove. Mary Gove had been married to an older man whom she despised and had devoted her life to demonstrating for feminist and reform causes. For her it was love at first sight. Soon enough the handsome former headmaster of Alcott House was gone, moved to the parlor of Mary Gove's parents' house in Lynn, leaving his devotion to the future of mankind behind him.

Bronson Alcott's authority was being questioned in his own family, the one place where he had always had a natural and absolute authority. Although less crowded with Wright gone, the Hosmer Cottage atmosphere seemed to breed delusions. Writing of an Edenic, Utopian community, Alcott had speculated, "Providence seems to have ordained the United States of America, more especially New England, as the field wherein this idea is to be realized in actual experience."

The Transcendentalist idea of God, a God who can be found in the song of the thrush or the smile of a friend or the innocent question of a child, was profoundly revolutionary in times when most people felt that God was located firmly in churches, the Bible, and perhaps in an unimaginable afterlife.

But destabilizing God seems to have occasionally been too much for Bronson Alcott; at the Temple School it was the Gospels, taught with a portrait of Jesus at his back that started the trouble. Now, in search of his own earthly kingdom, Alcott seemed to get loonier and loonier. He refused to pay his taxes — much as his friend Thoreau would do two years later — and was arrested by a local official, Sam Staples, who held him in jail until a neighbor bailed him out.

In theory, Bronson Alcott and his family were embarked on the dream of a harmonious community. In practice, they were living in a Yankee version of a banana republic ruled by a petty despot who decreed that plates were a silly luxury, so the family meal of apples and bread was eaten off napkins. Lane also commanded that no one should eat cheese or milk or sugar, and that the family must continue to feed a poor neighbor family even when their own stomachs were growling. Abba Alcott was treated like a servant, responsible for arranging laundry and housekeeping. Then in the evenings, she was expected to listen to Mr. Lane lecturing on the barbarism of the family unit and the predatory nature of women and the evil intoxications of maternal love. Lane decided that he would write for *The Dial.* The dark Hosmer parlor was often filled with men eating Abba Alcott's thrifty cooking, messing up the place, and furiously talking to Charles Lane and planning the future.

Lane and Alcott were part of a movement called Associationism, which originated in France with a philosopher named Charles Fourier. Fourier had laid out very specific plans for communities in which people's best selves would enable them to thrive in an atmosphere of new freedoms and a closer connection with the land. The Hosmer parlor was often crowded with men who might live in the New Eden once it was established: one Mr. Larned who had lived for a year on crackers and another year on apples, and another man who had just been released from an insane asylum, where he had been unjustly imprisoned by his relatives, he said.

Since their marriage, Abba Alcott had been steadfast in supporting her husband. No matter what her husband had done, no matter how often her father warned her away, no matter what her feelings about moving from Germantown to Boston and Boston to Concord in order to accommodate her husband's dreams, Abba Alcott had always believed in Bronson Alcott's genius. Abba hadn't forgotten their courtship, his reticence and the happiness of their connection at a time when she had been all but relegated to the disenfranchised class of Boston spinster. He still dazzled her with his confident looks, his surprising ideas, and his profound moral sense.

Abba and Bronson had a deep connection that would not be severed, but it could be altered. Now, jammed into a tiny isolated cottage with an interloper who despised her and everything she stood for, Abba's feelings began to shift. Her father's last wish had been to separate his money from Bronson's dreams. Torn between two powerful charismatic men, Abba wavered. Whatever she thought of her husband, Abba did not like being contemptuously bossed around by Charles Lane. Things got so bad that on Christmas Eve of 1842, Abba walked out of the Hosmer Cottage and headed for Boston, leaving her four daughters and husband behind. This was the first time that the pressure of Bronson's associates drove Abba out of her own home, but it was not to be the last. In good times, her passionate marriage to Bronson superseded Abba Alcott's devotion to her children. In bad times her anger and disappointment with her husband also eclipsed her obligations to her four daughters.

Abba's departure was a domestic disaster.

Without her, there was no one to care for the children or cook or do the laundry and keep house, all chores which Abba had been doing with no thanks and little respect. Charles Lane took it upon himself to visit the May family in Boston, where Abba had retreated for comfort. Lane charmed the family. Bronson then sat down and wrote a pleading letter to his wife. It worked, and after the New Year, Abba returned to the Hosmer Cottage. Lane treated her with much more respect, writing her persuasive and loving notes, but there was still no question that he had taken over the running of the house and family from its rightful masters. Bronson, a natural autocrat, was somehow in thrall to Lane, perhaps because of his money, perhaps because of his experience, and perhaps because Lane claimed to be a fervent admirer of all things Alcott.

The misery at the Hosmer Cottage that winter also had a profound effect on the lively, irrepressible Louisa. She began to write. On her tenth birthday at the end of November, as the leaves left the trees naked and the cold settled in for good, as the ponds froze over and the wind began to feel like an enemy, her mother gave her a pencil case. Forced inward by Mr. Lane's restrictions and the crowded unhappiness around her, she started with poetry and soon enough began creating a series of gorgeous fantasy tales that she and her sisters would act out when Mr. Lane permitted it. When a child is ten, adult behavior appears to be mysterious, but it is sharply noticed and remembered. Until this winter, whatever else had happened, her father had been the authority in the family and her mother his fan, his believer, and his biggest supporter. As this family constellation began to shift and the family power leeched away from Bronson Alcott into the hands of a stranger, a normal child might respond with anxiety and fear. Louisa began her career as a storyteller. In her stories, for the first time, she christened the Alcotts "the pathetic family."

As soon as the ground began to thaw, Alcott and Lane started looking at possible places where they might reestablish their new world order. They traveled to Lincoln and Milton and Roxbury, and finally in May, Mr. Lane found what he had apparently been looking for: the Wyman Farm in Harvard, Massachusetts, twelve miles west of Concord, a place that made the isolated Hosmer Cottage seem like an urban hub. The farm, with its run-down house and outbuildings, was on a hillside that had a lovely view from the top and not much else. The soil that would feed the colonists in their new world was rocky and sour; there were no roads in the vicinity of the house, and no neighbors close by.

Lane bought the place on May 20, and the deed was signed on May 25. Lane and Bronson named it Fruitlands, and the family started packing to leave Concord. For once, Emerson refused to help financially. In spite of her increasing doubts, Abba Alcott followed her husband's lead. It was a long way from following the man who had recently been the toast of Boston, the educator of the children of the families with whom she had grown up while living in Federal Court, but Abba went willingly one last time. This would be the last time the Alcott family moved in pursuit of an idea. Until Fruitlands, Abba and Bronson had been united in their dreams of educational reform, community reform, and even new ways of raising their children. After Fruitlands the family would change from being devoted to ideals to being devoted to survival. Bronson's high-mindedness would continue, but instead of supporting him emotionally, the women around him had to focus on supporting him and themselves financially.

On an unseasonably cold June 1, 1843, the family packed up their books and the ubiquitous bust of Socrates that had once overlooked the triumphant Temple School and had failed to sell at the auction of the school's effects. Mr. Lane paid off some of the family debts to the villagers of Concord. Abba's brother Sam was persuaded to sign a note for $300 for remaining debts and to become a trustee of Fruitlands, and everything was loaded into a horse-drawn carriage for the trip west.

# 3
# FRUITLANDS. FAMILY IN CRISIS.
## 1843–1848

Good biography scrupulously sticks to the facts. These facts are found in libraries and archives where journals and letters are kept — primary sources, and in other biographies and published books — secondary sources. Yet in spite of this necessary limitation, in spite of the facts, every biography has a story imposed on the facts by the biographer: Bronson Alcott was a genius who loved his girls but couldn't manage to make a living, or Bronson Alcott was a punitive father who traumatized his daughters. Both are true according to the facts. *Little Women* is a great novel, the pouring forth of yearning and talent that came together for a mature woman at the height of her creative power, or *Little Women* was written by a writer who had caved into intense and accumulated financial pressure.

In its own way, biography is more imaginative than the novel and more intimate than memoir. Every biographer reads letters, journals, contemporary accounts, and other biographies to discover the story of their subject's life. Then they illustrate the story they have imagined using the facts that fit. To me the story of Louisa May Alcott is the story of how a woman finds her place in the world. How can women choose between love and work, or should they gamble that they can have both?

There are many biographies of Louisa May Alcott, Bronson Alcott, Abba Alcott, and of the Alcott family. They are piled next to me as I write, bristling with the Post-its I use for notations. As I read them again and again, I come on different versions of events. One biographer will take a letter out of context and move it ten years forward so that its meaning is altered. Another will speculate openly, while a third lines up facts in a way that suggests a different conclusion. Even autobiography is storytelling; facts *chosen* can manipulate the narrative as powerfully as facts *imagined* manipulate the narrative of a fictional story.

Nowhere is this malleability of actual events more evident than in various biographers' descriptions of what happened to Louisa May Alcott and her family between June 1843 and January 1844 when Louisa was ten and eleven and they traveled with the Englishman Charles Lane and his son to a remote farm in Harvard, Massachusetts. Thirty years after the fact, Louisa wrote *Transcendental Wild Oats,* a cheeky, eloquent account of the time between June 1, when the family arrived on a beautiful hillside with a group of colonists and high hopes, to January 6, when they hastily decamped to rented rooms in a neighbor's already crowded house in the tiny crossroads nearby called Still River. Her account features a Charles Lane–like tyrant, Timon Lion, and a Bronson Alcott–like follower and patriarch, Abel Lamb.[1]

Bronson Alcott had wanted to start his community closer to Concord, but Charles Lane insisted on the Wyman Farm, perhaps to get his protégé out of the reach of Emerson's ideas and Emerson's skepticism and Emerson's generosity. At Fruitlands there would be only one patron — Charles Lane.

In 1843 the Wyman Farm was approached by a cart track. These days the road to the farm runs along a ridge well above the farmhouse. In the distance, you can see the mountains of New Hampshire, while nearby Mount Wachussett appears in one of the many folds of green and blue landscape stretching away to the north. But the Fruitlands farmhouse does not have this view. The farmhouse at the top of the ridge belongs to someone else, it wasn't there in 1843, and a road winds down the hill into what feels like a deep green pit or ravine, with the faded red Fruitlands farmhouse at the bottom. Bronson Alcott called this situation "the bowl of Heaven." On a summer day, the air is stifling. On snowbound winter days, this must have seemed to be literally the end of the world.

The Fruitlands farmhouse is only twelve miles due west of the Hosmer Cottage, but it feels as if it is on another planet. For the Alcott girls, there would be no more running down to the edge of the meandering Concord River or walking into town; instead, a wild clamber up a steep 500-foot ridge brought them to a place where they could see and feel their isolation. On arrival, Abba was so surprised by the size of the house that she compared it to a pigsty. The four girls lived under the roof in a crawl space around the central chimney so small that visitors today can only peer into the darkness of it from the top of a narrow staircase.

Still, they were all young — Anna was twelve, Louisa ten, May eight, and Lizzie just two — and soon enough it was the height of a glorious New England summer. In the morning, after a five-thirty cold bath and lessons with Mr. Lane, Louisa was free to hike up the ridge from the house and admire the amazing view. Although to the people at Fruitlands, the outside world seemed impossibly far away, history proceeded with a grim, inexorable pace. The antislavery Liberty Party held its first convention. Alcott family birthdays were always big occasions, and for Lizzie's birthday the family made a woodland bower filled with small presents to which they escorted the happy girl.

Members of the Consociate family began to arrive to crowd into the narrow beds in the small farmhouse and create Bronson Alcott's and Charles Lane's new community. Another Englishman, Samuel Bower, came, hoping to practice his nudist principles in freedom. He was joined by Isaac Hecker, a refugee from Brook Farm, George Ripley's community, which Hecker thought was far too worldly. Hecker, who heard imaginary voices and sometimes suffered from nervous fits — he may have been schizophrenic — had once upon a time been a New York banker. He abandoned the fleshpots of Brook Farm, where residents ate meat and wore leather, for the ascetic valley run by Bronson Alcott and Charles Lane. Ultimately, Hecker became a Roman Catholic priest, but his months at Fruitlands seem to have been a time of mental instability.

Another member of this asylum in the woods was Abraham Everett, who had rechristened himself Wood Abram. Samuel Larned came from the community in Providence that had admired Alcott from afar. For most of the months at Fruitlands, Abba Alcott was the only woman in residence in a world where women did all domestic work without help — now a particularly overwhelming load. Ann Page was the one woman who arrived as company for Abba. "Are there any beasts of burden on the place?" Louisa has her ask Abba Alcott in *Transcendental Wild Oats*. "Only one woman!"[2] replies the exhausted Abba.

But in Louisa's story Ann Page was soon enough expelled from Eden for having sneaked a serving of fish while visiting a neighbor. Eating fish was a flagrant violation of the strict vegan principles at Fruitlands. When questioned about her infraction, Ann Page protested that she had only eaten a bit of the tail of the fish. Louisa May Alcott's Timon Lion turned Old Testament on her. "The whole fish had to be tortured and slain that you might tempt your carnal appetite with one taste of tail."[3]

Another Fruitlands recruit was Joseph Palmer, a neighboring farmer who owned land and ran a butchering business in Fitchburg. Alcott and Lane chose to ignore Palmer's profession in the light of his fervor for their community. Palmer had been jailed for refusing to cut off his beard at some point, and at Fruitlands he found the hirsute freedom he was seeking.

In July, Ralph Waldo Emerson and William Ellery Channing paid a visit to the farmhouse, where things were still going well. But all this excitement was a distraction from the crops that were planned to feed the entire community in the long months of winter. Using an unmatched team of ox and horse — two animals that had presumably given their express permission to be used — Bronson, Lane, and their recruits started planting; but there were so many other things to do. In New England, by the beginning of August, there are cool days in which a slight shift of the light forecasts the deadly cold winter to come. In the end, the only crop that grew at Fruitlands was barley. By the time it had to be picked, the men were off visiting other like-minded communities. The barley had to be haphazardly harvested by Abba and the children using sheets and their own clothing.

By that time, Fruitlands and its eccentricities had become a rich source of local gossip. People said that Bronson would only eat fruits and vegetables that grew above the ground, reaching for heaven, while he disdained the root vegetables that grew downward. Perhaps they exaggerated, but it would have been hard to exaggerate the lengths to which Bronson went in pursuit of the idea of purity. The pathetic family had never been conventional, but dressed in their linen frocks and shoes and living on fruits, vegetables, and grains while only provisionally using animals to plow, the Consociate family certainly reached new heights of weirdness. "[He] held that all the emotions of the soul should be freely expressed," Louisa Alcott wrote later of Isaac Hecker in *Transcendental Wild Oats,* "and illustrated his theory by antics that would have sent him to a lunatic asylum, if, as one unregenerate wag said, he had not already been in one."[4]

By November, Anna, Louisa's older sister, had been shipped off to her grandparents in Boston — it was hard for Abba to part with her and the extra pair of hands, but even one less body to care for was a relief. As soon as the cold set in, both Louisa and William Lane got sick. Bodies exposed to tremendous physical stress and the teeming bacteria colonies of other bodies often break down, and this is what happened to the children at Fruitlands that autumn. The colonists who had been happy to populate this new Eden in the summer fled from the cramped house in the cold months, and Bronson Alcott and Charles Lane were off on their long trips to visit other communities.

In the hope of fostering familial honesty, Abba instituted a family tradition that would survive the Consociate experiment and reappear in *Little Women* — the family post office. Everyone was encouraged to use it to communicate with each other and the group. Abba also used it for little notes of praise and encouragement for those who deserved them. Part suggestion box, part reward system, this box was her way of keeping the family together on many days when it seemed to be flying apart.

Some historians write about Fruitlands and the other Edenic communities fostered by Associationism as part of a desperate, eccentric reaction to the coming of industrialism. By December of 1843, something more important than Lane's ideas had happened in the Alcotts' world — the new railroad had been built as far as Waltham, and it would extend to Concord on the way to Fitchburg by June of 1844. The railroad would bring factories. It would end the real agricultural life that was all Bronson Alcott had known. In reaction, he created a fantasy agricultural life. "Industrialism had spread its first great wave across the countryside," writes Bernard De Voto in his brilliant book *The Year of Decision, 1846*. "The sensitive found only two courses: they could flee from industrialism or they could master it with virtue. . . . The sensitive had reached perihelion at Fruitlands, where the Great Inane voiced thoughts while Mrs. Alcott and the children gathered in the barley, a poor wench was excommunicated for eating a shred of vile flesh, and in the end Alcott turned his face to the wall and hoped to die because virtue had failed."[5]

Whether or not it was a reflection of the end of the agricultural world as they knew it, at Fruitlands that winter the Alcott family had their existential crisis, their long dark night of the soul. Whatever happened there came close to splitting the family apart, causing a permanent emotional distance between Bronson and Abba and the children and further bankrupting them. There on a snowy hillside where they had enjoyed a lovely summer, the family came to a sexual, emotional, and financial turning point that almost destroyed them. On this, all biographers agree. How much of the crisis was sexual and how much domestic and emotional is not as clear. Before Fruitlands, Abba Alcott adored her husband enough to follow him where he led in spite of doubts and disagreements; she worshiped him.

Before Fruitlands, both Abba and Bronson lived in pursuit of a finer world, whether that was expressed in progressive ideas about education or Utopian ideas about community. After Fruitlands, Abba never again overrode her own doubts in order to do what he suggested. Bronson's idealism was no longer the engine of the family but rather an eccentric, sometimes lovable, quirk. The pursuit of ideas and the ability to change the world were modified to become a pursuit of service to others, a worthy goal with less disruption and fewer expenses. Ultimately though, Abba's dedication to service brought on a disaster worse than bankruptcy.

Before Fruitlands, Abba and Bronson had had an apparently happy, straightforward sexual connection. Both agreed with Sylvester Graham that ejaculation was a dangerous loss of male fluids and that sex should occur only once a month; the experience of Fruitlands threatened to darken and distort this forever. As a ten-year-old, Louisa watched and absorbed this radical shift in the power balance of her parents' marriage.

One of the earliest and best biographies of Bronson Alcott, Odell Shepard's 1937 *Pedlar's Progress,* sketches out the problem between the three adults in power at Fruitlands. After visiting a nearby Shaker community run on the principles of the eighteenth-century Shaker leader Mother Ann Lee, Charles Lane's belief that family and marital love are destructive came to a head. Lane felt that Alcott's ties to Abba and his daughters were holding him back. On their long walks from Fruitlands to Providence and Boston, Lane tried to argue Alcott into his own belief that no one could achieve transcendence unless they severed all earthly bonds and lived without family ties as the Shakers did. In the celibate Shaker community, everything was shared, including families. (The Shakers' belief in celibacy is one reason why the once-thriving Shaker communities of New England are no longer with us.)

Charles Lane's conviction, expressed

again and again in the haylofts and spare rooms where the two men slept, was that only by abandoning all temporal and earthly loves could a man ever rise to what Lane called the *love which is divine.* Lane owned Fruitlands and had recently helped pay many of Bronson's debts, and this gave his argument force. He was also a man whose intellect Bronson had much admired and not only because Lane was such a huge admirer of Bronson's ideas.

When Bronson was in residence, Abba Alcott argued the opposite case as if her life depended on it. It did. Family and marriage were the path to spiritual transcendence, she pointed out. In describing this battle for the body and soul of Bronson Alcott, Shepard admits what he doesn't know about the sexual aspects of the struggle. "If the dark truth must be told, they were definitely reticent on this topic," he writes.

At some point, Bronson was forced to choose between what he felt were his higher ideals and his earthly family. "It was a real Gethsemane for Bronson," writes Sandford Salyer in his 1949 biography of Abba, *Marmee.*[6] Both Shepard and Salyer also make the point that the disagreement between Bronson and Lane had broader implications, and was a clash between the community-minded ideas of Europe and the reverence for the individual of the new world. This was a clash that had already led to the American Revolution and was now being relived in the shabby old Wyman Farm that had become Fruitlands. Both biographies suggest that Lane urged Bronson to become celibate, while Abba understood that her sexual relationship with her husband was the basis of the connection that had held them together so long and under so many pressures.

In Madeleine Stern's 1950 biography *Louisa May Alcott,* Stern sidesteps the issue of sex but reports that things at Fruitlands got so heated that Abba Alcott refused to sit down to dinner with Charles Lane even though she had cooked the dinner in question. A family conference in December, described in the young Louisa May Alcott's journal, brought up the question of the family's separation and left Louisa and her sisters going to bed in tears. "In the eve father and mother and Anna and I had a long talk," Louisa wrote in her journal on December 10. "I was very unhappy and we all cried. Anna and I cried in bed, and I prayed God to keep us all together."[7]

A few days later, Abba Alcott played her ace. She announced, with a courage that is

131

hard to imagine, that it was over. She was planning to take the girls and all the furniture that she had donated to Fruitlands. They would move to rented rooms in nearby Still River that her brother had helped her acquire. Would Bronson go with them or would he join Charles Lane in a search for divinity on earth?

"I see no clean, healthy, safe course here in connection with Mr. L.," Abba wrote to her beloved brother Sam in that dreadful winter, adding in another letter to her brother Charles, "I am not dead yet either to life or love, but the last few weeks here have been filled with experiences of the deepest interest to me and my family."[8]

What did she mean? There is no question that Charles Lane and Abba Alcott were fighting for the soul of Bronson Alcott, but were they also fighting for the body of Bronson Alcott?

In her 1980 book *The Alcotts,* Madelon Bedell writes more directly about the possible sexual implications of the Fruitlands struggle. "We must conclude that Abby had begun to suspect that there was an attraction between her husband and Charles Lane that was personal and sexual as well as intellectual,"[9] she writes. In Bedell's account, Bronson was forced to choose between the man he loved and his family — certainly a difficult moment. Instead of being urged to be celibate, he is being urged to leave his wife for his teacher.

Martha Saxton's *Louisa May Alcott,* originally published in 1977, takes a different tack with the same set of letters and journals. Saxton tells a story of a marriage in trouble because of Bronson's desire for sexual freedom. Many biographers have concluded that Bronson was a highly sexual man, partly from his veiled descriptions of male orgasm. Geraldine Brooks's contemporary novel *March* about a fictionalized Bronson Alcott describes him as a man easily and deliciously swayed by women's bodies. Saxton agrees.

Of a visit Bronson paid to Emerson in December, Saxton writes that Emerson was amused by the grandeur of Bronson's manner even in the face of failure and rejection. "Alcott was casting about for new roads to perfection," she writes. "Not for the first time, he talked about abandoning the institution of marriage in favor of free love." Emerson advised him against it. "Bronson wanted the freedom to experiment communally, spiritually and physically," Saxton writes. "He discussed with his family the possibility of breaking up on many occasions."[10] In this version, the problem is not an American passion for individual freedoms, nor is it a sexual attraction to the fiercely intelligent and intolerant Lane. Instead, Bronson wanted permission to be free. He doesn't seem to have had any specific woman in mind, although he had almost certainly met many interesting women on his recent travels with Lane.

A more recent biography speculates that Lane wanted to sleep with Abba Alcott, not her husband. "Bronson Alcott had been driven to the most important decision he would ever make," writes John Matteson of the events at Fruitlands in his Pulitzer Prize–winning biography of Louisa and her father, *Eden's Outcast.* But what was that decision? "Perhaps Lane had decided that the spirit of community extended to the bedroom and was arguing for conjugal privileges," Matteson writes. "No less likely, given Lane's high regard for all forms of self-denial, he was urging Bronson and Abba to abstain from relations with each other. Whether or not Bronson's chastity was at issue, Abba plainly feared for his sanity."[11]

Faced with this decision, whatever it was, Bronson completely collapsed. He took to his bed, turned his face to the wall, and refused to eat for days. But at some point, his optimistic nature reasserted itself, and he asked for bread and water. In her account of Fruitlands, Louisa May Alcott describes his rising like a Phoenix from the ashes of his old self. "My faithful wife, my little girls, — they have not forsaken me, they are mine by ties that none can break. What right have I to leave them alone? What right to escape from the burden and the sorrow I have helped bring?"[12] Louisa has Abel Lamb exclaiming in *Transcendental Wild Oats.*

Louisa's version of the Fruitlands story is bitter and funny. "With the frosts, the butterflies, who had sunned themselves in the new light through the summer, took flight," she writes of the people who had been happy to stay at Fruitlands in the summer months. But for those who were stuck there, "Precious little appeared beyond the satisfaction of a few months of holy living. At first it seemed as if a chance to try holy dying also was to be offered to them." Instead of blaming the disaster on her father or the despised Charles Lane, Louisa reserved her bitterness for those old friends who had deserted them. "Then the tragedy began for the forsaken little family," she wrote. "Desolation and despair fell upon Abel. As his wife said, his new beliefs had alienated many friends. . . . All stood aloof saying, 'Let him work out his own ideas, and see what they are worth.' "[13]

As the dream of Fruitlands vanished, even Emerson kept his distance. After his summer visit, he had written that the experiment that was doing well in July might not be thriving in December. His prophecy had come true. From twelve miles to the east he watched with an admiration that was useless to the starving, beleaguered family. Emerson admired Alcott for his honesty and intellectual ambition; he couldn't help but notice that Alcott had been unable to provide for his family or even for himself. "The plight of Mr. Alcott!" Emerson wrote later. "The most refined and the most advanced soul we have had in New England; who makes all other souls appear slow and cheap and mechanical; a man of such courtesy and greatness that in conversation all others, even the intellectual, seem sharp, and fighting for victory and angry, — while he has the unalterable sweetness of a muse!"[14]

On January 6, Lane and his son, under pressure of the Alcotts' impending departure, left to live with the Shaker community. Abba wrote her brother exultantly, "All Mr.

Lane's efforts have been to disunite us. But Mr. Alcott's conjugal and paternal instincts were too strong for him."[15] Abba had beaten Lane. Her husband once again belonged to her and her daughters, but the shifts that occurred in that remote snow-bound farmhouse would be played out for the rest of their lives together.

By the middle of January, Fruitlands was abandoned; the Alcott family moved to a house on Hog Street in Still River rented from the Lovejoy family and paid for with labor from Bronson, who chopped wood, and Abba, who took in sewing. (Later, Lane was able to sell the Wyman farmhouse to former Consociate family member Joseph Palmer.) During the summer and autumn months, Abba had befriended the Lovejoys, and the move was financed by her sale of a silver piece that had been a gift from a friend, a cloak, and a $10 bill sent by her brother Sam. The Lovejoys had been stalwart friends during the last months at Fruitlands, visiting back and forth with Abba and her daughters and refusing to believe any of the local gossip about the weird doings at the old Wyman farmhouse.

By spring Abba had moved her family, which still included Bronson, from the rented rooms to a larger place, half a house in Still River called the Brick Ends. Louisa and Anna were enrolled in Miss Chase's village school, where the neighborhood children, and games and lessons appropriate to children, seemed more Edenic than anything at Fruitlands. Hundreds of pages have been written by biographers about the six months the Alcotts spent at Fruitlands, but the eight months the family spent recovering in Still River are usually given only a few paragraphs. Not much happened to the family in this peaceful interlude of rest and recuperation from the dreadful last days at Fruitlands. For once, the Alcotts had a chance to behave like a normal family, and Louisa seemed to relish this. Children love children, and in Still River the Lovejoys and the Gardner family children as well as the children at the school were supplemented by Llewellyn Willis, a boarder at the school who was taken in by Abba. Even in a crisis, she never stopped being as hospitable as if she were running an inn.

By July of 1844, Bronson was off again, but this time he took the thirteen-year-old Anna along with him as a companion, traveling to western New York to visit his mother and, as he wrote back, to investigate other possible communities that might interest him. It's not hard to imagine Abba's feelings of dismay when she got a letter from Bronson saying that he was planning to visit Mottville, a Utopian community in Onondaga County run by a man named John Collins. "At the latter place are a few persons whose plans deeply interest me."[16]

When we make mistakes, we often blame them on a decision we made, a road not taken. If only we had not listened to this friend or been swayed by that one. If only we had not swept aside our reservations about something in the enthusiasm of the moment. Bronson, a chastened idealist, was torn between loyalty to his old idea of a perfect community and regret for what he had lost. Remorse was never a powerful feeling for this optimist, who had invented himself whole-cloth as an intellectual complete with broad-brimmed hat. Still he confided in his brother Junius that the failure of Fruitlands had made him feel abandoned. "For I am all alone again; and you seem the sole person in the wide world, designed as faithful coadjutor — a lover of the Excellent and willing to join in the attainment of the same day by day." Even surrounded by his own adoring, resilient family, he seems to have felt alone. He hadn't given up his idea of a perfect community and, as he wrote to Junius sounding very much like his old self, he considered joining some of the other communities in Massachusetts but "they aim at little, and are but new phases of the spirit of the Old Society."[17] As the humbling days at Still River rolled into summer, a summer that was worlds away from the victorious summer before at Fruitlands, Bronson wondered if his mistake had been in leaving Concord. Concord understood him; Concord was a place where ideas and idealism were honored.

So in November the Alcott family headed back to Concord. They had moved from Fruitlands to Still River in the middle of winter by ox sled. Now they boarded the stagecoach that ran from town to town pulled by four lackadaisical post horses; the coach went about 10 miles an hour. Louisa sat on the roof of the coach above the huge wheels and between the carriage lamps next to the bench for the driver.

About halfway from Still River to Concord, the Alcott family made a change that may well have symbolized their entrance into the modern world. They left behind an agricultural, patriarchal past; they entered an industrial future where women's power would often equal, if only quietly, the power of their husbands. They unloaded themselves from the stagecoach and boarded the train — their first train ride. The train on the Fitchburg Line, which had opened with great fanfare on Bunker Hill Day, June 17, provided four trains a day at a third the cost of Deacon Brown's old stage and at more than twice the speed. The train, still traveling at a pokey 20 miles an hour, would eventually bring the world to Concord, but on that day it only brought the Alcotts.

In the war between the old agricultural ways and the new mechanized ways, the train was the decisive weapon. When the train came through town, first in the form of a swarm of workers who laid the track, and then in the form of the actual cars, Concord's intellectuals all wrote obligatory attacks on the railroad. At Walden Pond, part of which had been filled in to accommodate the tracks which he could see from his hut, Henry David Thoreau wrote that "the iron horse makes the hills echo with his snort like thunder, shaking the earth with his feet, and breathing fire and smoke from his nostrils."[18] Ralph Waldo Emerson wrote a jeremiad about men being transported in boxes. Then he shrewdly also bought some railroad stock. Emerson, Alcott, and a council of the town's leaders wrote a furious complaint to the railroad's general manager while the tracks were being laid. "The No. branch of the Concord River is our 'Central Park' and one of the most beautiful pieces of simple scenery in New England. We feel it is bad enough to have a railroad at all in that place, but the ruthless destruction of a single tree, or shrub, for fire wood or any purpose not absolutely necessary . . . will be viewed by all as barbarism."[19]

Concord's intellectuals could see that industrialization might also be a blessing for them, bringing their Cambridge and Boston friends closer and, in Emerson's case, broadening the scope of his lecture circuit, which was now his primary source of income. In fact, most of Concord found it hard to resist the seductions of the new, especially since in this case the railroad made it possible to go to Boston for the day. The trip, once a dusty and miserable three to four hours, was reduced to a relatively comfortable hour.

Agricultural Concord, once an isolated hub for the Concord and Assabet river valleys, soon became connected to a network of providers and buyers; by 1846 a milk train had been added to the morning train and Concord farmers began shipping their milk to Boston. In the winter, the ice on Walden Pond was stacked up on straw and sent off to the city on the afternoon train. The railroad also developed an area of Concord that not many tourists see. Its history is not that of the American Revolution but of the Industrial Revolution. Just west of town, the combination of water power from the Assabet and the new railroad line came together in a small cluster of mills, two sawmills, a factory which made lead pipe, Damon's fabric mills, and a powder mill, which occasionally exploded. Although West Concord never approached the scale of Lowell, Massachusetts, or Manchester, New Hampshire, to the north, it changed the feel of the center of Concord from being at the heart of a world of farmers to being at the edge of a world of manufacturing.

By Thanksgiving, the Alcott family had resettled in Concord, renting rooms from the Edmund Hosmer family again in the big house next to their old cottage. But the family who returned from Fruitlands and Still River was a different family than the one that had disappeared to the west just a little more than a year earlier. Bronson's blond hair had turned to gray and he was stooped over. He had not stopped feeling

sorry for himself. Some introductory enqui-
ries that he made about starting a school in
Concord were soundly rebuffed. Later the
Teacher's Institute, led by another educational reformer, Horace Mann, who had
married Mary Peabody, met at the Concord
courthouse for a ten-day session. Had Mary
forgotten what had happened between the
Alcotts and her sister Elizabeth? Alcott
eagerly went to the meetings and was told
that he was not welcome. The brilliant
educator of 1837 was an outcast. "I am
looked upon with distrust," he confided to
his journal. "And while there is little hope
of aiding forward mankind save by forming
the young, I am prohibited from com-
munication with these. How am I to work?"
And later, "O God! How long wilt thou not
permit me to be useful to my fellowmen,"
he wrote. "How Long, O Lord! How long
wilt thou try me."[20]

Of course, the biggest change was in the
four Alcott daughters. "It was the children
who had changed the most. Marked, all of
them by the drama of separation and recon-
ciliation that had taken place at Fruitlands,
they were, as children brought up in isolated
families often are, older and more sophisti-
cated,"[21] writes Madelon Bedell in *The Alcotts.*

The sisters were Alcotts first and girls second. Louisa took this literally, acting whenever she could as if she had been born a boy. She climbed trees, ran and jumped, and took dares — once rubbing red peppers in her eyes. In a rage, she could destroy a friend's pen or pour whale oil on her hair. She loved all animals, especially spiders, those creepy, crawly creatures that make most girls scream.[22]

Louisa was the clear leader, the one who organized games and plays and the one who told stories. In looks and temperament, she was like her mother, who often gave her gentle talks about controlling her temper. This had always been a problem. In the detailed notes he took about his infant children, her father had written about Louisa's obstinacy of temper. Like her mother, she had a sense of herself as an aristocrat in temporarily straitened circumstances.

By now, as a mature thirteen-year-old, Louisa was writing stories to add to her journals and letters. She would be a writer; she would be an actress. Louisa wanted to be famous, as famous as Jenny Lind, she said, and her sisters believed that one day she would be.

In May of 1845, after a winter with the

Hosmers, Abba got a letter from her cousin Samuel Sewall that once again changed everything. Her father's will had been settled and what was left of his estate ready to be distributed. His wish that none of his money would be used to pay Bronson's debts had been successfully skirted. In return for a percentage of what they were owed — $2,000 on a $6,000 debt — Bronson's Temple School creditors had agreed to drop their claims. After that, what was left of Abba's remaining small legacy was actually hers. Enlisting their friend and neighbor Emerson as a scout and a lender — he offered to contribute an additional $500 this time — the family began to look for a new house in Concord. For the first time in almost a decade, they were actually solvent.

At first Emerson offered them one of his new woodlots on Walden Pond, but eventually the family settled on a run-down house for sale by Horatio Cogswell, a wheelwright. This house on the Lexington Road had a fine pedigree; it had been owned by Samuel Whitney, the muster master of the Minutemen during the Revolution. Yet the house had known hard times in the intervening years; it had served as a trading post and, more recently, as a pig farm. It fronted directly on the road half a mile uphill from the Emerson's house, with 10 feet of shoulder separating it from the traffic between Concord and Boston.

Frustrated by his inability to teach, Bronson Alcott threw his energy into improving the new house, and it certainly needed improvement. He cut the old wheelwright building in two, hoisted it up on a set of wheels, and moved one-half to the other side of the house. He began extensive planting and terracing. He moved a barn from the other side of the road to a spot next to the kitchen end of the half of the wheelwright shed. Twenty fruit trees were rooted in the sandy soil. The land on the other side of the road was turned into a thriving vegetable garden.

On the steep hillside behind the house, Bronson began what would be one of his largest and most lasting projects, a dozen terraces dotted with benches and fanciful shelters. At the top of the ridge he built a larger gazebo, a curved shape that he wove, basketlike, out of saplings and osier so that its curved lines seemed to grow out of the surrounding landscape. That ridge and its transformation into a picturesque spot was one of the things that enchanted everyone who lived in the house after the Alcotts had left. In the new house, at Hillside, Louisa got something she had wanted for a long time — a room of her own. It was a small dark room with one window at the back of the house, perfectly situated for bursting out the back door and scrambling up the bank into the woods.

Louisa was an intense, intelligent girl on the verge of womanhood. Dark-haired and tall, she had not yet learned — she would never learn — the arts of femininity. "I have at last got the little room I have wanted so long, and I am very happy about it," she wrote in her March journal after the family move. "It does me good to be alone. . . . I have made a plan for my life, as I am in my teens, and no-more a child. I am old for my age and don't care much for girls' things. People think I am wild and queer, but Mother understands and helps me."[23] She was outspoken, well read, and prone to temper tantrums. She was smarter than almost everyone else, and she didn't mind letting them know that. In spite of her mother's support, she was often in trouble with her parents.

The Alcott family had already moved ten times, and Louisa could look back on at least three triumphant starts that had slowly turned to desperate failures. She revered her father, but in the family hierarchy even Louisa — especially Louisa — must have sensed that his masculine, intellectual idealism had failed so dramatically that the women must now take over. Abba Alcott was very good at taking over, and she raised at least one daughter who was also a born leader. But what is it like to be a thirteen-year-old on the brink of sexuality who is better equipped to lead a family than to settle down with a husband?

Anna at fifteen was already beautiful and attracting the notice of the men who visited the family or who saw her in Boston. Blond and accommodating, she was able to appear fascinated — or actually be fascinated — by the men who crossed her path. Louisa had no such gift. If a man said something idiotic, it was hard for her to hold her tongue. Her erotic idols were men who would never fully reciprocate: the dreamy naturalist Thoreau and the older, thrillingly powerful and intelligent Emerson.

Then as now, thirteen is a critical age for a girl. It is at this age, as feminist writer Carol Gilligan among others has explained, that girls begin to lose their original voices. They are mercilessly pressured by the world around them, the impossible models provided by society, their parents' expectations, and the landslide of feelings and opinions released by their emerging, delicious, and unconscious sexuality. Under this onslaught of expectation, many young girls are pushed away from their original childhood selves and become silent hybrids, creatures molded so much by their environment that it is hard to recognize who they really are. "Girls in our society learn early on that they are expected to behave in certain ways," writes pediatrician Berry Brazelton in an analysis that might apply to Louisa as well as anyone in the twenty-first century. "Girls are expected to be compliant, quiet and introspective. They soon learn that they should suppress any open expression of aggression or even strong non-compliant feelings. They also learn . . . to value relationships more than rules."[24]

In 1845 the pressures on young women to conform to a feminine ideal that would be attractive to men were more severe than they are now. At puberty both the older Alcott girls understood that in some people's eyes they were the family's greatest assets. By marrying the right man, either of them could end the financial pressures that still clouded every family decision.

Louisa May Alcott resisted these pressures, and her resistance was made easier because she lived in a family that was laughed at and pilloried by the forces that sought to mold her. The Alcotts relished being different and unconventional. They were the pathetic family and proud of it. After an afternoon in which her new tutor, Sophia Foord, and her sisters went tramping through the woods destroying their clothes and getting thoroughly wet, Louisa wrote her friend Sophia Gardner back in Still River, "We are dreadful wild people here in Concord, we do all the sinful things you can think of."[25]

One of the "sinful" things that happened in the winter of 1846, a sin of which her family was especially proud, was sheltering a runaway slave on his way from Maryland to Canada. The slave's name was John. Bronson described him as "an amiable intelligent man just seven weeks from the House of Bondage."[26] The Alcotts welcomed the fugitive, and he lived, more or less hidden, at the house until arrangements could be made for him to travel north. While he was there, Emerson dropped by. Bronson probably took John along on one of his regular Sunday visits to Thoreau's hut at Walden Pond. Some biographers speculate that Thoreau used his cabin on Walden Pond as a stop on the Underground, although clearly it did not provide good hiding places. "Some who had more wits than they knew what to do with," Thoreau writes of his visitors to Walden, "run-away slaves with plantation manners, who listened from time to time, like the fox in the fable, as if they heard the hounds a baying on their track."[27]

Many in Concord were not sympathetic to the abolitionist cause at the time. This was before the Fugitive Slave Act of 1850 made it possible to break the law in your own house by practicing hospitality. That revised act made it a crime not to turn in a man's property — an escaped slave — even if the slave had made it as far as Massachusetts. Before then, to many people it seemed as if the best thing to do with the problems of the South was to let the South solve them. Bronson Alcott and Henry David Thoreau never wavered. They were always ready to help the runaways and always fiercely clear about the value of human life whatever the color of the human's skin or the "ownership" the person might officially have to deal with. Both men knew that no one owns anyone, and they were pioneers in this furious, beneficent belief. In education and in human rights, Bronson Alcott was a man whose convictions — convictions formed somehow in the progress from farmer to schoolmaster — were way ahead of his time. No one could budge him. This courage was one of the things that Emerson so admired.

While Bronson worked on conversations and sayings in his front parlor, his moody, romantic, daughter poured her energy into stories in the back room. Beset with feverish dreams of fame and love, Louisa came into her own as a woman while the family lived at Hillside. At first, when the dreaded Charles Lane returned to visit for a few weeks, she found Hillside to be too crowded. "More people coming to live with us," she wrote in her journal. "I wish we could be alone and no one else. I don't see who is to clothe and feed us all, when we are so poor now." But a few days later, after a run in the Concord woods, she felt her heart lift in the rustling of the pines and the view of the hills. "My romantic period began," she wrote later of this time in Concord, "when I fell to writing poetry, keeping a heart-journal and wandering by moonlight instead of sleeping quietly."[28]

In her own room at last, Louisa mooned to think of Emerson sleeping in his solid white house down the way. In his library, Emerson pointed out to the impressionable Louisa Goethe's recently published *Cor-*

*respondence with a Child,* a book of letters from the thirteen-year-old Bettina von Arnim to her "master," Johann Wolfgang von Goethe. This book, about a presumably platonic love affair between a young teenager and her much older love, was a sensation in New England in 1843. Many young girls wrote "Bettina" letters to older men. Louisa began wandering dreamily down to the Emerson's house at all hours of the day and night, and haunting the library. At home she read and began her own writing and dreamed of Emerson. Emerson, although he probably didn't respond to Louisa with the physical hugs and kisses that Goethe lavished on his Bettina, seems to have been affected by his neighbor's longing. "Give all to love," he wrote that fall, although he may have been thinking more of the elusive, sexual adult Margaret Fuller than of the all-too-present adolescent Louisa.

Obey thy heart:
Friends, kindred, days,
Estate, good-fame,
Plans, credit and the Muse —
Nothing refuse.[29]

In and out of school and tutored by

anyone who volunteered, the four Alcott girls had enough time to write stories and put on increasingly elaborate plays for anyone who cared to attend. "Love, despair, witchcraft, villainy, fairy intervention, triumphant right, held sway in turn," remembered Edward Emerson, one of the Emerson children who eagerly played along with the Alcott girls. "In those days a red scarf, a long cloak, a big hat with a plume stolen from a bonnet, a paper-knife dagger, a scrap of tinsel from a button card, a little gold paper for royalty, tissue paper stretched on wire hoops for fairy wings, produced superb effects."[30] The new barn became Louisa's Globe Theater and the residents of Concord her audience.

The barn is now the visitor center of the National Park Service, and the ranger who gives tours of the house repeatedly emphasizes that Louisa May Alcott was indeed Jo March. Certainly the events that became the basis for *Little Women* happened at Hillside — later renamed the Wayside — in the three and a half years the Alcott family lived there, years in which Louisa spent a lot of her time writing in the little room at the back of the house.

When she went to write about these years, twenty years later, she transposed the events of the 1840s to the house next door, Orchard House, which has now become a shrine to *Little Women.* She made the Alcotts the Marches. She would be more famous than Jenny Lind, and that fame would be tied to a ramshackle clapboard house she passed hundreds of times without noticing it. It was the Moores' house in those days, surrounded by elms and too close to the busy road.

When Emerson was away, Louisa's longing had another, shaggier object, Henry Thoreau, who was also a hero and close friend of her father's. In the spring of 1845, at Emerson's suggestion, Thoreau began building a hut on a woodlot of Emerson's on the shore of Walden Pond. The Alcotts and the Hosmers were among the neighbors who helped Thoreau raise the timbers. From July 4, 1845, to September 6 of 1847, with time out for a trip to Maine, Thoreau lived at the northwest edge of Walden Pond in the hut he built in a clearing near Wyman's Meadow. The site was in a small rise looking out at the deepest part of the pond, which legend contended was bottomless but which Thoreau had measured at 102 feet.

To the west, Thoreau had a clear view of the shoreline that had been filled in to accommodate the new railroad track. To the east, he looked into the woods where Route 2 now funnels drivers on their way to Boston. Some of his nearest neighbors as the crow flies were the Alcotts at Hillside. A series of well-worn paths led to their house at the bottom of a ridge, and he often dropped in on them on his walks into town. Their three and a half years at Hillside — critical years in Louisa's young life — coincided with his two years, two months, and two days at Walden. Bronson Alcott and his daughter often returned Thoreau's visits. What seemed like a short walk — just over a mile — brought this passionate young woman face-to-face with the man who had first shown her the miracles of nature, a man who reminded her of the perspective of the natural world. "Young women seemed glad to be in the woods," Thoreau wrote after a visit. "They looked in the pond and at the flowers and improved their time."[31]

Bronson also made many visits to Walden that Thoreau wrote about in the journal that became his book. "I should not forget that during my last winter at the pond there was another welcome visitor, who at one time came through the village, through snow and rain and darkness, till he saw my lamp through the trees, and shared with me some long winter evenings," Thoreau wrote. Alcott provided good company; Thoreau provided some much-needed admiration. "One of the last of the philosophers — Connecticut gave him to the world," Thoreau wrote. "He peddled first her wares, afterwards as he declares, his brains. . . . I think that he must be the man of the most faith of any alive. His words and attitude always suppose a better state of things than other men are acquainted with."[32]

Alcott and Thoreau, in spite of their differences in background, had a common love of upbeat aphorisms. Some of the phrases in *Walden* read like clearer, better-written versions of Alcott's "Orphic Sayings." "However mean your life is, meet it and live it. . . . It looks poorest when you are richest."[33] Thoreau did not move to Walden Pond to write *Walden;* while living at Walden Pond, he planned to work on his book about a river trip with his beloved brother John, who had died in 1842.

In the winter of 1846, after the move to Walden, Thoreau gave a lecture on Emerson's friend the English writer Thomas Carlyle. Like Emerson, Carlyle believed that the world was populated with great men from whom all others might learn. Thoreau began to form a more universal idea of what a hero might be. "Are we not all great men?" he wrote, as he developed the idea of a hero as an ordinary man, a man who would represent everyone. "Working himself slowly free of the still-admired friends, Thoreau's next book presented himself as American hero," explains Robert Richardson in his wonderful biography of Thoreau. Thoreau and Emerson; Thoreau and Bronson Alcott; Emerson and Hawthorne — each of the brilliant writers and thinkers in the Concord community had inestimable effects on each other's work. Louisa May Alcott was there, soaking up information about the simplicity of great writing and the possibility of an ordinary character becoming a hero or heroine.

By 1848, the wolf again appeared at the door of the Alcott house. Abba's inheritance had been spent on the original purchase of Hillside, but not enough money had been set aside for the family living expenses. Bronson's garden produce was delicious but scarce even in the summer. Abba and her daughters' sewing and teaching were not enough to support the family. As the winter approached in New England, as the air began to cool and the leaves turn their brilliant golds and reds, as the light began to fade earlier in the day and the apples ripened and fell from the trees, Abba Alcott became more and more determined to move.

Visiting friends who were shocked at the poverty of the Alcott family in Concord organized a job for Abba in Boston as the head of a new charity. The job would enable her to support her family — a task that her husband was clearly unable to accomplish even with income from his daughters. In October, a former patron of Bronson's, Mrs. James Savage, visited the family in Concord and urged them to move. Would they leave Hillside empty? That week a tenant offered to rent the house for $150 a year. Abba and Bronson had talked of splitting the family again, but this way they could all be together in Boston.

Louisa, visiting friends, found out about the move when she got a letter from her father announcing that her family had left Concord and settled in three cramped rooms on Dedham Street, and that he would be giving Conversations on West Street above Elizabeth Peabody's bookstore.

No one thought to consider Louisa, nor did she think of herself, either as a sixteen-year-old girl or later as a fifty-year-old woman. With the Alcotts, family came first and individuals came second. Bronson had created a powerful family myth, and individual problems were swept away when it came to the good of the family or the survival of the family. They were Alcotts. So Louisa gave up her favorite thinking place, an old cart wheel half hidden in the grass where she used to go to work out her stories or rail at her fate and promise the gods that she would amount to something, somewhere, somehow. She gave up the space to run free and her friendships and her connection to the natural world, all without thinking twice. Although she was still the age of many students, she resolved to be a teacher in the city.

"My sister and I had cherished fine dreams of a home in the city," she wrote in her *Recollections* years later, "but when we found ourselves in a small house in the South End with not a tree in sight, and no money to buy any of the splendors before us, we all rebelled. I was left to keep house, feeling like a caged sea-gull as I washed dishes and cooked in the basement kitchen where my prospect was limited to a succession of muddy boots."[34] Until the move to Boston, Louisa had somehow avoided feeling the straitened circumstances and desperate scrimping and saving and occasional brinksmanship by which Abba and Bronson kept the family going. Now, she understood.

All the family theatricals and stories written for fun could not obscure the family poverty.

"We were now beginning to play our parts on a real stage," she wrote, "and to know something of the pathetic side of life with its hard facts, irksome duties, many temptations and daily sacrifice of self."[35]

# 4

# BOSTON. "STICK TO YOUR TEACHING."

## 1848–1858

Eighteen forty-eight was a year of European revolution and colonial expansion. In France the workers revolted and unseated Louis-Philippe. In Austria, Italy, and Germany, liberal revolutions unseated emperors and kings, and Karl Marx and Friedrich Engels issued *The Communist Manifesto,* an appeal to workers everywhere to throw off their chains. The workers responded. The spirit of revolution swept right across the Atlantic and inspired the second-most-oppressed class of Americans — women.

Although the domestic slavery of women in the nineteenth century was hidden by the institution of marriage and family, and not as severe as the institution of southern slavery, it was an appalling source of injustice. American women had almost no legal privileges. They could not own property or vote. They were essentially owned by their fathers, who passed them on to their husbands as if they were possessions. The disaster of the Civil War would sweep away all talk of women's rights for at least a decade, but in the 1840s women were as eager to work for justice at home as they were to fight for justice in the South.

In July of 1848, while the Alcotts ate produce from Bronson's garden, a convention of 300 women and a few men gathered in the Wesleyan Chapel at Seneca Falls, New York, to issue their own manifesto. Led by Lucretia Mott and Elizabeth Cady Stanton, and inspired by Margaret Fuller's *The Great Lawsuit: Man versus Men, Woman versus Women,* first published in *The Dial,* the convention issued a Declaration of Sentiments. This was based on the Declaration of Independence, replacing that declaration's anger at King George with an indictment of "all men."

The sentiments in this declaration are not polite, accusing men of oppression of all kinds, including the denial of the right to vote, and the imposition of laws in the formation of which women had no voice. "He has withheld from her rights which are given to the most ignorant and degraded men," it reads. "He has made her, if married, in the eye of the law, civilly dead."[1] Inspired by Quaker teachings and by Tran-

164

scendentalism, the women of Seneca Falls began a movement that would parallel abolition in fits and starts during the second half of the century.

For Louisa May Alcott, female equality was both a longed-for dream and a foregone conclusion. She lived in a family of women run by a woman; by this time Bronson's power as the head of the family had been diminished to almost nothing. Yet she had no formal education, and college was not open to her. The jobs available for a young single woman were domestic and often demeaning. Even teaching was often glorified babysitting. It required no formal degree and was usually done by young women.

The Boston to which the family returned was a different city than the one they had left for Concord when Louisa was a little girl. No longer a protected agricultural provincial capital and sleepy seaport, Boston had become a swirling center of world events. The Alcotts returned to Boston on the promise of a salary Abba could make by running a mission for the poor. The mission also became an employment office. The community of poor families Abba knew from doing good works as a girl from Federal Court were very different than the poor who flooded Boston in the early 1840s. Industry had created thousands of low-level jobs in the mills and factories both in Boston and in outlying towns, and these jobs attracted families who were then barely able to support themselves. At the same time, these industries had created new wealth for a few owners and managers, and as the slums expanded, so did the mansions of the new rich as they marched down Commonwealth Avenue and up Beacon Hill.

Nearly 50,000 refugees from the Irish potato famine flooded the city, almost doubling its population in just a few years. By 1850, 26 percent of the population of this once high-minded, homogeneous city was made up of uneducated, untrained Irish immigrants and immigrant families. In Boston they lived in appalling conditions, often fourteen people to a room. The exiled Irish were farmers who had only agrarian skills, illiterate people who often had nothing to lose and brought with them their foreign religion — Roman Catholicism. Many of them made scant livings legally selling liquor — this in a city where temperance had previously thrived. Because of the crowded quarters and unsanitary living conditions of the immigrants, smallpox and cholera, which had been well controlled, now swept the city in a series of epidemics.

Earlier in the century, a different kind of Irish immigrant had built the railroad and helped construct the thriving city of Boston. In those days, in the 1830s and early 1840s, Boston was being built on land reclaimed from the sea, and a building boom depended on cheap labor. The immigrants of 1848 were a new and desperate kind who had fled from their own country after witnessing the horrors of the potato famine, a holocaust of starvation.

The potato blight had begun at the end of the summer of 1846, spreading through Ireland and rotting potatoes before they could be pulled from the ground in the harvest months of August and September. Thousands of Irish families left, many on infamous "coffin ships"; hulks so heavily insured by their British owners that they were worth more if they sank than if they survived. Nevertheless, so many ships made it to Canada that the St. Lawrence River was backed up with ships and floating bodies.

Then in the summer of 1848 when Irish farmers, thinking the blight had passed, planted nothing but potatoes, the blight came back with a vengeance. This time tens of thousands of the remaining people who weren't too sick or debilitated to move boarded ships for new ports, one of them being Boston.

Abba Alcott arrived in Boston and opened her Mission and Relief Room on Washington Street just in time to receive the masses of new, starving poor. This flood of strangers with their insuperable problems threatened to overwhelm even the great and charitable heart of Abba Alcott. As a Protestant from Puritan stock, she was prejudiced against the Catholic Church, yet she couldn't turn her back on the needy Irish families.

In Boston, cooped up in tiny rooms in a crowded city, the Alcott family's robust psychological health again began to break apart under the force of circumstance. There was no gorgeous natural world to balance the indignities and ugliness of the city, no distinguished and loving Emerson and playful Thoreau to talk with about what was happening. Daily teaching that Louisa took on as well as the housework was exhausting. "Every day is a battle, and I'm so tired I don't want to live; only it's cowardly to die till you have done something. I can't talk to anyone but my mother about my troubles, and she has so many now to bear I try not to add any more. I know God is always ready to hear, but heaven's so far away in the city."[2] She was of an age when another girl might be thinking of parties, frocks, and eligible men, but the Alcotts' situation instead compelled her to think about how they would eat and pay the rent.

Bronson Alcott, although he pulled himself together to give his Conversations on West Street, had patched up things with Elizabeth Peabody, and had even been made the librarian of a new intellectual club — the Town and Country Club — began to veer toward the emotional extremes that were all too familiar to his family. Abba could do little more than provide physical support as her husband began to unravel. He began working feverishly on a series of arcane charts showing invisible forces. He refused to sleep or eat. He thought he was God. "Bronson was experiencing mental states and visions that suggest a frighteningly disturbed mind,"[3] writes biographer John Matteson in his chapter about these years, titled "Destitution."

Louisa's only respite was the family gatherings of parents and sisters at the end of the day, gatherings that she often enlivened with a drama performed by the four girls: *The Captive of Castile,* or *The Moorish*

169

*Maiden's Vow.* Sometimes the sisters acted out Shakespeare, memorizing long speeches for these evening performances. Louisa began to dream of acting her way out of poverty. Her other dream, which gathered steam during the first desperate winter in Boston, was to be a writer. She began keeping a record of everything she earned each week.

Louisa May Alcott's first novel, *The Inheritance,* was written before she was twenty. A short romantic Cinderella story written in girlish, sentimental prose, it is weirdly enlivened by the desperate feelings of its author. The heroine of the novel, Edith Adelon is a penniless orphan working on an English country estate for the fabulously wealthy Hamilton family. As it turns out — as it so often turns out in fiction about penniless young women — Edith is the true heir to the Hamilton estate, where she has been working as a servant. Yet the family has treated her lovingly. When the document proving her legitimacy comes to light, Edith tears the document to pieces. "She tore the will and, with a calm smile on her pale face and a holy light in her soft eyes that shone through falling tears, she dropped the fragments saying, 'Now I am the poor orphan girl again. Can you love me for myself alone?' " Of course they can, and a handy nobleman stands by to rescue Edith from her self-imposed poverty.

This fantasy of a double rescue from poverty and from the mindless adoration accorded the wealthy reflects Louisa's deep confusion about both money and fame. In a contest between money and her family's love, including her father's often ambivalent feelings, family would win every time. At the same time, the Alcott family was starving to death. And the Alcotts were as proud as they were poor.

Bronson had made a kind of religion out of the family, and his daughter Louisa was one of the principal worshipers at that sometimes bankrupt shrine. After all, in not going with Charles Lane after Fruitlands ended, Bronson had chosen his family. Only by elevating that choice to spiritual status was he able to make sense of his life.

No matter what their circumstances, Alcotts always remembered their principles. Although many women like the Alcott sisters might have angled to marry for money or security, that was not what Alcotts did. Although thousands of young women at this time in history entered the indentured servitude offered by the factories and mills of the Industrial Revolution, such work was not for the Alcott girls. They might starve, but they would starve as gentlewomen and as intellectuals, as farmers who revered the land or teachers who understood Plato, not as illiterate millworkers or factory girls. The family often was as close as Louisa got to God in those difficult years.

In the meantime, the passionate national argument about the continuation of slavery grew more heated. In 1848, the Treaty of Guadalupe-Hidalgo ended the Mexican War and added territory that is now all or part of Texas, California, Arizona, Nevada, Utah, Colorado, and Wyoming to the United States. This treaty roughly doubled the size of the United States and in doing so doubled the size of the dispute about the existence of slavery. Suddenly there were half a dozen new states and territories that might tip the balance of whether the United States was a slave country or not. The suspense and acrimony grew. Would they allow slavery, or would they be "free states."

Zachary Taylor, a southern slave owner with moderate views who had earned the nickname "Old Rough and Ready" for his valor in the war with Mexico, was elected president with Millard Fillmore his vice president. Taylor would die of a mysterious intestinal disorder in 1850 while the Fugitive Slave Act was being debated in the U.S. Senate.

The passage of the Fugitive Slave Act set both sides angrily against each other in a way that presaged the impossibility of keeping a union of all the states. The Yankees were outraged. What business did southerners have telling them how to treat men, women, and children who had been subjected to unjust laws? How could the South reach into their own New England woods and rail lines?

This self-righteousness was matched in the South. What business did northerners, who knew nothing about slavery, have telling the South that they should eliminate slavery? Property was property. Neither side could tolerate the encroachments of the other. The stubbornness and fierce love of freedom that had motivated Americans to fight a war against England now turned them against each other.

This was a national moment that required great diplomacy and superb skills, but instead, Taylor's sudden death left Millard Fillmore to negotiate one of the most important pieces of legislation ever passed.

Passed in September, the Compromise of

1850 slightly soothed the agitated feelings of the southern states. In New England, it created a furor for abolition. By 1851, antislavery sentiment in Boston was passionate, especially among citizens like the Alcotts, who had personal experience with helping runaway slaves. Louisa had seen the intelligence and humanity of the men her father sheltered, and whom her friend Thoreau spirited out of town under cover of night. Her heart connected with their distress. "Fugitive slaves were sheltered under our roof," she wrote years later, "and my first pupil was a very black George Washington whom I taught to write on the hearth with charcoal, his big fingers finding pen and pencil unmanageable."[4]

Louisa and her family had exulted when a Boston mob rescued Shadrach Minkins, an accused fugitive slave, from a Boston jail and led him to freedom eventually in Canada. They had been horrified when a similar mob, including her father, failed to rescue a slave named Thomas Sims who had escaped from Mississippi and been arrested and was now — according to the new law — about to be shipped back to his owner in Mississippi.

In June of 1851, the Washington newspaper *National Era* had begun serializing

*Uncle Tom's Cabin,* in which Harriet Beecher Stowe demonized the evil slave catchers loosed by the new laws. For the first time in American literature, Stowe portrayed blacks as serious and sympathetic protagonists. The book was a huge bestseller. Adapted for the stage, it immediately became one of the most popular plays of all time. On the evening of April 8, Louisa took time off from her teaching and sewing to hear abolitionist speakers Dr. William Channing and Wendell Phillips. "We went to a meeting, and heard splendid speaking. . . . People were much excited and cheered 'Shadrach and Liberty,' groaned for 'Webster and Slavery,' and made a great noise. I felt ready to do anything — fight or work or hoot or cry, — and aid plans to free Sims. I shall be horribly ashamed of my country if this thing happens and the slave is taken back," she wrote.[5] Sims was returned to his owners in spite of Boston protests and the plans of the Anti-Slavery League to help him escape as they had helped Shadrach escape.

When a cholera epidemic hit the city, a May brother offered to board the family for a while in his roomy house on Atkinson Street. With a few months of having more light and space, Louisa's spirits rebounded.

She organized a family newspaper called the *Olive Branch,* a handwritten Pickwickian rag that presented her own hymns to her beloved cat[6] and her mother's reports on the progress of her charity work. When the epidemic passed and the family moved to another dark apartment in Groton Street, Louisa went to work helping with Anna's teaching. Louisa's ally in the family, her mother, was often so debilitated from the stresses of her overwhelming work and her difficult family life that she would start crying and be unable to stop. This bad situation got worse. Abba welcomed some starving children into the small garden of the house for some scraps of food that the family could hardly spare, and the whole Alcott family came down with smallpox.

Medical treatment in the 1840s and '50s was a primitive combination of experience and guesswork. There was no understanding of how disease spread or how it could be cured. There were no antibiotics, and a few progressive doctors were just beginning to talk about washing their hands before performing surgery. Surgery was almost always fatal. In the face of illness, the Alcott family creed served them well. No doctors were called. Instead, the family washed, rested, and consulted Hahnemann's homeopathic bible *Organon of the Healing Art.* In spite of having no medical treatment, or perhaps because of it, the family began to recover.

Although the Alcotts' health improved, their finances continued to spiral downward. The Alcotts moved again to an even worse building on High Street, two blocks from the wharves. As Louisa wrote, the family was "poor as rats and apparently quite forgotten by everyone except the Lord."[7] Every day Louisa walked down to the wharves and took a horsecar to Suffolk Street to teach. The Alcott girls dressed in shabby hand-me-down and made-over clothes, which were far from comfortable.[8] Women in nineteenth-century Boston staggered under the weight of a series of long skirts and layers of clothing. Poor women dressed in at least three layers of heavy fabric, while the well-dressed often smothered themselves in almost forty pounds of horsehair, crinoline, and whalebone with tight lacing inhibiting their breathing and steel hoops inhibiting their skirts.

Still, Louisa had recently experienced at least one triumphant moment. Llewellyn Willis, the young boy Abba had befriended back in Still River when the Alcott family left Fruitlands, had returned to board with the Alcott family while he went to Harvard. His room and board was paid by his family, and this was a part of the Alcott income. Willis was a family friend as well as a boarder and his rent was necessary, although it eliminated a badly needed bedroom.

Willis admired Louisa, and he had privately submitted a poem of Louisa's, "Sunlight," written under the pseudonym Flora Fairfield, to *Peterson's Magazine.* The poem was accepted. The magazine had been established to compete with the treacly, conventional *Godey's Lady's Book,* and it had quickly become the bestselling magazine in the country. They paid Louisa $5 and published the poem in September 1851. It was the first money Louisa May Alcott made as a writer.

Abba Alcott took as her personal and professional mission the protection of the flood of young girls who came to Boston from the "lust and sharks that wait," she wrote in her journal. She was apparently too busy to pay attention to protecting one young girl in particular, a tall girl with masses of shiny chestnut hair, glowing skin, and large deep-set eyes that often looked angry or sad. Louisa had no skills at flirting or small talk, and she was hungry for affection as well as for books and music and for all the things that had once made her life a series of private pleasures. As time passed, she retreated more and more into fantasy, and this made her more vulnerable to loneliness and the idea of rescue.

Bronson was equally distracted. At the age of fifty, having realized that many of his dreams would never come true, reduced to giving Conversations to sometimes sleepy audiences, he did what men sometimes do under the circumstances — he fell in love with a younger woman. The object of Bronson's affections was the twenty-four-year-old, Ednah Dow Littlehale, the youngest daughter of a successful Boston merchant. Littlehale became Bronson's secretary, faithfully recording his Conversations, and by the summer of 1851 the two met every morning for a sunrise walk on the Boston Common. "Love is the blossom where there blows. Everything that lives or grows,"[9] he ecstatically quoted in his journal. "Only bend the knee to me. My wooing shall thy winning be." Did Littlehale return his passion? It's hard to tell, and no one in the Alcott family seemed to guess what was going on. Certainly the arrival of trouble could not have chosen a better moment in a household in which both parents were entirely distracted and one was mooning after a girl young enough to be his daughter.

One day at the end of the summer, an elderly lawyer named James Richardson from Dedham applied to Abba's office looking for a young woman to help care for his sister. Louisa happened to be in the office when he made his request. Tired of teaching and sewing, the energetic nineteen-year-old offered herself for the job. "Going out to service," as such a companion job was called, was a rung below teaching and sewing on the social ladder, and Abba was surprised that Louisa had volunteered. Nevertheless, she was too preoccupied to ask many questions. For the hungry Louisa, time in Dedham promised an adventure, a trip away from a home.

"When I was eighteen I wanted something to do," she wrote later. "I had tried teaching for two years, and hated it; I had tried sewing, and could not earn my bread that way, at cost of health; I tried story-writing and got five dollars for stories which now bring a hundred; I had thought seriously of going on the stage, but certain highly respectable relatives were so shocked at the mere idea that I relinquished my dramatic aspirations."[10] At that moment, those "highly respectable relatives" — her parents — who were shocked at the idea of a stage career and certainly might have drawn the line at being a paid companion, were not paying attention. Instead of a sympathetic query from her mother, Louisa got more criticism. "I fancied you were rather too proud for this sort of thing,"[11] Abba warned her daughter.

Richardson, as Louisa noted, described his home as a sort of heaven on earth with books, pictures, a piano, and many distinguished visitors. Even before the job began, he started writing the young woman long letters with worrisome overtones. He imagined her coming to his room after the day's work so that he could "minister to her young and cheerful nature." Presumably, Abba and Bronson, who read everything in their house, read these letters, but no alarms were sounded. So Louisa packed her three homemade dresses and a few aprons and set off in January for her new job in Dedham. There had been no written agreement about duties and wages; enticed by her own vivid fantasies, Louisa was sure all would be well.

"The romance opens well," she thought as she peered into Richardson's comfortable book-lined study.[12] But what Louisa meant by romance was quite different than what Richardson meant. He watched her obsessively, and when she tried to avoid him, he remarked on the pleasure of "something tasteful, young and womanly." His elderly sister was a silent figure wrapped in shawls. Their ancient father never spoke, and the housekeeper avoided all contact.

At the end of each day, Richardson asked Louisa to join him in his study, the room where she had imagined being left to read in a beautiful place. Instead of reading, she was ordered to listen as Richardson complained about his life and read aloud from a variety of texts. She became "a passive bucket, into which he was to pour all manner of philosophic, metaphysical and sentimental rubbish,"[13] she wrote. When she protested, Richardson reacted with rage. He ordered her to black his boots and do the most menial work available.

The Dedham idyll quickly became a nightmare, and although Louisa lasted seven weeks, she finally was able to escape with her possessions in a wheelbarrow and her salary envelope in her pocket. At least she had hoped to make some substantial money. When she discovered that the payment she received for the entire seven weeks had been $4 she was outraged. Her family welcomed her home and their anger at the meager payment, perhaps colored by guilt, was greater than hers. Bronson was sent to return the $4 to the odious Richardson and to tell anyone he ran into about Richardson's proclivities and cheapness. Richardson's response to this scolding from Bronson Alcott has not been recorded.

The Alcotts' four years of Boston misery, years of illness and hunger and incessant work, were awful, but her seven weeks in Dedham particularly stuck in Louisa's imagination — perhaps because it was an adventure which she had without her family. Perhaps it was such a vivid memory because it had been traumatic, or perhaps it stood out because of the strong feelings of fear, sexuality, and disgust just under the surface of the story. In her scant spare time, she sat down and began to write a short essay about it.

In the spring of 1852, the Alcotts were once again saved financially at the last possible moment — this time by Nathaniel Hawthorne. Hawthorne and his wife, the former Sophia Peabody, who had once replaced her sister Elizabeth at Bronson Alcott's Temple School, had first come to Concord as newlyweds in 1843.

Hawthorne and Sophia's courtship had been as dark and secretive as a character in one of Hawthorne's early stories. In Salem, where he and the Peabody family were neighbors, Hawthorne had been friends with Elizabeth Peabody, who encouraged him and helped get him published before anyone else had acknowledged him as a serious writer. One day, while Hawthorne was visiting Elizabeth, her slender, sickly sister Sophia came downstairs. Soon she and Hawthorne were secretly engaged. He saved her from a life of being a bedridden spinster, and she never stopped being grateful, even when it looked as if he would never be able to support his family, even when it looked as if he might be in love with Margaret Fuller.

Like the Alcotts, the Hawthornes were first invited to Concord by the munificent Emerson. Their engagement had remained secret until they could find a way to set up a household together. This was a difficult task, since both were living with their parents and neither of them had any money. Emerson's invitation to Concord made it possible for them to marry and start to keep house. There at the Old Manse, which they rented from Emerson's step-uncle George Ripley, Hawthorne and Sophia had been very happy. On a few successive evenings they had carved their sentiments in the windowpanes with Sophia's engagement diamond.

But man's accidents sometimes seemed disastrous even if they were God's purposes. Jealousy over Margaret Fuller — who was passionately involved with both Hawthorne and Emerson — had ended the cozy arrangement by which the Hawthornes lived at the Old Manse for a token rent. Fuller, an intellectual who had assisted Bronson Alcott at the Temple School and edited the Transcendentalist magazine *The Dial,* was an object of erotic delight for both Emerson and Hawthorne although there is scant evidence that she slept with either of them. She had been staying at the Emerson House and taking long walks with Hawthorne when Emerson discovered the two of them lying languidly on a mossy bank in the woods. Soon after that, the Hawthornes had been summarily exiled from Concord.

Now in 1852 it was almost ten years later and everything had changed. The Hawthornes, a family led by the famous author of *The Scarlet Letter, The House of the Seven Gables,* and *The Blithedale Romance,* decided to return to Concord. They had moved enough, from Concord to Salem to the Berkshires and back to Salem. Recently they had been living in Newton, where they stayed with Sophia's sister and her husband — Mary and Horace Mann. By then Margaret Fuller was dead. Perhaps gently guided by their old friend Emerson, they zeroed in on Hillside, the dear old wreck that was the Alcotts' only asset in the world. In April, Hawthorne made arrangements with Abba's executor Sam Sewall and with Emerson, who owned the eight-acre plot across the road from the house, to buy the place for $1,500 with a down payment of $750 to be set up by Emerson and Sewall as trusts for Bronson and Abba, and the balance to be paid within a year.

The Hawthornes were appalled by the condition of the house and employed a dozen carpenters to remodel it, but Bronson Alcott's landscaping and gardening was one of the things that attracted them. Hawthorne, a tall, remarkably handsome man who stayed mysterious and distant even to those who knew him best, came to love the walks along the terraces on the hill behind the house and the high ridge that looked out over the fields and town. "I have bought a house," Hawthorne wrote, "and feel myself for the first time in my life, at home. . . . Alcott called it Hillside as it stands close at the base of a steep ascent; but, as it is also in proximity (too nigh, indeed) to the road leading to the village, I have re-baptized it "The Wayside.' "[14]

By 1852 the Hawthornes' early troubles were behind them, and they had settled into the sympathetic, considerate married love, chronicled later by their son Julian, in a way that was both touching and romantic. Sophia guarded her husband's time and serenity as if they were her own most precious possessions. When visitors came to the front door of the house, as Sophia welcomed them, Hawthorne used the back door, the door of Louisa's old bedroom, to escape as she had to the natural wonderland created by the man who had failed at every other thing he had tried.

Both Hawthornes, for the first time, found themselves in touch with the delicious consequences of nature tamed by an imaginative human hand. "The clearest picture in my mind is that of my father and mother stepping side by side about the grounds," wrote the Hawthornes' daughter, Rose, in a later memoir. "He talked then. Her head was almost always lifted; she was looking straight ahead or up at a height of summer loveliness."[15] The Hawthornes left the house in 1853 when Hawthorne's good friend from Bowdoin College Franklin Pierce became president and rewarded Hawthorne

— who had written his campaign biography — with the consulship at Liverpool, England. When they returned in 1860, Hawthorne dramatically changed Wayside architecturally, building a "sky parlor," a room at the top of the house with long windows facing in all four directions from which he could see Walden Pond to the south and the spires of Concord to the west.

Eventually, after the Hawthornes and their children had lived in the house, and after her parents' deaths, Rose Hawthorne sold it in 1883 to Daniel Lothrop, a well-known publisher. Lothrop's wife, Harriet, who met him when he agreed to publish her work, was the author of *The Five Little Peppers* and other children's books under the pen name Margaret Sidney. *Little Women* was the historical precedent for the Peppers in more ways than one. That the five little Peppers and the four little Alcotts and Marches and the three little Hawthornes had all played and learned under the same roof, albeit in different decades, seems more like God's purposes than man's accidents, as Sophia Peabody might have thought.

Touring the house in the summer of 2008 with a group of professors, I imagine that we are all looking for some kind of air pocket that will release the secret to the creativity that drove all the families who lived here. The house is dark, with low ceilings and all shades drawn against the light. In the kitchen, we hear about the shower Bronson Alcott rigged up for his family's frigid morning ablutions. On the wall, we squint at the original of Bronson's beautifully handwritten "Order of In-door Duties," a schedule for his four daughters — even when Bronson Alcott wasn't running a school, he was running a school for his family. (The National Park ranger explains that the "Order of In-door Duties" at Orchard House next door is a copy.) At 5 A.M. the girls were to rise, bathe, and dress, and at 9 join their father in the parlor for studies. After dinner at noon, they were to sew, read, and have conversations with their mother and Miss Foord, and after supper at 6 there were more conversations and instruction in music.

The schedule's largest admonition seems directed at Louisa, reminding her of the importance of vigilance, punctuality, perseverance, and prompt, cheerful unquestioning obedience. The girls are also urged to remember government of temper, hands, and tongue and gentle manners and words. There was to be no playing during work times. All this rigidity must have been a tall order for a young woman who was so wild that she thought she was born to be a horse, a girl in love with an older neighbor, a girl just finding ways to channel her prodigious energy into the writing she began at the table in her private bedroom.

Our group crowds into the sky parlor at the top of the house, leaving our guide at the foot of the narrow stairs. It's a warm afternoon and the air seems thick in the enclosed space. Although Hawthorne wrote nothing of note in this parlor or at the standing desk he built for himself, the room seems haunted by his ambition, by the wild intention of a great man building an Italianate tower at the top of a New England farmhouse. This man dreamed great dreams. I am standing at the desk, a simple shelf against the chimney, when someone lifts a window shade to peer into the woods and the thing snaps open and up with a bang. We all jump, and for a moment the room seems to vibrate with spirits.

Another day I climb to the top of the ridge. Alcott's careful terracing has almost been obscured; the terraces are only visible if you know what to look for. The rangers warn about poison ivy, but as I slide on the pine needles, it's the trees that seem villainous. Forest sprawl has taken over New

England, which was once pasture and meadow cleared with the blood, sweat, and tears of the first settlers. I find myself hating the railroad that brought the industry that eventually eliminated the picturesque agricultural way of life. At the top of the ridge, with my back to the Alcott and Hawthorne house at the bottom, I stand looking at what would be the view if it weren't for the trees. I stand where Hawthorne often stood. Ahead of me is a large, new yellow house. Can I blame the builder? What could be better than owning a house at the edge of land owned by the National Park Service? In the backyard a gleaming basketball net reminds me how different childhood is now from the nineteenth-century childhood I have left behind at the bottom of the hill.

The money from the Hawthornes' purchase of their old house saved the Alcotts once again. Just at the time that Abba had concluded that her mission to help the poor in Boston had failed, the family was able to move out of the High Street slum and into far nicer rooms in a four-story brick house on Pinckney Street on the back side of Beacon Hill, near the dome of the Massachusetts State House.

The financial brinksmanship that had characterized their lives had taken its toll.

After the move in 1852, an exhausted and depressed Abba Alcott collapsed into despair. She thought that nothing she had done for the poor made any difference; her employment agency had failed. "It makes me feel sad that so much time is irrevocably gone,"[16] she wrote. Suddenly she was a tired old woman.

Since Fruitlands, Louisa had often dreamed of fame, or riches, or at least of earning enough money to comfortably support the beloved six people she referred to as the pathetic family. She longed for some kind of creative self-expression. Sometime during the years of deprivation and illness and discouragement in the family's second decade of living in Boston, during bitter days of remembering Bronson Alcott's triumphant Temple School as she walked across Boston Common to this or that demeaning job, the dream of becoming a writer began to take over Louisa's idea of her own future. In the resuscitated family newspaper, she published a full-fledged melodrama, "The Rival Painters." Slowly the $5 and $10 payments she got for her shorter published pieces in magazines began to catch up with her earnings as a seamstress and a teacher. Reading Harriet Beecher Stowe's sentimental, affecting *Uncle Tom's*

*Cabin,* written by the unprepossessing wife of a Bowdoin College professor, inspired Louisa as an abolitionist. It also inspired her as a young woman writer, providing a thrilling model of a woman with no distinguished degrees writing a popular and financially successful book.

While Abba sewed and cooked and organized paying lodgers in their new house on Beacon Hill, Louisa wrote new melodramas under the pseudonym A. M. Barnard in the spare time from her own sewing and teaching. One, "The Masked Marriage," was published in December in *Dodge's Literary Museum,* and she was paid $10 — this in a year when she made $80 sewing and teaching. Another, "Pauline's Passion and Punishment," exemplifies Louisa's melodrama style. "To and fro, like a wild creature in its cage, paced that handsome woman, with bent head, locked hands and restless steps. Some mental storm, swift and sudden as a tempest of the tropics, had swept over her."

What makes someone want to be a writer? Clearly, one thing this dream requires is a ferocious hunger, a hunger for recognition, a yearning to be heard that roars through the soul with a sound so great that the stories often feel as if they are discovered rather than invented. Writing also requires a kind of divine perversity. The writer stands outside the conventional world looking in with a vision sharp enough to describe things in ways that are both recognizable and entirely surprising. Good writing is almost always subversive. It uses the nuts and bolts of the texture of everyday life to communicate truths that may be as disturbing as they are original. There is often a lot of anger in great writing; no one likes to be outside, the one left behind to tell the story, but a writer must learn to live out there in the cold, warmed only by her ability to write.

In 1853, when she was still mired in making money from teaching and had started a school for young girls in the parlor on Pinckney Street, Louisa was partway to being a writer but not quite there. She was beginning to sell her short melodramatic tales, but disdained them and dreamed of a more serious kind of writing like Mrs. Stowe's or even Emerson's or Thoreau's. She wanted to write in a way that would confront the world and try to change it. Her moneymaking stories, potboilers, seemed beneath her even as she churned them out and walked them down to Frank Leslie, one of her publishers.

Louisa wrote her friend Alf Whitman that

her stories were "blood & thunder tale[s] . . . easy to compose & are better paid than moral and elaborate works of Shakespear so don't be shocked if I send you a paper containing a picture of indians, pirates wolves bears 7 distressed damsels in a grand tableau over a title like this 'The Maniac Bride' or 'The Bath of Blood, a Thrilling Tale of Passion.' "[17] Ashamed, Louisa May Alcott did everything she could to hide her tracks as a melodrama writer. She always used the name of A. M. Barnard and never acknowledged authorship after the stories were published, not even much later when anything she wrote was assured of an adoring audience. She systematically destroyed as much of her own correspondence as she could find. She asked others to destroy the letters she had written. The fact that A. M. Barnard was, in fact, Louisa May Alcott was not discovered until almost a hundred years later by Alcott biographer Madeleine Stern and her researcher Leona Rostenberg while researching for Stern's book in Harvard's Houghton Library.[18]

Louisa May Alcott had written and rewritten her essay about her time with the dreadful Richardson in Dedham. This was serious writing, not the ramped-up melodrama of her other pieces with their Paulines in

195

peril, their diabolical lovers, their natural disasters, and their wild landscapes. In writing "How I Went Out to Service," Alcott had her first try at the detailed, textured realism that would end up more than ten years later as the basis of her greatest book. This time, however, she failed.

The essay reads as if Louisa is still whining about how badly she was treated. Her account brings up many unanswered questions about Richardson's intentions. "At first I innocently accepted the fraternal invitations to visit the study," she writes of her employer, after a few days "feeling that when my day's work was done I had earned the right to rest and read. But I soon found that this was not the idea. I was not to read: but to be read to. I was not to enjoy the flowers, pictures, fire, and books; but to keep them in order for my lord to enjoy."[19]

Where a reader expects resolution, there is more complaining. The essay does not clarify what was really going on, and the reader suspects that Louisa wasn't sure herself. She's a very unreliable narrator. Bad writing is often driven by resentment, and good writing is based on authority. The essay has little authority. Although this first serious essay by Louisa May Alcott is not one that anyone reads now, it is her first foray into memoir and into a simple authorial voice that would become the empathetic, brilliant voice of her greatest books.

The Alcott family was living in relative comfort in the house on Pinckney Street (a plaque on the house today incorrectly identifies it as a house where Louisa May Alcott lived as a young girl, but she was in her twenties when the family lived there). Louisa's life was beginning to be the money-earning patchwork of companion, tutor, teacher, seamstress, and writer that made her feel quite happy and successful as the numbers in her ledger went from two to three digits.

Success often breeds ambition. In the spring of 1854, Louisa decided to pay a visit to James T. Fields, a venerable editor who stood for serious writing by serious writers. Perhaps he would give her some encouragement. He had gone to work as a clerk for the Old Corner Bookstore when he was fourteen, and by the time Louisa went to see him, he was a partner in the publishing venture Ticknor & Fields. He was in his thirties and had already published Thomas De Quincey's *Confessions of an English Opium Eater* and Hawthorne's *The Scarlet Letter,* and he would soon publish Emerson, Thoreau, Longfellow, Dickens, Thackeray and Wordsworth.

Or perhaps Louisa was provoked into visiting James T. Fields by her father's most recent failure. Bronson had gone on a lecture tour that took him as far as Cleveland. Financed, as always, by Emerson, he had sent back good news at first. So far he had $25 saved from giving Conversations, and there would be much, much more. It's astonishing that anyone in his family actually believed him enough to be disappointed. On his return, he was warmly welcomed, and after the hugging and kissing had died down, he opened his wallet to reveal his earnings with a rueful smile — $1. It was all other people's fault as it always was, he explained. His overcoat was stolen, promises were not kept, and traveling was expensive. "I shall never forget how beautifully mother answered him, though the dear, hopeful soul had built much on his success, but with a beaming face she kissed him saying, 'I call that doing very well. Since you are safely home dear. We don't ask anything more,' " Louisa wrote of that disappointing night in her journals. We "took a lesson in real love which we never forgot, nor the look that the tired man and the tender woman gave one another."[20]

Certainly the key to a successful marriage

is a kind and tender acceptance of another's failures, and certainly this was a situation in which Abba Alcott had plenty of practice. At the same time, as biographer Martha Saxton points out about Louisa's reaction to Bronson's habitual insolvency, "rage, anger, and disappointment were not allowed, so she had to reduce everyone, and especially her father, to the stature of a large, bumbling, adorable baby. By making him like an infant, Louisa justified his outrageous irresponsibility."[21]

Someone had to be responsible for supporting the family, and Louisa reached for the role. James Fields had already met Louisa when he visited her father at the Emerson's house in Concord, and Louisa hoped he would be a friendly audience. That morning Louisa took the mile-long walk from the family house on Pinckney Street on the back side of Beacon Hill over the rise, and through the open passage under the State House. She went down the steep hill past the Masonic Temple where her father had had a school so long ago.

She passed the Boston Common and turned into the bustling center of downtown. There the spire of the Old South Church presided like a disapproving Puritan dowager over the teeming business of the new Boston. There was the bookshop, next to Mrs. Abner's Coffee House, where Fields took authors and colleagues for coffee and hot buns. There was the gorgeous palace of the Music Hall with its golden gaslit interiors, where Louisa had already been to see Madame Henriette Sontag sing Rossini (the Willis family had provided the tickets) and where she had recently gone to hear Theodore Parker, one of her favorite speakers and a fervent abolitionist, demand equality for women.

Now Louisa headed for the second floor of the Old Corner Bookshop, where Fields had his office behind a green curtain that separated him from his young assistant, Thomas Niles, and the piles of manuscripts he had yet to read. She handed him the manuscript, her first and last memoir essay, "How I Went Out to Service." He motioned her to sit and began to read. She could hear the noise of Thomas Niles's pen scratching and the chatter in the bookstore downstairs. The air smelled of paper and ink.

Finally the great James T. Fields looked up at her and delivered the verdict that she would remember for the rest of her life. "Stick to your teaching, Miss Alcott. You can't write."[22] Perhaps Fields, who later became a friend of Louisa's, understood her well enough to think his criticism might push her to another level of writing. Perhaps Louisa was too different from the middle-aged men who were the key to Fields's success for him to recognize her potential as a writer. Perhaps he thought of her as Bronson's daughter in a way that blinded him to her talent. Louisa May Alcott wrote about what it was like to be a woman in the world, and Fields had not read anything else on that subject. Perhaps the piece didn't engage him at all. At any rate, it was at that moment in Fields's office that Louisa May Alcott became definitely and certainly a writer. A stubborn girl who had to fight for every privilege she had in her young life, Alcott was inspired rather than discouraged by Fields's dismissal.

Psychological studies have recently shown that adversity can be a more powerful motivator than support. Successful people often remember being told that they could not do what they have, in fact, done brilliantly. Stubbornness drove them. Their parents or teachers have told them they will never make any money, or that they will never get a college degree, or that they will never marry and have children. The urge to prove authority wrong has often spurred human beings to unusual success. In 1854 there were no psychological studies of this kind, but it's easy to see how a woman like Louisa May Alcott, told that she couldn't write, vowed to write. "He could hardly have hit on a surer way to stoke her determination," writes John Matteson.

In describing this moment, however, Louisa May Alcott's biographers vary markedly on when it happened. In the prestigious Library of America volume of Louisa May Alcott, Princeton Professor Elaine Showalter has this scene located in 1854, when Louisa was twenty-two and had yet to publish anything under her own name. She had recently been to Dedham and the experience of being trapped as a paid companion was fresh in her mind as she wrote the essay. Yet John Matteson in *Eden's Outcast* has the same incident happening almost a decade later in 1862. Indeed, it appears in Louisa May's journals in May of that year. Was she writing as a moneymaking writer and remembering the slight when she wrote, "Mr F. did say 'Stick to your teaching you can't write.' " In the 1862 journal, she adds, "Being willful, I said, 'I won't teach and I can write and I'll prove it.' " That she did.

Writing reveals character. A sentence or paragraph of writing can be like a fingerprint, so idiosyncratic and individual that a person's character and eccentricities can be read there by an astute critic. Louisa's essay about Dedham is the essay of a young woman, still upset and confused by Richardson's behavior, a woman who isn't sure exactly what happened to her in that cold, unwelcoming house. "My honored mother was a city missionary that winter," the essay goes, "and not only served the clamorous poor, but found it in her power to help decayed gentlefolk by quietly placing them where they could earn their bread without the entire sacrifice of taste and talent which makes poverty so hard for such to bear." In 1854, Louisa knew a great deal about such sacrifices of taste and talent. If Fields delivered his verdict in the spring, she showed him he was wrong by December when another publisher, George W. Briggs, published her book *Flower Fables* in an edition of 1,600, and it "did well," as she noted in her journals.

The *Flower Fables* combine the melodramatic inclination of the stories and plays Louisa had written for her family with naturalism and a powerful yearning for love — the elements that would mark Louisa May Alcott's mature work. Moral fables originally written for Ellen Emerson, they feature flower fairy heroines and an evil Frost King. In the last story, a girl named Annie abuses a flower she has been given to help her be good and is enslaved by the nightmarish spirits of pride, selfishness, and anger. "Each tale is a pathetically simple fulfillment of a wistful desire for love," writes Martha Saxton.

The chronology of Louisa May Alcott's work is clear from "How I Went Out to Service" to *Flower Fables,* from melodramas to the more serious autobiographical novel *Moods* that combines domestic detail with a melodramatic shipwreck. In fact, the scene in which Fields discouraged Louisa from writing must have taken place in 1854, before Fields took over the editorship of the *Atlantic Monthly* in 1856. By 1862, James Fields had changed his mind about Louisa May Alcott — he now thought she *could* write. By 1862 he had already published at least one of Louisa's stories about "the pathetic family": "A Modern Cinderella; or, The Little Old Shoe" in his magazine, a story Louisa based on her sister Anna's romance with the Alcott family friend John Pratt.

In 1862, Louisa was thirty, a woman who had suffered through a few crushes and turned down at least one marriage proposal and who had dedicated most of her time with a great deal of success to becoming a writer who could help support her family with her earnings. By then the Alcott family had returned to Concord, and they had suffered another great loss, a loss that put all Bronson's eccentricities and Abba's tears in a new perspective. But all that and a lot more were in the future. How many people in Boston could guess that the Civil War was the disaster for which they were headed, or that her participation in the war would change Louisa's life forever. Who could know on that day when Louisa May Alcott first visited James T. Fields that she would become one of the most famous women in the world, while Henriette Sontag, the Willis family, and even the great James T. Fields are only remembered because of their connection to her?

# 5

# ORCHARD HOUSE.

## 1858–1862

Greening, Porter, Northern Spy, Winesap,
Baldwin, Pearmain: the Alcotts decided to
name their new place Orchard House for
the varieties of apple trees that grow on its
east side. It's one of the oldest houses on
Concord, built in the 1600s by John Hoar
as a workshop for Christian Indians of the
Wampanoag tribe. In 1857 when the Alcotts
bought its twelve acres for $945 — once
more with a $500 loan from Emerson, who
would again be their neighbor across the
street — the house was such a dilapidated
wreck that it was thrown in for free with the
land by the owner John Moore.

Even from the comfort of Beacon Hill,
Bronson and Abba Alcott had begun missing Concord, which had come to seem like
home. Louisa disliked the town, she said,
but she was old enough to live anywhere
she pleased. On September 22, Bronson Alcott took the train to Concord, signed the

papers drawn up by S. E. Sewall to acquire the new house, had dinner with Thoreau, and spent the night with the Emersons.

Even better, the new place was next door to what had once been Hillside, the Alcotts' former home in Concord. It was too close to the same road and backed by the same steep ridge. "I walk down Hawthorne's Lane with my wife," Bronson Alcott wrote with unusual clarity of approaching the new house from their old house through the woods. As always he was an optimist. To him the wreck was a gold mine of architectural potential. "Surveying our place from that perspective, and seeing how the prospect will be opened and improved when the barn opposite is removed to give full view of the willows by Mill brook and of the landscape beyond. It seems the fittest spot for a house," he added, "protected so by the hills on all sides from round East to West, and enjoying the south so pleasantly. And the house standing quietly apart from the roadside to give room for the overshadowing elms to lend their dignity and beauty to the scene and bring out its homely aspects; the brown porches, many gables, architectural chimney tops; the hills through which winds the grassy lane. . . . Tis a pretty retreat, and ours; a family mansion to take pride in."[1]

Emerson was pleased to have his friend Bronson back; Thoreau was delighted. Even Hawthorne, who was in England when he heard that the Alcotts had bought the wreck next door, was pleased in his own, slightly less affectionate way. His delight was in the prospect of another Alcott failure that might benefit him as a landowner. He wrote his friend Howard Ticknor asking him to keep an eye on the possibility of the Alcotts being forced to move again. "I should be very glad to take it off his hands,"[2] he wrote of the acres next to his own house.

The Alcott family, although used to discomfort, was not quite pathetic enough to move into the new house as it was. While they oversaw the renovations, they rented half a house near the railroad station on the other side of town, on Bedford Street. May and Louisa both spent a great deal of time in Boston, and Anna was helping out at a nearby farm owned by a family named Pratt. Lizzie and Abba sometimes stayed with the Peabodys, who had rented the Alcotts' old house from the Hawthornes, who were in England.

Orchard House was to be the family's final refuge, the place that would come to be the symbol of their family life and which still stands there at the bottom of the steep hill today. In many ways, it is Bronson Alcott's accidental masterpiece. At a time when few Americans valued anything for its age — the word "antique" had a very different and negative meaning in 1857 — Bronson Alcott understood how history could be written through objects. He studied the town records to learn the history of the old house and quarreled endlessly with the "unconquerably stupid" carpenters he hired to be sure that the renovation was done with respect. In return, the townspeople mocked him, saying that he had used enough wood on the graceful split-wood fence at the front of the house to build an entire new house. Bronson quoted Thomas Fuller: "He that alters an old house is tied as a translator to the original."

Orchard House today is a mecca to those who tour through the rooms where Louisa May Alcott set the scenes of *Little Women* even though, of course, the "real" scenes of the sisters' teenage years happened in the yellow house down the street. The pilgrims who line up to go up the narrow staircase and look hungrily at the small bed in Louisa's room and the minute desk between two windows where she wrote *Little Women* seem to be searching for something in the books on the shelf, in the party dress laid out on the bed.

Perhaps because the impossible choices that faced Louisa May Alcott are still the impossible choices facing most women, Orchard House still vibrates with significance. The ghosts seem to be there in the very angles and doors of the place, the narrow staircase and the small scale of everything from the beds that are half the size of modern beds and the tiny rooms — hardly large enough to accommodate a modern walk-in closet.

The young women who come to Orchard House, dressed in low riders and halter tops in the summer, sweaters and puffy parkas in the winter, are looking for a way to honor their awkward, tomboy Louisa May Alcott and Jo March selves and to succeed as women at the same time. How can they be girls without being the simpering, obedient, sexually dressed image of what we still call *femininity?*

More than 150 years have passed since the Alcott family moved into Orchard House. The girls who chuckle at seeing Louisa's "mood pillow" would be unrecognizable to the Alcott sisters or the fictional March girls. Their inner lives might look very familiar. If marriage is a woman's goal, her primary job is to make herself attractive to men. A look at clothes and advice we give young girls makes it clear that attracting a man who will be a provider is still one of the major jobs a young woman has in our culture. We give them Barbie dolls and makeup. We tell them to be calm and quiet and to remember that men are predatory hunters so that successful women must pretend to be tantalizing, elusive prey.

Yet Louisa May Alcott somehow escaped this fate. We know that it was a combination of accident, intelligence, world events, and focus on her family that facilitated her. She loved men, but she refused to marry. She had at least one proposal, one she apparently considered because the man in question (we don't know who it was) might have been able to help the family financially. Louisa would have been happy to marry for the sake of the family, but she was unable to marry for the sake of herself. After a long talk with her mother — no, she did not love the man in question — Louisa turned the man down.

On another occasion, when she was twenty-eight, the vibrant Louisa attracted a Southern gentleman of forty whom she met on the train from Boston. "A Southerner, and very demonstrative and gushing," Louisa wrote in her journal, "called and wished to pay his addresses, and being told I did not wish to see him, returned to write letters and haunt the road. . . . He went at last and peace reigned."[3]

Louisa May Alcott now seems heroic for her refusal to compromise who she was — a rebel, a tree climber, a girl who loved to be free — free of the house, free of the schoolroom, free of the expectations of her family and her society. She was a woman, but she refused to be falsely feminine. Yet she triumphed, and her great novel, a novel in which a girl just like herself is beloved and successful, is still read and reread.

In 1855, two years before the Alcotts moved back to Concord, yet another May relative had offered a house rent-free for the summer in Walpole, New Hampshire. At first Walpole, a small town on the Connecticut River, seemed a piece of good luck. The picturesque town with its central green and white-spired churches is now famous for being the home of Burdick Chocolate and one of the best restaurants in New Hampshire. But in 1857, it was the sticks, a town in the middle of nowhere. Open to the green New England summers and the glorious autumn foliage, it was definitely country living. Louisa felt isolated and quickly left for a job in Boston.

In Walpole, Abba continued her charity work and in June started ministering to the Hall family, a mother and children who lived in a room above what had once been a pigpen. Outraged at the filth in the family's rented rooms, Abba sued the landlord, a deacon, as Louisa angrily noted in her journal. Pigs and swine were thought to cause disease, and the Halls and the Alcotts all came down with scarlet fever — much as the Alcotts had in 1850, but this time it was a far more serious case. The two Hall children died, and May and Lizzie were very sick. Louisa came home to help with the nursing.[4]

Lizzie Alcott's heart began weakening, although overall it seemed that she was improving. Louisa, reassured, returned to Boston, where she lived in an attic room of a pleasant boardinghouse run by Alice Reed. Bronson started off on a lecture tour — his Conversations were becoming slowly more popular, and he was in some demand.

By the time the family had decided to return to live in Concord at the beginning of 1858, Lizzie Alcott's illness had caught up with her. The family had bought Orchard House. It was in their temporary quarters, the rented house on Bedford Street, a house that has long since been torn down, that the Alcott family as Louisa knew it — and as millions of readers would come to know it — began to come to an end. Life hadn't been easy for the family of four sisters led by an impractical seer and held together by a solid, sometimes depressed woman who struggled with her own anger. But looking back even on the hardest times, it seemed that Louisa's first twenty-six years were spent in a golden dream of family. It was a life where adversities were less difficult because the family dealt with them together and the whole world was cushioned by the family that, although pathetic, was also somehow divine.

A room had been set up in the rented house for Lizzie, who was now too weak to continue pretending that she was not sick as she had been doing for months. In January a doctor who had finally been consulted in Concord, Dr. Geist, told the family that there was no hope for a recovery. It was no consolation that there had never been anything that the doctors or the medicine of that time could have done. The family gathered in the small rooms — the twenty-ninth place where they had lived in Louisa's twenty-six years. Everything else was put on hold as snow piled up outside and the family poured its considerable energy into Lizzie's last days, during which her suffering was slightly alleviated by ether and opium.

In *Little Women,* Beth has a quiet, dignified death, a fictional death. Although young Lizzie Alcott was a graceful, quiet woman, she was not so lucky. A twenty-two-year-old whose disease had wasted her body so that she looked like a middle-aged woman, she lashed out at her family and her fate with an anger she had never before expressed. They responded with love. Louisa acted out stories and comic scenes from conversations with her Boston landlady to make her sister laugh. Bronson sat by her upstairs bed and had an intimate conversation with her. Always the curious one, even at his daughter's deathbed, he asked if she had any idea where she would be going after death. "Have you some notions of your state after the change?" he asked gently. "Not so clear as I would wish," replied his daughter, as always an Alcott. Her physical pain was forgotten in a moment of intellectual examination, she told him, "but I prefer going as soon as may be."[5] Thoreau dropped by to visit the invalid and talk about Nature with Bronson.

Bronson distracted himself from his youngest daughter's illness with the renovations of Orchard House on the other side of town. The run-down place became a member of the family during this time. As Lizzie faded, the new house took on a vivid life. It would be a safe place, ending the years of nomadic risk. On March 13, he noted in his journal that "bricklayer builds the west parlour fireplace, fashioning it after my design, the bricks projecting from the jambs and forming an arch."[6] Then on March 14, his journal continues in the same tone: "This morning is clear and calm and so our daughter Elizabeth ascended with transfigured features to the heavenly airs she had sought so long."[7]

Louisa and her mother were at Lizzie's bedside when she took her last breath at around three in the morning. "A curious thing happened," Louisa wrote in her journal, "and I will tell it here for Dr. G. said it was a fact. A few moments after the last breath came, as Mother and I sat silently watching the shadow fall on the dear little face, I saw a light mist rise from the body and float up and vanish in the air. Mother's eyes followed mine, and when I said, 'What do you see?' she described the same light mist. Dr. G. said it was the life departing visibly."[8]

On March 15, a beautiful early spring day, the Emersons, the Alcotts, Thoreau, Anna and her employers the Pratt family, and Concord's new schoolmaster, Franklin Sanborn, invited to town by Emerson — all gathered for Lizzie's funeral and burial in the new Sleepy Hollow Cemetery, just established, on a ridge near Concord. The cemetery, a short walk from town, replaced the crowded old Concord Cemetery across from the village green. It was built along modern lines as a parklike Eden where visitors to the dead might be uplifted by the idea of natural beauty.

The Bedford Street house was abandoned, and in April, with Anna still at the Pratts and May back in Boston, what was left of the Alcott family — Louisa and her parents — moved into Hawthorne's Wayside, the better to oversee the renovations at Orchard House next door. "Came to occupy one wing of Hawthorne's house (once ours) while the new one was being repaired,"[9] Louisa wrote in her journals with typical terseness. Living in a house they had left ten years earlier, a house in which all four girls had been bursting with life and energy, a house that had been another of those places which seemed to be the solution for the pathetic family, evoked deep feelings for at least one of the Alcotts. "It suggests memories of busy days spent within these walls, and pleasing experiences in times past when Thoreau and [William Ellery] Channing and Emerson sometimes honored me with their sittings,"[10] Bronson mused on the past.

Then on April 7, less than a month after Lizzie's death, the family cohesiveness and the golden band of sisters was dealt another fatal blow, this time in the form of happy, happy news. Anna Alcott came back from living at the Pratt farm with John Pratt and announced that she was in love and that they were engaged. Even for Bronson, this departure of another daughter — to marriage instead of death — was complicated. "The thought is more than I am ready for at this moment,"[11] he wrote. But for Louisa, this "happy" announcement was a dreadful betrayal. In public Louisa congratulated the happy couple. "I moaned in private over my great loss and said I'd never forgive J. for taking Anna from me."[12]

In some ways, Anna's engagement to John Pratt, which was the only conventional marriage among the four sisters, was harder to bear than Lizzie's death. The death was awful and everyone agreed that it was awful. Sitting by Lizzie's bedside, desperately trying to amuse her as she cycled in and out of unbearable pain, giving her ether, watching her sleep, were all satisfying in their own sad way. We all grieve when we lose someone close; sadness is normal.

An engagement is supposed to be a happy occasion. Love makes the world go around. Our community gathers to rejoice with us even as, after a death, they gather to mourn. We are supposed to be thrilled. Presumably, Anna's engagement was a happy thing for *her;* but for Louisa it felt like another death, a death that she was not allowed to mourn.

Lizzie's death and Anna's engagement signaled the end of the Alcott family as Louisa had known it. The golden band of four sisters was now down to two, and May was often away. When a family creates its own intimate mythology, such shifts are hard. As long as Louisa was one of four sisters, sisters devoted to each other and to the family, her inability to connect with an appropriate man, and her own inability to conform to a feminine ideal was obscured. Anna's engagement threw Louisa's emotional isolation into sharp relief. At the same time, Louisa's mother was profoundly distracted by the death of her youngest daughter and the betrothal of her oldest. Once again she didn't have time to comfort the daughter who always seemed competent and able to take care of herself.

Louisa's other passions had seemed fine when they were the dreams of a young girl: her father's older friends, those Olympian married men, or younger men who were happy to climb trees, plan practical jokes, and take the lesser parts in the dramas she wrote and directed. That had all been happily normal when it was part of the fabric of the pathetic family.

Louisa may have been ambivalent sexually. She often referred to her masculine traits and her "mannish" looks. She did not, however, seem attracted to other women; quite the contrary. It seems more likely that, growing up in a family rocked by the throes of a passionate and stormy marriage between two people she adored, she formed a deep and abiding distrust of the state of holy matrimony. Later, when *Little Women* was a success, she refused to marry Jo to Laurie because she didn't want to represent marriage as a happy ending when she had abundant evidence that it was no such thing. Louisa as a child had watched the Hawthornes come to an accommodation of Hawthorne's friendship with Margaret Fuller; she had seen Lidian Emerson's pain over her husband's emotional and physical absences. She had watched the admirable Thoreau repel advances, and of course she was an astute observer of her own parents' struggles.

Whether because of her nature or because of the environment in which she grew up, Louisa May Alcott was deeply practical and able to suppress most of her feelings. Her focus was on helping the family survive and earning the money to ensure this, rather than with planning her own individual future. Louisa May Alcott kept journals during these difficult years. Later, when she was an older, wealthier, and well-known writer, she annotated the journals. As a result, her surviving journals are a fascinating study in perspective. In the passage written in 1858, she cried out in the written word over the loss of Anna to John Pratt.

The mature Louisa May Alcott had a different point of view. "Now that John is dead, I can truly say that we all had cause to bless the day he came into the family, for we gained a son and a brother and Anna the best husband ever known," she wrote in a footnote in 1873, fifteen years later.[13] For Alcott's readers, John Pratt was certainly a benefit, since Louisa's closeness to Anna enabled her to write a laser-sharp portrait of the stresses of young marriage in *Little*

That was later; the fall of 1858 found Louisa, as she approached her birthday at the end of November, feeling abandoned and useless in a way she had not anticipated. With much fanfare, the Alcott family moved into Orchard House and began to receive visitors. Their Monday night open houses featuring bowls of Bronson's apples were often crowded with old friends like the Hawthornes and the Emersons. "Much company to see the new house. All seem to be glad that the wandering family is anchored at last. We won't move again for twenty years if I can help it. The old people need an abiding place, and now that death and love have taken two of us away, I can, I hope, soon manage to care for the remaining four,"[14] wrote Louisa in her journal. But what was left of the wandering family?

There are three bedrooms at the top of the narrow stairs in Orchard House, laid out by Bronson Alcott. Moving into her little room at the front of the house was very different from the rough-and-tumble of life in the places the family had previously moved. May was in Boston and Louisa was the only child left at home. Before, they had been crowded. Now, suddenly, there was too much space. The possibility loomed that

Louisa would become the spinster sister.

In many New England families, one sibling ended up in the unenviable position of being the maiden aunt, the one who spent her life caring for the parents who had brought them all up. Louisa didn't want this position, but she seemed to be veering toward it. Her powerful dreams of finding fame and fortune as a writer — of being as famous as Jenny Lind or as talented as Charlotte Brontë — seemed to be slowly devoured by circumstance.

Louisa had come to dislike Concord. She wasn't even enchanted by Orchard House, which she called "Apple Slump." The railroad had changed the sleepy, isolated country town into a bustling business hub. The once-picturesque Milldam, Concord's eccentric Main Street, which is still on a dam built over the river — like a Yankee version of the Ponte Vecchio in Florence — was a busy thoroughfare crowded with shops like Holden's grocery, Reynolds's apothecary, and Jonas Hastings's boot shop.

When winter loomed, Louisa planned her escape. Her spirits were at their lowest ebb, and she decided to go to Boston to stay with her cousin Thomas Sewall on Chestnut Street and see if she could once again bring in some cash for the family and relaunch her literary career. "I am not needed at home and seem to be the only bread-winner just now,"[15] she wrote. After this entry, Louisa seems to have plunged into a loneliness and despair that were new for her. What she refers to later as her "fit of despair" passed, and Louisa wrote of suicide that "it seemed so cowardly to run away before the battle was over."[16] Buttressed by her Boston friends the Parkers and an offer of work as a governess for the charming child Alice Lovering, Louisa recovered. "There is work for me and I will have it," she wrote. She "resolved to take Fate by the throat and shake a living out of her."[17] Had she known what the next decade would hold for her and for her country, would she have been heartened or further depressed?

There are dozens of theories about what started the Civil War. How could it have been avoided? Was it the election of Hawthorne's friend Franklin Pierce, who hadn't the skills to find a way to bring the states together, or the passage of the 1850 Compromise, or the Dred Scott decision in 1857? Was it the local civil war in Kansas fought between the men who wanted the new state to sanction slavery and the men — many of them transplanted New Englanders — who abhorred slavery and wanted Kansas to be a free state? Was it the day that South Carolina Representative Preston Brooks used his cane to protest an antislavery speech by beating Massachusetts Senator Charles Sumner unconscious on the floor of the United States Senate, or was it the liberation of Shadrach Minkins, or was it Stowe's *Uncle Tom's Cabin*? A few years later, when Stowe was introduced to President Abraham Lincoln, the story goes he looked down at her from his great height and joked, "So you're the little lady who started this big war."

Many of these factors were more than hearsay to Louisa May Alcott and her family. None brought them closer to an understanding of the causes of the war than the short, violent career of a man named John Brown. Was John Brown a madman who kept his wife and children in an Adirondack hideout while he went about fomenting unnecessary revolution? Did he want slaves to rise up and murder their owners? Or was he a courageous freedom fighter, willing to give his own life for the equality guaranteed in the United States Constitution — an equality that would extend to all men no matter what their color?

In 1857, John Brown, a Connecticut native who had become a loud voice for abolition, came to Boston to raise money and made his first visit to Concord. He was contemptuous of the Concord intellectuals who were safe in their pretty houses while the world came apart. Yet he spoke to a packed meeting at the Concord Town Hall and won over Emerson and Thoreau. John Brown reflected the passion of the Alcotts and their friends, a passion that in their case had come from the very personal experience of helping frightened runaways to freedom.

Brown moved with his five sons to Kansas in order to fight against those who would have slaves there. He had become an outlaw and had organized a secret committee to raise money, called the Secret Six, that included Concord schoolmaster Franklin Sanborn and Emerson's friend Thomas Wentworth Higginson. President Buchanan put a price of $250 on Brown's head, and Brown mocked him by offering $2.50 for Buchanan's.

In May of 1856, after the town of Lawrence, Kansas, had been sacked and burned by proslavery men, Brown and his sons went on a killing spree among the families who lived along the banks of Pottawattomie Creek. They hacked one man to death and shot another execution-style. Five men were killed.

By the next summer, Brown was back in Concord giving another lecture to his fans, a lecture punctuated by waving the Bowie knife he had used in the Pottawattomie massacres. Few of the Concord townspeople gave money, but they were all enchanted with Brown. How did this group of nonviolent men and women reconcile their admiration for Brown with his barbaric actions? His fiery rhetoric combined with their passionate beliefs in individual freedom seemed to ignite in a way that obscured the moral landscape.

"Thoreau and Emerson took John Brown at the value he set himself," explains Robert Penn Warren in his brilliant biography of John Brown. "They didn't give him money, but they gave to the world his own definition of himself. . . . Emerson spent his life trying to find something which would correspond to (his) fine ideas. In John Brown Emerson thought he had found his man."[18]

Then at midnight of Sunday, October 16, 1859, a year and a half after the death of Lizzie Alcott, John Brown and his men took over the United States Armory in Harpers Ferry, Virginia, and waited for a revolution among the slaves from the neighboring plantations, a revolution that never came. Instead, U.S. Marines led by Colonel Robert E. Lee arrived, killed ten of the conspirators, and captured Brown and killed two of his sons. The events at Harpers Ferry were as important in Concord as if they had happened next door. "We have a daily stampede for papers & a nightly indignation meeting over the wickedness of our country, & the cowardice of the human race,"[19] Louisa wrote another casual friend from her Concord childhood, Alf Whitman.

Brown was hanged as a traitor in Charlestown, Virginia, on December 2. Thoreau and Emerson and Bronson Alcott all referred to him as a Christ-like martyr, and Louisa, who by this time was spending most of her time in Boston, even wrote a poem about his death. The poem demonstrates that as independent and clear-thinking as Louisa usually was, she was capable of sentimental lapses and was sometimes able to follow those she admired without being disturbed by the facts.

No monument of quarried stone,
No eloquence of speech,
Can grave the lessons on the land
His martyrdom will teach.[20]

In one of the annotations that Alcott wrote in her own journals years later, the wry Louisa reasserts herself, pointing out that her patriotism was better than her poetry.

John Brown's execution also became the subject of a more popular verse, "John Brown's body Lies a'mouldering in the grave," which in turn became the unofficial anthem of the Union Army a few years later. By then Robert E. Lee had turned down an offer to lead the Union Army and was leading the Army of Northern Virginia. After his execution, two of John Brown's daughters came to stay with the Alcotts for a few months, and Anne Brown later wrote a short memoir about staying in the house that she described as filled with fun and a happy family.

"One day Miss Louisa came bounding in, whirled around and clapped her hands above her head, exclaiming, 'I came, I saw, I've conquered,' " Brown wrote.[21] Louisa explained to her surprised houseguest that she had been trying to get the Alcotts' cranky next-door neighbor, Nathaniel Hawthorne, to let her have a look at the new sky tower which he had built onto the top of his house — once the Alcott house. He didn't seem inclined to let his boisterous young neighbor up the narrow flight of stairs, which had been built as an extension of the hallway above where she had once had a treasured first room of her own. Louisa kept asking for the loans of books that she knew were in the sky tower. Finally he had told her to go look for herself.

Brown also described playing games with the Alcotts, Nine Men's Morris, cribbage, casino, and Old Maid. When Brown asked Louisa why she had turned down a proposal, Louisa answered that she would have shocked her husband too much for the marriage to work.

In 1859, as war approached, Abba Alcott got sick, as she was to be almost every winter. Louisa went home to nurse her, and this hardship, a week nursing even a beloved old lady in a town she hated, opened another path for her. "Wonder if I ought to be a nurse, as I seem to have a gift for it," she wrote. "If I couldn't act or write I would try it. May yet."[22] As the war approached, Boston filled with soldiers and rumors. Louisa, still caught up in her round of story submissions and sewing and teaching jobs, watched the preparations swirl around her.

In May, Anna Alcott married John Bridge Pratt in a simple ceremony at Orchard House. Smiling on the outside, Louisa could not stop grieving on the inside. "We are in grey thin stuff and roses," she wrote of Anna's bridal party and dresses. "Sack-cloth I called it and ashes of roses, for I mourn the loss of my Nan, and am not comforted."[23] Still it was interesting to see some of the benefits of being married, Louisa wrote. "Mr. Emerson kissed her, and I thought that honor would make even matrimony endurable, for he is the god of my idolatry and has been for years."

Louisa's career finally seemed to be taking off. The *Atlantic Monthly* bought her melodramatic story about an orphan with a heart of gold, "Love and Self-Love." Louisa had been rejected by the *Atlantic* and its editors, James T. Fields and James Russell Lowell, so many times that she had despaired. But she never gave up. She had the endurance that is as much a necessity for a successful writing career as is talent. Her story appeared under her own name in the magazine in March 1860. Encouraged, she began to work on her first serious novel. The title was *Moods,* after an Emersonian epigram from his essay "Experience." "Life is a chain of moods like a string of beads, and as we pass through them they prove to be many colored lenses, which paint the world their own hue, and each shows us only what lies in its own focus."

In *Moods,* Alcott told a story that was quintessentially Concord. Her young heroine, Sylvia Yule, is torn between two loves; a Thoreau-like Adam who is at one with nature, and an Emerson-like fellow who is as elegant as he is desirable. Mistakenly thinking that the Thoreau character is lost to her — that he is married to someone else — Sylvia accepts the proposal of the other man. This love triangle, set on river trips and at country houses, obsessed Louisa all through the summer. "I was perfectly happy and seemed to have no wants,"[24] she wrote in her journal. By November, when her shared birthday with her father passed pleasantly, Abraham Lincoln had been elected president, and three weeks later South Carolina officially seceded from the Union, followed by Mississippi, Florida, Alabama, Georgia, Louisiana, and Texas.

Soon after Lincoln's inauguration, a stalemate that had been coming a long time developed over the United States' Fort Sumter in the bay off Charleston, South Carolina. Sumter was a federal fort and therefore, according to the Yankees, the property of the Union. Sumter was in South Carolina, and therefore the property of the southern states according to what had recently become the Confederacy under the leadership of Jefferson Davis.

In April 1861, the standoff at far-away Fort Sumter would have consequences for everyone in Concord and Boston. War in those days was still considered a gentleman's game, and few seemed to realize the carnage and heartbreak that would be released by a few shots on an obscure federal garrison. Louisa turned out to wave good-bye to the Concord Artillery of the State Regiment, Massachusetts Volunteer Militia, that was ordered to Washington along with all other volunteer units. "I've often longed to see a war, and now I have my wish," Louisa wrote with an innocence that in retrospect seems sad and mistaken. "I long to be a man, but as I can't fight, I will content myself working for those who can."

Fort Sumter was under the command of Major Robert Anderson, a career soldier from Kentucky who had owned slaves but had joined the Union at the start of the war. Opposite him manning the batteries onshore was General P. T. Beauregard, a man who had been one of Anderson's students when they were both back in a classroom at the United States Military Academy at West Point. At first the standoff was a series of strategy exercises right out of the West Point classrooms. Anderson snuck his troops into Fort Sumter under cover of night. Beauregard, as he had been taught, had thrown up a blockade at the entrance to Charleston Harbor. By April, Anderson's company was being starved out, and on April 12 the standoff broke. Beauregard's army shelled the Fort until Anderson and his men surrendered fourteen hours later. No one was killed. Perhaps this made it all seem even more unreal. In May, Louisa May Alcott took a sail out into the forts in Boston Harbor. "Felt very martial and Joan-of-Arcy, as I stood on the walls with the flag flying over me and cannon all about."[25]

The summer seemed to pass in a lazy haze. Louisa and her father were both concerned because their friend Thoreau had gone to Minnesota in the spring for his health. He was having trouble breathing. His health was not getting better. In July, Bronson sprained his ankle. This was an excuse for him to spend weeks at home reading, while Louisa visited her married sister Anna in her "sweet little nest" and worked on *Moods*. In Concord the roses bloomed, Thoreau got worse, and Bronson Alcott read and wrote in his journals.

Near the equally sleepy little town of Centreville, Virginia, about twenty miles south-west of Washington, D.C., where President Abraham Lincoln was now in the White House, the Confederate Army had camped at Manassas, Virginia, under the Confederate hero of Fort Sumter, P. T. Beauregard. The Union Army camped to the east and planned an attack to drive the southern armies away from Washington. This attack, many hoped, would be sufficiently decisive to win the war or at least to make it clear that the rebels could not win the war.

Because the attack was planned for a summer Sunday in July — July 21 — and because Washington, D.C., was a place where news traveled fast, and because there wasn't much to do on that particular day, many people had packed picnic lunches and ridden on horseback or in carriages down to Centreville to spread out on the gentle slopes above Bull Run and have a firsthand look at the pageantry of war. How thrilling to see our boys drive those Confederate soldiers back where they came from! There were ladies in bright-colored summer crinolines and senators and congressmen in shirt sleeves and newspaper reporters. Settling down in full holiday mode, they watched puffs of gun smoke from beyond the hills and approvingly observed Union soldiers march this way and that on the Warrenton

Turnpike below them.

Until that beautiful summer Sunday, war had sometimes been a spectator sport as well as a way of settling arguments. No one realized that this war would be the first modern war, the first war that was less like a duel between gentlemen and more like a vast natural disaster. Union General Irvin McDowell dithered while reinforcements arrived for Beauregard. The back-and-forth of the battle on July 21 was a series of strategic moves in which both generals made many mistakes, but the Union general made more.

What were the senators and ladies doing there picnicking on a battlefield? "They were there . . . because it never occurred to the authorities to keep them from coming," wrote Bruce Catton in *The Coming Fury*. "They were there, in short, because America did not yet know what it was all about; and because they were there they contributed mightily to the fact that an overstrained army driven from the field in defeat dissolved into a wild and disorderly rout which no man could stop."[26]

When the Union Army retreat began, the Sunday picnickers realized that something was amiss. They started to stampede for the bridge over Bull Run. They created a level of hysteria and traffic that finished off the Union strategy and which also, as if it had been calculated to do so, spread word of the terrible defeat faster than the uninvented telephone. Screaming women, terrified of rebel soldiers, shrieked and horses plunged into the water as the retreating army ploughed into the tourists who had come to see them win the war. Horace Greeley, editor of the *New York Tribune,* all but surrendered to the Confederacy in a letter he wrote to the president. "On every brow, sits sullen, scorching, black despair."[27] For two days, the *Tribune* had been predicting a glorious victory at Bull Run. Now, Greeley wrote, "we have fought and been beaten."

In Concord the summer went on quietly, but the news from Virginia was the cloud on the horizon that would build to the perfect storm. The Concord River would wind down through the pastures to meet the Assabet; the cows would come home at nightfall; the finches would sing and the ponds would shimmer; there would be strawberry parties and games of Nine Men's Morris — but even Concord would never be the same. Within three years, Thoreau and Hawthorne would both be dead, one of lung disease, the other of stomach cancer probably exacerbated by the terrible disagreements brought to the community by the war. Families would be decimated. Louisa would be gravely ill, and her life would never go back to what seemed in retrospect to be the carefree days of her youth.

*The young Louisa May Alcott.*

*Amos Bronson Alcott at the Concord School of Philosophy, c. 1880.*

*The Alcotts and Orchard House, c. 1865.*

*Orchard House and School of Philosophy, c. 1905.*

*May Alcott drawing of her sister Louisa as "The Golden Goose," c. 1870.*

Illustration by May Alcott from
the first edition of Little Women.

Frontispiece from first edition of Little Women, 1868.

*Louisa May Alcott, c. 1858.*

*Alcott in her bedroom at Orchard House, the room where she wrote* Little Women.

*Louisa May Alcott on the porch of her Main Street home (the Thoreau-Alcott House) with her niece Lulu's rocking horse, c. 1880–85.*

*Louisa May Alcott, c. 1870.*

*Louisa May Alcott and her niece Lulu,
c. 1882.*

*Louisa May Alcott after her literary success, c. 1879.*

*Louisa May Alcott with the actor James Edward Murdoch, c. 1886.*

# 6
# FREDERICKSBURG. AT THE UNION HOSPITAL.
## 1863–1865

Even after the humiliating rout at Bull Run, the war seemed like a skirmish, especially to the faraway Concord Yankees, comfortable with the righteousness of their abolitionist beliefs. The army and God were on their side; with such allies, many people in New England believed that a war could not be too serious. The South was equally blind; South Carolina Senator James Chestnut facetiously promised to drink all the blood that was shed if war was declared.

"Southern secessionists believed northerners would never mobilize to halt national division or that they would mount nothing more than brief and ineffective resistance," writes historian Drew Gilpin Faust in *This Republic of Suffering*. "Neither side could have imagined the magnitude and length of the conflict that unfolded, nor the death tolls that proved its terrible cost."[1] Three million men took up arms between 1861 and 1865, Faust points out. During the American Revolution less than a hundred years earlier, the army numbered 30,000 men at most.

Reading the history of 1860 and 1861 induces a strange kind of vertigo. It's like watching someone head pell-mell for the edge of a cliff that they just don't see. Even President Abraham Lincoln, elected in November of 1860, didn't seem to understand what was happening. The future Civil War General William Tecumseh Sherman, visiting Washington as a civilian, was profoundly disturbed by Lincoln's equanimity in the face of disaster. "The country is sleeping on a volcano," he wrote in his memoirs.[2]

The men of this country were not only unprepared for war, Faust writes, they were unprepared for it in a lopsided way. Many young men, ardent in what they believed was the cause of justice, went to war ready to die. Very few of them had thought about what it would feel like to kill. Dying for a great cause was the right thing to do, but they had been taught that killing was wrong.

Although Lincoln himself may have underestimated the stubbornness and animosity of his detractors (he was elected without appearing on some Southern ballots), his election by the forces of abolition was the first in a line of political dominoes that led straight to perdition. By February eleven states named themselves the Confederacy. In April, Fort Sumter fell.

In Concord, life went on more placidly. John Brown's family came to stay at Orchard House, but they were treated like any welcome houseguests. Louisa was obsessed with working on her novel *Moods,* the story of a young girl very much like her younger self named Sylvia Yule. Throughout her writing life, Louisa had written two kinds of stories. The first, which she called her "blood and thunder" stories, were written, at least consciously, entirely for money.

During the time she was writing *Moods,* for instance, being interrupted by her dozens of domestic obligations — sewing, hostessing, nursing her mother — she also found time to churn out one of the melodramas that she sent primarily to *Frank Leslie's Illustrated Weekly* under her pseudonym, A. M. Barnard. "Pauline's Passion and Punishment" is a short story about a beautiful woman who has been summarily dumped by her true love for a younger woman. She plots revenge — a revenge involving a much younger man — and the whole thing ends in a florid disaster. The two younger people

241

fall in love and jump off a cliff.

It's easy to see Louisa May Alcott in both the melodramas that she was writing and in what she thought of as her more serious work. When Pauline is in love, "some mental storm, swift and sudden as a tempest of the tropics, had swept over her and left its marks behind."[3]

When Sylvia Yule is in love, which happens as she cards wool with Adam Warwick in a scene of exaggerated domestic tranquillity, "Sylvia had quite forgotten herself, when suddenly Warwick's eyes were fixed full open upon her own . . . human eye had never shed such summer over her. Admiration was not in it, for it did not agitate; nor audacity, for it did not abash; but something that thrilled warm through blood and nerves, that filled her with a glad submission to some power, absolute yet tender, and caused her to turn . . ."[4]

In "Pauline," Alcott's writing is less guarded, and the bones of her argument push right through the prose. Revenge is not a good idea. In both her "rubbishy" writing and her earlier serious writing, Alcott's work is flawed by her intellectual ambitions. She lived in a house where ideas were all-important, in a community that made its living from ideas. But these ideas sabotaged her prose and her plots for a long time. No one reads novels for ideas alone. We all read for storytelling and if, when we have finished a lovely story in which the writer has taken us by the hand and gently guided us to places we have never seen before, our ideas are slightly changed then we are grateful. It was not until six years later that her storytelling skills caught up to her thinking.

*Moods* was to be her first novel, the kind of book that might get her attention from the James T. Fieldses of this world; she thought it would be the kind of book that would put her in the company of the great men who had always been her inspiration. At first *Moods* was a novel that seemed to have a life of its own. It obsessed Alcott for months, during which she forgot to eat or sleep and stayed up all night at her small desk scratching away with a quill pen. At least she had the support of her family. "Mother wandered in and out with cordial cups of tea," she wrote in her journals, "worried because I couldn't eat. Father thought it fine, and brought his reddest apples and hardest cider for my Pegasus to feed on. . . . I didn't care if the world turned to chaos if I and my inkstand only 'lit' in the same place."[5]

All writing is an act of obsession, but fiction writing requires a higher level of intensity. To write fiction, a writer must let the subconscious bubble up into full view and then tame and shape the images into some kind of coherent story and some kind of coherent theme. The descent into the subconscious can be terrifying and time-consuming. For a novelist, the real world falls away and the world of the novel takes on a vividness and fascination that can't be matched by people or happenings in the pale, ordinary, slow-moving actual world. The characters of the imagination seem to have a mysterious claim on the writer's time and attention. In this kind of trance, it is extremely hard to perform as a good wife, daughter, or mother.

Different writers find this trancelike state in different ways. The trance in which Louisa was writing *Moods* was interrupted by war news, by her mother's illness, and by the arrival of the Brown family as houseguests. Louisa's journals during these months alternate between times when she is sunk in a creative fervor, leading the vivid parallel life of her own novel, and times when she emerges to express her desire to fight in a real war. She longs "for battle like a warhorse when he smells powder," writes this sheltered twenty-eight-year-old.[6]

When it came to writing a novel, Louisa May Alcott was much more of an expert than she was on the matter of war. She was an obsessive reader who had imbibed Dickens's novels and memorized speeches from *Pickwick Papers,* a reader who so completely identified with one of Dickens's characters that she often called herself Sairy Gamp after the tipsy, outrageous, eye-rolling Mrs. Gamp, who serves as a comic nurse in *Martin Chuzzlewit.* From Dickens she had learned that even unimportant people with little money could be made important in literature. From this master too she had learned the difference between sentimentality — which he used to great effect — and melodrama. She also read the novels of Samuel Richardson and Henry Fielding as if they were how-to manuals for a writer. Her reading of *Jane Fyre,* by the English Charlotte Brontë and published by Harper & Brothers in the United States in 1848, profoundly influenced her own ideas about what women should and could write. Charlotte and her sister Emily also taught Alcott a valuable lesson about the kinds of women who make arresting characters.

Writing and reading were the two activities in which the difficult Louisa had also managed to please her father. In many ways, he was disappointed in his large-boned, temper-prone, passionate, hyperactive daughter, but when it came to books, they shared a voracious intellectual curiosity. Louisa's reading was wide and careful. In one typical month, June of 1861, she read Thomas Carlyle's *French Revolution* ("his earthquake style suits me," she wrote in her journal);[7] W. S. R. Hodson's *Twelve Years of a Soldier's Life in India,* which Emerson had recommended to her; and a life of Thomas More, which he also lent; as well as three contemporary novels: *Charles Auchester* by Elizabeth-Sara Sheppard ("charming"), *Evelina* by Fanny Burney (an eighteenth-century novel that Alcott reread), and Henry Fielding's *Amelia,* which she thought "coarse and queer," remembering what someone had written of Fielding's contemporary Richardson — that "the virtues of his heroes are the vices of decent men."[8]

Her father also approved unequivocally of her writing. There were still things about Louisa — including her dark looks and her abundant energy and her propensity to challenge almost any statement — which clearly displeased him. Nevertheless, she was the reader and the writer of the girls, and therefore often the only one who could be his companion in discovering interesting new works and in talking about things they had both read. Bronson had always wanted to be more successful as a writer than he was; Louisa shared his ambition and his passion for prose.

When she finished her first draft of *Moods*, she called the family together and held them spellbound in the parlor as she read. "It was worth something to have my three dearest sit up till midnight listening with wide open eyes to Lu's first novel," she wrote.[9] Even better, her reluctant father said two lovely things: "Emerson must see this." And "Where did you get your metaphysics?" All the discouragement in the world from the likes of editor James T. Fields could not have made a dent in the deliciousness of being the approved center of her own family.

In January of 1862, Louisa May Alcott took another teaching job. Unlike her father, she had never enjoyed teaching, but the success of Elizabeth Peabody's new Boston school that was based, as Bronson Alcott's schools had been, on the progressive principles of the Swiss educator Johann Pestalozzi was so successful that an additional school for poorer children was needed. The Peabody school charged $10 a pupil, the school being offered to Louisa May Alcott as headmistress and chief teacher would charge $6 and convene in a room at the Warren Street Chapel.

The school wasn't making enough to provide room and board, so Alcott stayed with whoever invited her or, often, commuted home to Concord after school on the train. It was an ordeal, from the social pretensions of her erstwhile hostesses to the teaching itself, and Louisa longed for her writing. "Hate to visit people who ask me to amuse others," she wrote in her journal, "and often longed for a crust in a garret with freedom and a pen."

For a while during the school year, she even stayed with James T. Fields and his wife, Annie, and their family. Fields had enrolled a nephew in the school, and he also lent Alcott $40 for books and supplies. His admonition that she should stick to her teaching because she couldn't write must have resounded bitterly in her head as she dragged herself through the dreary days of teaching. This semester, although she didn't know it, was mercifully the end of her teaching career. She would never preside over another classroom.

After school let out, she spent the summer in Concord, writing the lurid stories that embarrassed her but thrilled Frank Leslie. At Orchard House, she slept in her low-ceilinged upstairs bedroom and tried to make herself useful domestically as well as financially. She planted a vegetable garden and did the sewing. July was spent with the Willis family in the White Mountains, taking hikes and reveling in nature. In August her story "Debby's Debut" was published in the *Atlantic Monthly,* and the editors sent a check for $50. The family celebrated "Marmee's birthday" in October, Louisa wrote, using her pet name for Abba, and Louisa visited her sister Anna and her new husband in the cottage they had rented.

Eventually, the war came home to the Alcotts. As their neighbor Nathaniel Hawthorne wrote in an article in the *Atlantic,* "There is no remoteness of life and thought, no hermetically sealed seclusion, except, possibly that of the grave, into which the disturbing influence of this war does not penetrate."[10] As winter came on, with its premonitions of being shut in by the icy cold and snow, Louisa made a decision that would change her life. She was sick of knitting and sewing for the Concord boys who had joined the army, and her restlessness grew painful. "Wanted something to do," she wrote in her journal.[11] She had heard that nurses were needed, and she applied to be a Civil War nurse at a hospital in Washington, D.C.

The social reformer Dorothea Lynde Dix had been appointed the Union's superintendent of female nurses during the Civil War. The autocratic crusader had spent more than twenty years working for improved treatment of mentally ill patients and for better prison conditions. A week after the attack on Fort Sumter, Dix, at age fifty-nine, volunteered her services to the Union and received the appointment in June 1861, placing her in charge of all women nurses working in army hospitals.

Sometimes called "Dragon Dix" for her opinionated manner, Dix had definite ideas about who her nurses should be and what they should do. Previously women who followed armies had often been camp followers providing sex and companionship for the soldiers. Dix knew that she had to work against this stereotype. After convincing the army that women could serve as nurses, she recruited the plainest women she could find and dressed them in modest dark-colored clothing. She refused to have nurses younger than thirty years old and did not want women with children. Not only was she deeply concerned about the welfare of her nurses, she raised private money to supplement the meager funding the army gave her for her nurses and worked for nothing herself. Three thousand nurses served under her administration. One of them was Louisa May Alcott.

It was December 11 by the time Louisa received a letter telling her to start south. She was assigned to serve under Matron Hannah Ropes of Boston in the Union Hotel Hospital, a former hotel that had been commandeered by the Union. She wasted no time, spent the afternoon packing and saying an emotional but hurried good-bye to her parents, and by nightfall was off to the train station to take the train to Boston with her sister May and her neighbor Julian Hawthorne, who would travel with her on this first part of the journey. Hawthorne, the only son of Nathaniel and Sophia, was now living next door to the Alcotts in their old house. He remembered her before her trip to Washington as lively and generous. "A black-haired, red-cheeked, long-legged hobbledehoy of 26, though not looking or seeming near that age," he wrote.[12]

The young Edward Emerson, younger than Louisa, concurred. "The Civil War so kindled her that no one was astonished, or ventured to remonstrate, when she took the almost unheard of decision to volunteer as nurse behind the lines," he wrote, describing Louisa as tall, dark and "flashing." "She was a big, lovable, tender-hearted, generous girl, with black hair, thick and long, and flashing, humorous black eyes."[13]

In those playful days before the war changed everything, days of gardening and floating down the river under the willows and childhood games, the young Julian Hawthorne had a severe crush on May, the younger Alcott sister. Almost every day, he walked up the road to nearby Orchard House to visit the object of his enchantment. The two young people took walks together or worked in the garden or sat in the Alcott parlor. Julian thought May was also pleased to see him, but one week she made him nervous by mentioning that she was expecting a visit from a "cousin from England" who was coming to stay at Orchard House.

One summer afternoon, as Julian approached the house, he saw two figures standing by the Alcott fence in what looked like a very intimate conversation. One was his beloved May and the other a tall, elegant-looking gentleman with a monocle. No one even noticed Julian approach, the two seemed so engrossed with each other. He interrupted, and the two acted as if they were both disturbed in an important conversation. May blushed as she introduced him to the English cousin who glared through his monocle and spoke condescendingly with a clipped accent.

The young Hawthorne, increasingly jealous, wondered if he could beat the English cousin to a punch, when the gentleman put an arm around May's waist and drew her toward the house. "Come, my dear," the visitor murmured into May's shell-like ear. Furious, Julian began to sputter with rage and rush after them in protest when the English gentleman pulled off his hat and burst out laughing — the English gentleman was a cleverly disguised Louisa! That mischievous nature combined with an impressive acting talent was the Louisa Julian had grown up with. The war would change all that.

As Louisa hurriedly packed for her trip, Union soldiers 500 miles south of her began finally to assemble pontoon bridges over the Rappahannock River to the town of Fredericksburg. The bridges had been one reason for many, many delays in the Union Army advance. General Ambrose Burnside had insisted on waiting for the bridges, which took nearly a month to arrive. While he waited, he lost his ability to surprise the Confederate Army.

A handsome West Point graduate — his name and his flamboyant whiskers gave us the expression "sideburns" — Burnside had replaced the popular General George McClellan after the Union victory at Antietam, which had been the bloodiest day of the war and decimated the Union ranks. Unlike the confident McClellan, who was often compared to Napoleon, Burnside was a reluctant leader — he had twice turned down Lincoln's offer of command of the Army of the Potomac before he accepted it in the fall of 1862.

Burnside's army of 115,000 was much larger than the opposing southern force. Burnside positioned his men across the Rappahannock from the town of Fredericksburg, a town on the flatlands below the hills where the Confederate Army was encamped. As he waited a full month for the pontoon bridges, the Confederate Army had time to call for reinforcements and solidify its position. In fact, by the time the bridges arrived, the Army of Northern Virginia, led by General Robert E. Lee, was firmly entrenched with 78,000 men in the wooded hills above the town of Fredericksburg.

Before the official Union charge, Burnside ordered an artillery barrage that decimated the town of Fredericksburg but left the protected Confederate soldiers untouched.

Louisa May Alcott spent the day of December 12 in Boston doing errands, going to the dentist to get a tooth filled, and rushing from office to office, trying to unsnarl the bureaucratic obstacles to getting her credentials as a nurse and to buying her series of tickets for the trip. In order to get from Boston to Washington, she would travel by rail to New London, Connecticut, by steamship from New London to Jersey City, and then again by train to Washington, D.C.

As soon as she boarded the train to New London, Alcott returned to faithfully keeping the journal she had started at the beginning of her trip — a journal that later became a weekly letter home. These descriptions are written in a different voice than either of her previous writing voices. They do not have the melodramatic blood and thunder of the stories Alcott wrote for Frank Leslie, nor do they have the metaphysical underpinnings and ornate language of her more serious work. That day, on the train to New London, Louisa May Alcott came a long way toward finding the voice that would create Jo March. Her gentle self-mockery and willingness to be wry appear and reappear. "Put my tickets in every conceivable place . . . and finish by losing them entirely," she wrote. "Suffer agonies till a compassionate neighbor pokes them out of a crack with his pen-knife. Put them in the inmost corner of my purse, then in the deepest recesses of my pocket, pile a collection of miscellaneous articles atop and pin up the whole. Just get composed, feeling I've done my best to keep them safely, when the conductor appears."[14]

As Louisa May Alcott was bumbling through her trip in a way familiar to many travelers, General Ambrose Burnside was getting ready to make a far more serious series of blunders. Burnside's delay in taking command in the first place was closer to his nature than anyone realized. Later, in hindsight, the great Union General Ulysses S. Grant would describe Burnside as "an officer who was generally liked and respected. He was not, however, fitted to command an army. No one knew this better than himself." Burnside's stubbornness had been previously mistaken for courage. Having lost the opportunity to attack Lee's Army, commanded by Stonewall Jackson and James Longstreet, when they were not prepared, and having divided his own troops into three less effective sections, Burnside still delayed.

On December 12, the Union soldiers, having struggled to get the pontoon bridges into place and finally managed to cross the river, tore into the sleepy, charming southern town of Fredericksburg in a terrifying spree of looting and pillaging. Stores were gutted and soldiers trashed whatever could not be carried off. They entered houses, defaced walls with paint and graffiti that included their unit numbers, and tossed the contents of the gracious southern parlors and bedrooms into the street. Soldiers lounged in covered armchairs that had been dragged outdoors, and on Princess Anne Street a ragged group gathered around a stolen piano to sing. Mountains of household silver, women's jewelry, and anything of value were carried back across the Rappahannock to the Union lines and tents.

This ferocity on the part of the Union soldiers was presumably condoned at the highest levels, although a few officers ordered their men to stop. It stoked Confederate fury even before the two armies engaged. Many of the Confederate men, watching the looting of a Virginia town by Yankees, were from Virginia themselves. They were fighting to protect the virtue of their mothers and sisters and daughters and the sanctity of their own families. Local newspapers made much of the depredations inflicted by the Union Army, stressing how their women had been violated. Although the women of Fredericksburg were not raped or attacked physically, their boudoirs were stripped and muddied and the roads out of Fredericksburg were filled with fleeing, defenseless women and children.[15]

Further up the Atlantic Coast, Louisa May Alcott was taking her first trip beyond New England. She hadn't left Baltimore yet, but her journal is already more Dickensian than Richardsonian. Gone were the pacing beauties and mustachioed villains of her A. M. Barnard stories. Gone were the convoluted metaphysics of her more serious work. Instead, she wrote in a wry, direct voice. Just south of Baltimore, Alcott's train had an accident when a coupling iron broke, creating a small crash between two cars. "Hats flew off, bonnets were flattened, the stove skipped, the lamps fell down, the water jar turned a somersault," she wrote. "Of course it became necessary for all the men to get out and stand about in everybody's way, while repairs were made; and for the women to wrestle their heads out of the windows, asking nine foolish questions for one sensible one."[16]

Finally on the morning of December 13, Burnside gave the command to attack. The Union Army, two months late, started across the pontoon bridges with all possible pomp and fanfare. The blue columns crossed the river on the swaying bridges in vast, organized waves, flooding through the town and fanning out onto the open plain below the Army of Northern Virginia. "It moved with flags and with bands and with a great rumbling of moving cannon, making a display of might that impressed the waiting Confederates, impressed even Lee himself."[17] Looking down at the approaching army from Marye's Heights, Lee had an acute consciousness of history — he had been educated at West Point like Ambrose Burnside — and of the future. A brilliant strategist, he knew that the attack was hopeless and that the superior strength of the Union Army was unimportant because of the position and preparation of his own army. "It is well that we know how terrible war really is," he commented to an aide as the glorious but doomed Union Army approached, "else we would grow too fond of it."[18] Burnside's men swept across the river and through the remains of the town into the entrenched Confederate lines, where they were mowed down immediately.

As the dead of the Union Army began to pile up below the Confederate position at Marye's Heights, Burnside's men led another attack. The day wore on, and Burnside, sequestered in headquarters on the other side of the river, watched the battle from the second floor of a beautifully furnished Greek Revival house. The Union Army made sixteen attacks against a position that had been shown to be unbreachable earlier that day.

The waves of Union soldiers marching forward under a rain of fire and sometimes crawling over their fallen comrades to move ahead sickened even the Confederate troops who were mowing them down. The Battle of Fredericksburg was one of the worst defeats in the history of the United States Army; 12,700 men were killed that day as Burnside ordered his men over and over again into death and they obediently followed his orders. Fredericksburg quickly became a symbol of stubbornness in the face of unbeatable odds and of the resulting, almost incomprehensible, horror.

As the day waned, Burnside seemed to fall apart, and finally, at dusk, weeping, he announced he would lead the last charge himself. Instead, he was coaxed to retreat. As he left the field strewn with the Union dead, his aide called for three cheers; instead, there was an appalled silence from the men. "A battle is indescribable," a Union chaplain wrote after seeing the carnage at Fredericksburg, "but once seen it haunts a man till the day of his death."[19]

That night, defeated Union soldiers and their Confederate enemy looked out over acres of land that seemed to be carpeted with the Union dead and wounded, heaps of men groaning and screaming. Quiet figures moved among the wounded and dying, some Union and some Confederate. The wounded must be retrieved, the dead buried. The soldiers from the Twentieth Maine carved rude grave markers and dug shallow graves for the bodies they could find and identify. A Confederate doctor gave the dying remnants of men water from his canteen. Slowly the sky lit up and an extraordinary natural phenomenon illuminated the scene. Sheets of red and gold — an aurora borealis, usually called northern lights and very rare as far south as Virginia — threw curtains of lurid light down from the sky. Nature herself seemed to be shining a horrified spotlight on the events of that day.

Watching in exhausted wonder, the Union soldiers took the marvelous lights as a sign of their righteousness. "Firey lances and gold all pointing and beckoning upward. Befitting scene! Who would die a nobler death or dream of a more glorious burial?"[20] wrote a soldier in the Maine division. On the Confederate side, the heavenly lights were seen as God's approval of their victory. "We enthusiastic young fellows felt that the heavens were hanging out banners and streamers and setting off fireworks in honor of our victory," wrote Robert Stiles, a Confederate officer who had graduated from Yale a few years earlier.[21]

Does nature reflect the feelings we have? No. In literature this is called the "pathetic fallacy," the mistaken idea that there should be a storm when a character is furious or that the dawn arrives just as a character dies. The literature of the nineteenth century from Wordsworth to Louisa May Alcott leans heavily on this device. But here there was no literary device, unless you believe that God is a writer. Following one of the worst battles in history, the sky actually did light up with the kinds of lights and mysterious movements that seemed a reflection of divine response.

Walt Whitman's brother George had been one of Burnside's soldiers, a captain in the Union Army, and Whitman rushed from Brooklyn to the battlefield to see if he could find his brother. George Whitman survived with a superficial wound, but the sight of the battlefield at Fredericksburg and a pile of human parts — amputated legs and hands outside a hospital tent — changed Whitman's career. For the rest of the war, he devoted himself to the Union hospitals, starting at a hospital near Fredericksburg, where another Civil War nurse, Clara Barton, was also at work.

Whitman visited the wounded and dying, brought gifts of candy and rice pudding, and wrote sometimes dozens of letters a day home for soldiers who were unable to write letters for themselves. He always carried a pocketful of notebooks for his own observations. Even sadder, Whitman wrote letters to the families of soldiers who were dead or dying, trying to fold some kind of consolation into the words for those whose losses he understood would be unbearable.

Louisa May Alcott and Walt Whitman had never met, but Bronson Alcott had twice visited the burly author of *Leaves of Grass* in his mother's Brooklyn house on Classon

Avenue before the war. Emerson had been an early fan of the book, and his laudatory phrase "I greet you at the beginning of a great career" was emblazoned by the shameless, self-promoting Whitman on the jacket of the book. Some Bostonians were not forgiving of Whitman's bold voice. "It is no discredit to Walt Whitman that he wrote *Leaves of Grass*," Emerson's friend and Emily Dickinson's mentor Thomas Wentworth Higginson cracked, "only that he did not burn it afterwards."[22]

Given Whitman's address by Emerson, Alcott had taken Henry David Thoreau on a special visit to Brooklyn to visit in 1856. Whitman whisked the visitors through the house and up to his attic bedroom where the walls were covered with pictures of well-muscled half-naked men — images of Hercules and Bacchus. For the visit, Whitman then offered his guests a chair, while he reclined his 200-pound body, dressed in a red flannel undershirt, and lay back against his own bent elbow. Alcott had found Whitman "full of brute power" and his eyes "gray, un-imaginative, cautious yet sagacious: his voice deep. Sharp, tender sometimes and almost melting."[23]

Whitman, the sensual spider in his Brooklyn lair, was changed forever by his visit to his brother George at Fredericksburg. Feeling that the soldiers he saw represented the majesty of the American people, Whitman gave his help to them wholeheartedly. Although no Christian himself, he tried to comfort the families he addressed. "There is a text, 'God doeth all things well' — the meaning of which, after due time, appears to the soul," he wrote the family of one soldier, Frank Irwin.[24] In his greatest poems, like "When Lilacs Last in the Dooryard Bloom'd," Whitman's sense of loss and yearning seems to rise straight out of the men he helped. Louisa May Alcott was not the only writer whose mature prose was forged among the wounded of the Union Army. Whitman's Civil War journals became the poems in his book *Drum-Taps,* published in 1865.

Battlefields and hospitals go together, but the progress in weaponry that caused the Civil War slaughter had not been matched by progress in medicine. The only anesthetic available was chloroform, when it could be had; the idea that germs caused disease was not widely accepted, and doctors did not wash their hands as they went from patient to patient or when they performed surgery. There was no sterilization or even soap and water attendant on operations. The idea of antiseptic would not make it to our hospitals until after a British doctor, Joseph Lister, discovered the work of Louis Pasteur in 1865. No one understood that mosquitoes carried malaria, or that fecal matter could cause illness.

Disease was an enemy that took more lives than bullets. Hospitals were more dangerous than battlefields. Twice as many men died from disease during the Civil War as died of wounds from fighting the enemy. Even without war, illness was a fierce enemy in the nineteenth century. The Alcott family way of dealing with illness through rest and homeopathic medicines was probably more effective than most medication and less deadly. Nineteenth-century doctors subscribed to the theory that disease fed on whatever was in the body and that, therefore, the body must be emptied. The liver was thought usually to be the source of disease, and a mercury compound named calomel was believed to be a great healer of all liver ailments. We now know that mercury is poisonous, but doctors during the Civil War mistook the effects of the poison for signs of healing and continued to do so as their patients died. To become sick was often a death sentence.

As Burnside, shattered, retreated, Louisa

May Alcott arrived in Washington 45 miles north and took a horse-drawn cab to her destination, a hospital that turned out to be hardly changed from its former life as a hotel. A Union Hospital ward was still labeled "Ballroom," and the renovations had not removed fetid damp rooms, or peeling walls and leaking ceilings. The hospital was so disorganized that Alcott immediately gave it the Dickensian name Hurly-burly House and herself the name of Nurse Tribulation Periwinkle.

After a fitful first night, she was ordered to be superintendent of a ward with forty beds. Her duties would be washing the patients, serving meals, and giving medicine to men with pneumonia, diphtheria, and typhoid. A dozen "dilapidated patriots, hopping, lying and lounging about,"[25] looked on. Hannah Ropes, the matron of the hospital, wrote, "We are pleased by the arrival of Miss Alcott from Concord — the prospect of a really good nurse, a gentlewoman who can do more than merely keep the patients from falling out of bed."[26] Alcott and Ropes often worked together in the wards.

On the morning of December 16, everything changed. Louisa May Alcott looked out the window at what seemed to be rows and rows of farmers' market carts stretching as far as the eye could see. With growing horror, she realized that the carts were piled not with vegetables and produce but with men, wounded and dying men, survivors of the Battle of Fredericksburg on their way to her hospital, needing her care. "My ardor experienced a sudden chill," she wrote, "and I indulged in a most unpatriotic wish that I was safe at home again, with a quiet day before me."[27] Louisa May Alcott spent a total of six weeks working at the Union Hospital. She arrived December 13 and left at the end of January. In that six weeks, she lived a lifetime of experience, an experience that changed her forever, physically and as a writer. Fredericksburg was Louisa May Alcott's Fredericksburg.

"In they came, some on stretchers, some in men's arms, some feebly staggering along propped on rude crutches, and one lay stark and still with a covered face, as a comrade gave his name to be recorded before they carried him away to the death house."[28] Confronted with this army of the wounded, Alcott was unable at first to summon the courage the situation required. This bold woman whose brashness had often gotten her into trouble lost her nerve and hid behind a pile of clothing. Another matron spotted her in her hiding place, pulled her out, and told her to get to work and wash the men, many of whom were caked with mud and dirt from the battlefield and filth accumulated during their journey in the carts with piles of their fellow soldiers. Alcott noted that if she had been asked to dance a hornpipe on the stove funnel she would have been less staggered, "but to scrub some dozen lords of creation at a moment's notice was really — really — . However there was no time for nonsense, and having resolved when I came to do everything I was bid, I drowned my scruples in my washbowl . . ."[29]

Her first patient was an Irishman with a head wound, and as Louisa went after him with soap and water, he began to laugh, something he hadn't done for a few days, days that seemed like a lifetime, Alcott wrote in *Hospital Sketches,* her detailed account of her time at the Union Hotel Hospital. Something about being washed by a woman amused this Irish soldier. Soon, Alcott and her patient were laughing together, and later he rested his tired head against her shoulder like a sleepy child. Although Alcott had probably never seen a naked male body before this day, she overcame her inhibitions and became a compe-

269

tent and loving nurse. She washed off the layers of mud and gore and dressed their awful wounds, and most of all she listened to their stories. One was a sergeant who was worried that on Judgment Day there might be confusion among the thousands of amputated legs and arms and he might end up with the wrong ones. Another man from Michigan had his arm blown off at the shoulder. After washing the men, Alcott helped feed them from trays of bread, meat soup, and coffee that appeared from the kitchen. "Great trays of bread, meat, soup and coffee appeared," she wrote, "and both nurses and attendants turned waiters, serving bountiful rations to all who could eat."[30]

Now, at the Union Hospital in Washington, D.C., everything shifted for the protected Alcott. Dr. John Winslow, a Quaker who was the surgeon on Alcott's ward, took a romantic interest in her. "He comes often to our room with books, asks me to his (where I don't go,) & takes me to walk now & then. Quotes Browning copiously, is given to confidences in the twilight, & altogether is amiably amusing," she wrote in her journal.[31] Winslow's friendship was not confined to whispering sweet nothings in the twilight; he and Louisa walked all over Washington. They went to hear William Henry Channing, the chaplain of the House of Representatives, give a speech at the Capitol Building, which Louisa found boring, and they had dinner at a local German restaurant.

But it was the wounded and dying men who captured Louisa's attention and her heart in the first weeks after Fredericksburg. At first she was on the day shift; she began her morning by running through the ward and opening the windows. The men grumbled at the cold but Alcott was convinced — like all medical professionals at the time — that disease was carried by stale air. "A more perfect pestilence box than this house I never saw — cold, damp, dirty, full of vile odors from wounds, kitchens, washrooms, & stables. No competent head, male or female, to right matters," she wrote.[32] After a breakfast of fried beef, butter, grainy bread, and weak coffee taken with her coworkers, Alcott, a former vegetarian, ran around the hospital making beds, tending wounds, sewing bandages, and helping the surgeons who, she thought, were often too rough with her beloved patients. After a similar lunch, Alcott would continue working until 9 P.M. when the lights went down and she was free to retire to her own spartan room.

Louisa used every trick she knew to comfort and care for the men. She read Dickens to them and recited the parts of Sairy Gamp from *Martin Chuzzlewit.* She quoted poetry and told them stories. She listened to them. She wrote letters for them, and when they died and letters still had to be written, she did that too. "The answering of letters from friends after someone has died is the saddest and hardest duty a nurse has to do."[33]

In this setting where social conventions and class distinctions fell away, Alcott came to love many of the men she nursed. She was astonished by their quiet bravery and she grieved when they died. The stakes were high at the hospital. There was no time for chitchat or any place for all the things in life Louisa despised — phoniness, snobbism, the shame of being poor. Here where all was life and death, she found an intimacy with those who needed her that had eluded her in life, and she relished it. Later, when her shift changed from the day to the night shift — she first worked from noon to midnight, and then from 9 P.M. until dawn — she came even closer to the men she cared about as she hovered over them in the red head-scarf that was her nurse's uniform. "It was a strange life — asleep half the day, exploring Washington the other half, and all night hovering, like a massive cherubim, in a red rigolette over the slumbering sons of man."[34]

One 6-foot-tall New Hampshire man who could not sit up, asked Alcott to come and feed him the soup that was splattering on his face and beard when he tried to feed himself. As she did, he told her his version of the battle of Fredericksburg. This had been his first experience in combat. The man he fought next to, a friend, was killed early on and this angered him. As a result, he explained, "a lot of us larked around Fredericksburg, and give some of them houses a pretty consid'able of a rummage."[35] Later he was near a shell explosion that had ruined his leg.

In gratitude for her nursing and her help in feeding him, he offered Alcott two gorgeous pieces of jewelry purloined from a fine house in the looted city — earrings made to represent "corpulent grapes" and a pin made to look like a basket of fruit. She accepted the grapes but not the basket only because, as she wrote, she felt "delicate about depriving him of such valuable relics." Did she also feel delicate about taking part in the spoils of war?

One man who stood out in the ward of

dying men was a Virginia blacksmith named John Suhre. He had never married but devoted his life to helping his mother and family. Now he lay dying with a musket ball lodged in his lungs, but since his wound was in his back, he could hardly believe the pain he felt or understand his peril. Tall and extremely handsome, he was dying without complaint or remorse, and Alcott spent as much time with him as she could. "His mouth was grave and firm, with plenty of will and courage in its lines," Alcott wrote, "but a smile could make it as sweet as any woman's."[36] John Suhre wanted to live, and in spite of his pain, he believed he would. But when Alcott asked the surgeon what John's chances were, the doctor said that John was suffering more pain than anyone else in the ward and that he would be dead in a day or two. Then the surgeon gave Alcott the awful job of telling the handsome blacksmith, who was exactly her age, that he only had a few days longer on this earth.

Alcott was devastated and had no training or experience in such a task. Terrified and suppressing tears, she approached the bed of this dying man as his wounds were being dressed. She leaned in and offered him her hand and shoulder to help him bear the pain. After that, his eyes followed her everywhere, and she did everything she could for him, bringing flowers and writing a letter for him to his brother. Finally he asked her if this, his first battle, would be his last. She was able to tell him that yes, he had fought his last battle. This exchange brought the two of them even closer, and both waited for a letter that might reassure him that his mother and younger sister would be taken care of.

The night John died, Alcott sat grieving by his bed, wiping his brow, holding his hands, and listening to him — powerfully reminded of what it had felt like to sit next to her own sister Lizzie's bed as she had died. As John's body struggled to survive, futilely, the big man wept in Alcott's arms. "For a little while, there was no sound in the room but the drip of water, from a stump or two, and John's distressful gasps, as he slowly breathed his life away," Alcott wrote.[37] "I thought him nearly gone, and had just laid down the fan . . . when suddenly he rose up in his bed, and cried out with a bitter cry that broke the silence, sharply startling every one with its agonized appeal.

" 'For God's sake, give me air!'

"It was the only cry pain or death had wrung from him, the only boon he had asked; and none of us could grant it." When John Suhre's body finally failed, he was holding Alcott's hand so tightly that she could not pry his fingers away. After another patient helped her untangle her hand from the dead man's hand, she still had four white marks where his fingers had dug into her flesh as he died.

In the letter she wrote home about John Suhre's death, Louisa took a great story and embroidered it to reflect the vividness of her feelings. In her version, the blacksmith dies just as dawn's light floods the room. The letter from John's home arrives in time to be buried with him. And although Alcott had a special connection to John Suhre, many of the other men needed her ministrations just as much. In many ways, in spite of the smells and sleeplessness, in spite of the fear and grief, she had found a place in the world where her strength and boldness and outspoken ways were assets instead of liabilities.

Then she got sick.

Both Alcott and Hannah Ropes came down with pneumonia in the beginning of January. "Sharp pain in the side, cough, fever & dizziness. A pleasant prospect for a lonely soul 500 miles from home!" Alcott wrote.[38] The doctors gathered around their suffering comrade giving her doses of calomel, taking her pulse, and examining her lungs. John Winslow turned himself into a nurse and brought cologne, flowers, and wood for her fire. And the doctors advised her to give up and go home.

Louisa May Alcott was as stubborn as Ambrose Burnside. She refused to leave and stayed in her room nursing her fever, taking more calomel, sewing, and learning even more about hospitals and the way they work from being a patient in the place where she had been a nurse. "I was learning that one of the best methods of fitting oneself to be a nurse in a hospital, is to be a patient there; for then only can one wholly realize what the men suffer and sigh for; how acts of kindness touch and win; how much or little we are to those about us," she wrote.[39]

When President Lincoln's Emancipation proclamation was passed on New Year's Day, Alcott got out of bed and danced a little jig, but she was soon prostrate again. Decoding the signs and symptoms of nineteenth-century medicine is not an exact science, but Alcott seems to have contracted pneumonia and then typhoid, a disease carried through the drains or water that has been infected with fecal matter. Her illness started with a cough and soon progressed to the high fevers and delusional fever dreams that are typical of typhoid. Then, as the pneumonia and typhoid resolved, her body was racked by the effects of the mercury poisoning caused by the doses of calomel medicine that the kind doctors provided her with every day in the hospital. Mercury poisoning is insidious, damaging the central nervous system, distorting the mental processes and causing muscle weakness, salivation, sores on the gums and teeth as the patient's body begins to shut down.

The news of Hannah Ropes's death electrified the hospital staff, and the arrival of Bronson Alcott, summoned by Dorothea Dix herself, overcame all Louisa May Alcott's protests. Bronson had rushed south and arrived on the morning of January 16 to find an emaciated Louisa, semiconscious on a thin mattress, alone in a freezing cold room with broken windowpanes and rats scuttling in the walls. Five days passed before the doctors decreed she was well enough to travel. She was bundled up and shivering with fever when she and her father boarded the train to Boston, where they spent the night, and got to Concord the next day. "Louisa was faint and overcome by the long ride, but much better in the morning," her father wrote his daughter

Anna after the grueling journey.[40]

The Louisa who returned to Concord was dramatically different from the healthy eager girl who had left six weeks earlier. "The amount of pleasure and profit I got out of that month compensates for all after pangs," Alcott wrote later.[41] She may have learned everything she needed to know as a writer and as a woman, but the effort almost killed her. She was, Edward Emerson noted, a white, tragic mask of what she had once been. Julian Hawthorne was also shocked at the changes in the woman he had seen off less than two months earlier.

Not only was she a weak, shrunken version of her former robust, tall self, but also there seemed to be an emotional veil between her and the rest of the world, almost as if she had already left on the first stages of a long trip. Neighbors helped spell Abba at Louisa's bedside. Emerson provided as much household help as Abba would tolerate. Looking in the mirror, Louisa saw a queer, thin big-eyed face she didn't recognize. When she tried to walk, she found that her legs were useless and this made her weep. Concord's Dr. Bartlett ordered her head shaved to discourage the fever. Alcott complied and was glad, she wrote, to have given her hair for her country although she could not give her life. This thought, percolated into fiction, reappears in *Little Women* when Jo sells her hair.

During the weeks of illness and fever, Alcott's brain seemed to rebel against everything she had seen in Washington. She had a series of nightmares right out of the melodramas of A. M. Barnard. She would bolt up in bed muttering incoherently, and she failed to recognize her mother, who was desperately trying to find a way to care for her. In her delusions, she was married to a fat, handsome Spaniard dressed in black velvet who was continually saying "Lie still, my dear." This man terrified her and seemed to be everywhere, in the closets, at the windows of her front bedroom on the Lexington Road, and in the dark after night fell. She thought she had married him. Her appeals to the pope to intervene with the Spaniard didn't work.[42]

In another semiconscious dream, Alcott went to heaven and found it twilit and ordinary. "I thought it dark & 'slow' and wished I hadn't come," she recalled.[43] In other delusions, she was being pursued by a mob in Baltimore that was trying to break down the door to the room where she had taken refuge. Sometimes her mother or sister Anna found her crying out as a result of these visions. One night, hearing a crash from Louisa's bedroom, May rushed in to find her sister on the floor. Louisa scolded May for leaving her alone with so many men.

In her waking dreams, she was also burned, stoned, and hung as a witch, and she was tempted by John Winslow and two of the Union Hospital nurses who urged her to worship the devil. "Such long long nights — such feeble idle days, dozing, fretting about nothing, longing to eat and no mouth to do it with, mine being so sore and full of all manner of queer sensations it was nothing but a plague."[44] Outside the windows of her room, the Concord winter set in with its snowdrifts and icicles and impassable roads. Snow fell on the elms in front of the house and on the flower beds and on the ice of Walden Pond, where Thoreau had lived what seemed a century ago. February passed in a haze of illness, semiconsciousness, and unsuccessful efforts to do simple things like sewing or reading.

By the beginning of March, appropriately the beginning of an early New England spring, Alcott seemed to be getting better, and her father left her bedside to give some Conversations. It became clear that she wasn't going to die; it was also clear that

281

she was not the same person who had so blithely gone off to war. "At the hospital her duties collided with her fear of men," writes Martha Saxton. "She had to repress her terrors and be physically intimate with many males. . . . The imagery of Louisa's hallucinations was richly gothic. . . . The Spanish grandee, a character Louisa had used since childhood dramas, was a romantic but fearsome scoundrel, full of vitality and sexuality, who worked his way with women. Tamed, these fantasies were material for stories. Untamed, they were expressions of Louisa's deepest sexual and emotional horrors."[45]

Alcott would be sick for the rest of her life and very sick for the next decade, suffering debilitating headaches, dizziness, and strange pains in her legs as well as overwhelming exhaustion. She had left for the war a vigorous and energetic woman; she returned a true casualty. Yet the war also changed her writing style forever. The literary recognition that had eluded her, in spite of a killing amount of hard work, almost immediately began to come her way.

During the homesick watches of the night at the Union Hospital, Alcott had written a poem in memory of her friend Thoreau, who had died in 1862. Titled "Thoreau's

Flute," it already incorporates a leaner, more visual style in spite of being a flowery memorial poem:

> His pipe hangs mute beside the river
> Around it wistful sunbeams quiver,
> But music's airy voice is fled.

The poem, which Alcott promptly forgot, was discovered by her father in her luggage during her illness and passed on to the Hawthornes, who in turn passed it to Louisa's old friend and nemesis James T. Fields. In May he published it in the *Atlantic.*

Louisa had written detailed, vivid weekly letters home during her time in the hospital, and these letters were then published in the antislavery newspaper the *Commonwealth* and reprinted everywhere. In a world of slow, erratic communications, Alcott's sympathetic and heartbreaking descriptions of the cost of war were avidly read by the families of soldiers. By June, as Louisa began to be able to move around and think of writing again, both Roberts Brothers and James Redpath bid to make her letters into a book. She chose the publisher James Redpath, who paid her the amazing sum of $200 for the book, which was titled *Hospital Sketches* and printed in an edition of 1,000.

Alcott received 5 cents a copy and a percentage of the profits were donated by Redpath to the children of Civil War casualties. The book sold well and earned her a great deal of praise and a nice letter from her friend Henry James. "I find I've done a good thing without knowing it," she mused after the publication of letters she had written to her family in the heat of the moment, letters she had not been composing as she would compose a book.

Whitman and Alcott hadn't met in Washington, but their literary careers began to overlap when they got home. The success of *Hospital Sketches* got Whitman's attention because he too wanted Redpath to publish his account of helping in the Union hospitals, to be titled *Memoranda of a Year.* By August of 1863, he was writing to Redpath that his book would be something "considerably beyond mere Hospital Sketches."[46] Redpath declined. For the first time in her life, Louisa May Alcott was being asked for writing, more and more writing. Frank Leslie wanted more of her A. M. Barnard stories. James Redpath wanted another book, and Roberts Brothers also wanted a book from her. Even James T. Fields clamored for more stories for his magazine and for another book from Louisa May Alcott, formerly the teacher who couldn't write. The literary gods are fickle. Once they had belittled her; now they were fighting over her! "There is a sudden hoist for a meek & lowly scribbler who was told to 'stick to her teaching,' " Alcott exulted in October of 1863. She knew just which book would be the next, and by January she had gone back to work on *Moods.*

# 7
# THE WRITER.
## 1861–1867

*Moods* was Louisa May Alcott's first serious novel, although she had been writing seriously for more than ten years. Finished for the first time in 1861, and read in the evenings in the parlor aloud to her delighted and enthusiastic family, *Moods* has not survived as a popular favorite. Women who loved *Little Women* have often never even heard about *Moods*. With the exception of scholars who are interested in both Louisa May Alcott and feminist studies, little has been written about it.

Yet *Moods* was clearly of great importance to the author herself. Of all the books she wrote and published, *Moods* was the one she cared about the most. It delighted her in the writing, sending her into a vortex of creativity so intense she did not eat or sleep for days at a time. Its edited, shorter form came to her in a dream. With its twin topics of the connection between love and marriage and the destructive nature of impulse, it embodied her own preoccupations. It obsessed her long after it was done.

While she was originally working on it in 1861, her writing was interrupted first by the visit of John Brown's family to Concord, and then much more seriously by her own Civil War service and almost fatal illness. When she was finally able to work again after coming home from the Union Hospital, she turned to *Hospital Sketches*. The success of that book raised her hopes, and she returned to the manuscript of *Moods*. Yet getting the novel published turned out to be a lengthy and painful process — a process in which Louisa May Alcott's patience, tolerance, ability to accept criticism, and writing talent were all taxed to the limit.

Her first submission was to James Redpath. Although Alcott had some questions about the way Redpath had published *Hospital Sketches,* she yielded to the pressure of his desire to see her next book. She was thrilled at the passion this publisher showed for her work, a passion so unlike the reluctance or neutrality of previous publishers, including that of James T. Fields. At the beginning of February 1864, an excited Redpath himself appeared in person at Orchard House in Concord to collect the manuscript, promising to have it out in book form by May. The next day, he telegrammed Louisa, asking her to come down to Boston to see the printers about the book. When she got to Redpath's office, however, his news was quite different than what she expected. The book was too long to publish in one volume, he told her. Two-volume novels were almost impossible to sell. He liked the book, but would it be possible for her to cut it in half?

Alcott responded with the restrained fury of a writer who has been asked to eviscerate a book that has come to be like a child to her. No, she said. She took her manuscript and left for the train back to Concord. "I had rather have Fields or some other publisher get it out," she wrote in her journal. "Redpath does not suit me though he does his best I believe."[1]

But Fields and Niles and all the other publishers were suddenly scarce. Alcott had become quite famous at this point in her life. She was regularly feted, and fans had started coming to Concord to try to catch a glimpse of her. Yet this didn't help when it came to the publishing of the book that was her heart's desire. In April, Alcott sent her manuscript to Howard Ticknor, who had joined with the famous James T. Fields to create the already well-respected publishing house of Ticknor & Fields. Ticknor had a different but equally daunting reaction to the manuscript of *Moods.* He wrote Alcott a letter familiar to all writers who have received many rejections. He said that he found the book interesting but that the publishing house had so many books on hand that they could not publish her novel at the time.

By now Alcott's attitude toward publishers had taken a turn from the confidence and enthusiasm of a year before. She felt quite sure, she wrote, "if they wouldn't have it there must be something good about it. Don't despair *Moods,*" she wrote addressing the book directly, "we'll try again by & by." In a later annotation of her journals, Alcott scrawled next to this entry, "Alas, we did try again!"[2]

Then in September a friend of Bronson Alcott's named Caroline Dall, a writer and lecturer who also counted herself as a Transcendentalist — she had hosted one of Bronson's Conversations in her Boston home — came with her teenage daughter to spend the night in Concord at the Alcotts'. Always a woman of action, Dall had come on a series of missions to the Alcotts, a family once again famously on the brink of financial disaster. She was to try and get a job for Bronson, she would help May sell her artworks in Boston, and she would read the manuscript of Louisa May Alcott's *Moods,* critique it, and try to find a publisher. Dall loved the book. She became an ardent fan, writing Alcott of *Moods* that "no American author had showed so much promise, that the plan was admirable, the execution unequal but often magnificent," Louisa wrote in her journals.[3] Thus began a relationship that was to yield as much pain as pleasure.

Two letters discovered by scholar Helen Deese in the Caroline Dall papers at the Massachusetts Historical Society in the 1990s show that Alcott's connection with Dall was prickly almost from the start. In spite of Dall's approval, an approval great enough for her to have forwarded the manuscript with her recommendation to another publisher, A. K. Loring, she couldn't resist writing a long letter of criticisms and suggestions to which Alcott responded again as if protecting a vulnerable child. "You call Sylvia deceitful, . . ." Alcott wrote, "but how many girls of 18 would have done any better. . . . Women instinctively hide much of themselves, & are called brazen huzzies if they don't. Very few are clear in their minds, steady in their feelings, or wise in their judgments, & when in love, good heavens! What blind bats both men & women are."[4]

The manuscript went off to A. K. Loring, who liked it very much, he said, but he thought it was way too long for publication. Loring urged Louisa May Alcott to cut; again she refused. "Was much disappointed, said I'd never touch it again & tossed it into the spidery little cupboard where it had so often returned after fruitless trips," she wrote.[5] In the meantime, Alcott embarked on another one of her romances to be published under the pseudonym A. M. Barnard. Money was tight and she also worked on a volume of stories for children and on what she hoped would be a second serious novel, titled *Work*.

Then one night in October when the air was crisp with the coming of winter, Louisa suddenly saw a way to cut her beloved novel down in length without ruining it. She had gone to bed as usual in her little corner room. Startled wide awake in the middle of the night by her vision, she got up and started to write. By morning she had slipped back into what she called the vortex, in which she "wrote like a thinking machine in full operation."

It took a week of writing day and night to remove ten of the book's thirty chapters. At the end of that time, Alcott felt that she had improved the book that she had earlier thought could not be cut. Later, she came back to her original opinion.

Much of the drama surrounding the writing and publishing of *Moods* reappears a few years later as Chapter 27 of Alcott's masterpiece *Little Women,* a book she did not want to write as much as she wanted to write *Moods.* "Having copied her novel for the fourth time, read it to all her confidential friends, and submitted it with fear and trembling to three publishers, she at last disposed of it on condition that she would cut it down one-third, and omit the parts which she particularly admired," cracks Jo March as she submits her novel. Even then in fiction as in life, her editors were not satisfied. In another edit, Alcott writes, Jo March "laid her firstborn on her table, and chopped it up as ruthlessly as any ogre."[6] In *Little Women,* the novel is published to both praise and blame. Jo March is surprised to find that the parts she took from real life are reviewed as "impossible and absurd" while the parts she drew from her imagination are pronounced "tender and true."

Loring loved the cuts that Alcott sent him and proposed to publish the book immediately, which he did. At last! By Christmas of 1864, Alcott received ten copies of her novel, signed with her real name. Yet the novel's actual publication was close to traumatic. Having cut and recut it until she thought her ideas themselves had been made incomprehensible, she was amazed and abashed at the attention the book received. Many wrote to say how much they had liked it, including Thomas Wentworth Higginson, Emerson, and Franklin Sanborn.

The book got a good review in *Harper's Weekly* but was damned in the *North American Review* by a man Louisa thought of as a friend — Henry James. James, in his early twenties and making his literary mark, had good and bad things to say about the book, but the bad things he had to say were awful. After scolding Alcott for trying something that had already been done much better by Europeans, and saying that her professed subject, a doctrine of affinities, made no sense, he wrote, "We are utterly weary of stories about precocious little girls." The two most striking facts with regard to *Moods,* he concluded, "are the author's ignorance of human nature, and her self-confidence in spite of that igno-rance."[7]

Nevertheless, Alcott and James remained friends, and his close reading of *Moods* was the beginning of the deep influence her writing had on his writing. Of course, the very precocious little girls of whom James claimed to be weary are the heroines of many of his own novels: Daisy Miller in *Daisy Miller*, Isabel Archer in *Portrait of a Lady*, and Verena Tarrant in *The Bostonians*. Writing in the *Massachusetts Review*, Alfred Habegger points out that the heroine of James's first novel, *Watch and Ward*, is referred to twice as "precocious." It's easy to see Alcott's influence as it flowed from *Little Women*, with its feisty, outspoken American heroine Jo March, to James's *Portrait of a Lady*, with its feisty, outspoken American heroine Isabel Archer. The power-ful influence of Alcott on her young friend began earlier with *Moods*.[8]

What was it about this novel that Louisa May Alcott couldn't let go? Why did this book, of all her work, obsess her long after it was first published? In the first version, a simple story of a young girl who fails to obey the dictates of her heart — the man who made her feel like summer disappears and she's unable to wait for him — Alcott seemed to be writing about the differences between love and marriage.

Alcott often noted that marriage didn't seem to make people happy. She saw nineteenth-century marriage as a kind of domestic slavery for women, who were yoked by law to the financial and emotional whims of their husbands. "*Moods* is about the other civil war, in which the conflicts were the inner struggle for modern individuality and the simultaneous battle to win for women the rights of man," writes Professor Sarah Elbert in her introduction to a recent edition of *Moods*.[9]

The sense of liberation that swept the country in the 1840s and '50s had given rise to a new idea of marriage. The practical, colonial idea of marriage — a non-romantic agreement between two people whose obligations were to have children, keep house, and perhaps clear the land — had more or less been cast aside. In the rush of enthusiasm for emotional truth and freedom, some people began to believe that marriage was a pairing of soul mates, a coming together of two sympathetic beings joined by true love. Once women married, however, they were still expected to follow their husbands both physically and emotionally. It was this clash between the head and the heart that at first seemed to be the subject of *Moods.*

Whether the subject of *Moods* was the constriction of modern marriage or the destruction caused by moody impulsiveness, as Alcott later said, the writing of it brought intoxicating relief, a refuge in Louisa May Alcott's imagination where she could escape the desperate realities of the family's diminished life and the tremendous costs of war.

Although he expressed interest in the novel, Alcott was afraid to show it to Emerson before it was officially published. Geoffrey Moor with his library and his intellect might have been a little too recognizable to Emerson.

For Alcott, moods were an important topic. She was a creature of violent, often uncontrollable emotional ups and downs. By the time she wrote the book, she had clearly experienced, according to her own journals, many extreme states of mind. She had those few moments of absolute transcendence in the natural world, times that caused her to affirm the existence of God. She had also been seized by vortices of manic writing energy. At times, sometimes because of illness, she had been unable to leave her bed. At one point, she had become so despairing that she thought of suicide. Yet at other times, her rugged, durable cheeriness was the mainstay of her family.

In his biography of Louisa and her father, *Eden's Outcasts,* John Matteson suggests that Louisa May Alcott may have been bipolar or suffered from what we diagnose today as a mood disorder. "The question demands to be posed: if Louisa May Alcott were alive today, might she herself have been diagnosed with some form of manic-depressive illness?" he writes.[10]

Matteson marshals a lot of evidence for his diagnosis. Bipolar disorder, formerly known as manic-depression, is hereditary and the Alcotts were famously erratic. Louisa's Uncle Junius ultimately killed himself in 1852. He cites the brilliant Kay Redfield Jamison, who wrote, "Many lines of evidence indicate a strong relation between mood disorders and creative achievement." Then he quotes Jamison in an e-mail to him as writing, with an ambiguity of syntax worthy of Bronson Alcott, that his evidence "does not irrefutably show, but is consistent with, the strong likelihood that Louisa May Alcott suffered from a form of manic-depressive illness." When Matteson telephoned the late Alcott biographer Madeleine Stern, however, she disagreed with him, contending that there was not enough evidence to diagnose Alcott.

Whatever Louisa May Alcott's mental and physical illnesses may have been, this controversy points out the problems with what has become a subsidiary Alcott industry — twenty-first-century diagnoses of her nineteenth-century illnesses. Was she bipolar? Was her chronic illness after her Civil War experience all from the mercury poisons in her system that were periodically reawakened, as Martha Saxton has written? Or did her continuing symptoms, as Madeleine Stern has suggested in her biography of Alcott, stem from meningitis contracted on her dreadful trip home from Washington to Concord with her father in January of 1864?

In 2007, Dr. Norbert Hirschhorn and Ian Greaves from the University of Minnesota School of Public Health published a long, detailed paper that is a history of Louisa May Alcott's illnesses beginning with the pneumonia and then the typhoid and mercury poisoning contracted in Washington, D.C. Hirschhorn and Greaves conclude from contemporary descriptions that Louisa May Alcott's death at the age of fifty-five was from a cerebral brain hemorrhage suffered after years of ailments, headaches, generalized aches, and severe stomach and throat pain that caused her to write that she was a "prisoner to pain." The mercury that poisoned her in 1863, they point out, would have cleared her system within a year — although mercury can do permanent damage. Even though she took morphine and many other drugs to kill the pain, she was not addicted to painkillers.

Instead, Hirschhorn and Greaves propose that Louisa May Alcott was suffering from some kind of immune disease, probably systemic lupus erythematosus, a disease that attacks nerves, skin, bones, and joints and causes migraine headaches. Their evidentiary *pièce de résistance* is an 1870 portrait of Alcott that shows the characteristic malar, or butterfly, rash of lupus. It's a nice idea, but I have looked often at the same portrait, and I do not see what they see.

All of this brings up the question of how history and biography are best understood. Is it possible, for instance, to argue that Louisa May Alcott's friend Henry David Thoreau was homosexual? Does it matter if he was? Is it interesting to catalogue Alcott's various physical symptoms, push aside the way she explained them, and how she thought of them and come up with a more "informed," or at least more modern medical diagnosis? And what of the mental states of the men and women we study when we study biography? Is it important to know that Ulysses S. Grant was an alcoholic, that Ralph Waldo Emerson suffered from acute senile dementia in the last years of his life?

On the one hand, understanding the nineteenth century through the lens of twenty-first-century knowledge and understanding and research may throw more light on people we struggle to know because of their accomplishments. Their work speaks to us, and so we want to know who they were. We connect with them on the page and this makes us hunger to connect with them as people. Yet in our postcolonial world, there seems to be a kind of imperialism to this assumption that our context is the superior context. Instead of immersing ourselves in the context of Louisa May Alcott's life, we drag her into our own as if what we know about illness, say, is far superior to what was known in 1865. This is true in many ways.

Are we doing our subjects a favor when we transpose them into the modern world? Do we really understand them better by imposing our own patterns of knowledge onto them? The purest biographers struggle to re-create the context of the times they write about; they take their subjects on their own terms. Biography is a shifting form, and more and more writers supplement what they can't know — exactly what it felt like to live in 1864 — with what they can know — exactly what it feels like to live in 2010. This can shed light on the hearts and minds of their characters, but it can also obscure them.

Certainly physical diagnoses are easier to make in retrospect than those of mental illness. Physical symptoms are relatively static, while mental reactions and behaviors are deeply influenced by the culture and the family and the historical context in which they happen. In Alcott's case, the diagnoses out of context are further complicated by her status as an artist. What kind of abnormal perceptions of the world contribute to the making of art?

Alcott and her friends and inspirations Emerson and Thoreau were sharp exceptions to the modern observations that connect the creative impulse to excessive drinking and other kinds of self-destructive behavior. The American nineteenth-century writers, including Hawthorne, Thoreau, and Longfellow, were not a group of alcoholic womanizers, as some European and British writers at that time seemed to be and as some American writers later became. Many of the Concord group were vegetarians who leaned toward temperance. Nevertheless, their creative impulses may have been intertwined with abnormal mental states — Alcott's manic vortices, for instance.

How are these states to be understood? Those who would label them, the English critic Charles Lamb wrote, are in error.

The ground of the mistake is, that men, finding in the raptures of the higher poetry a condition of exaltation, to which they have no parallel in their own experience, besides the spurious resemblance of it in dreams and fevers, impute a state of dreaminess and fever to the poet. But the true poet dreams being awake. He is not possessed by his subject but has dominion over it. . . . Where he seems most to recede from humanity, he will be found the truest to it. From beyond the scope of nature if he summon possible exigencies, he subjugates them to the law of her consistency.[11]

*Moods* is a failure in many ways, although it's hard to discern from the surviving manuscripts what it may have been like in the original version. In the end, Alcott persisted in thinking that the problem with the novel was the cutting she had been urged to do in order to get it published. The shortened version seems to merge Alcott's more serious writing — the lean informative paragraphs of *Hospital Sketches* — with her old habits of melodrama and sentimentality.

In Chapter 1, two lovers meet in a shadowy room after a red sunset in dangerous, romantic Cuba. Adam Warwick tells his fiancée Ottila that he wants his freedom. "If he had lifted his strong arm and struck her, it would not have daunted with such pale dismay. An instant she stood like one who saw a chasm widening before her, which she had no power to cross . . . she seized the imploring hands in a grasp that turned them white with its passionate pressure." Shame burns Ottila's dark cheek, ire flames up in her eyes, but she gives Adam leave to go. With its melodrama and inflated language, this chapter might as well have been written by A. M. Barnard for Frank Leslie.

Chapter 2 of *Moods* is worlds away in tone and content. In simple, cozy language, it introduces Sylvia Yule, a spirited young girl who has just secretly visited a neighbor's garden and found herself browsing uninvited in his library. The neighbor is the older

Geoffrey Moor, who will eventually per-
suade the young Sylvia to marry him. She
agrees only because she is convinced that
the man she truly loves — Adam Warwick
— has gone away and married someone else
and is never coming back.

Reading this novel, it's hard not to hear
the clanking of metaphysical machinery going on in the background. Having set up
Sylvia as a ditzy young girl enraptured by
Adam Warwick, Alcott has to make Geoffrey
Moor gentlemanly and intellectual but in
no way an object of passion. At first Sylvia
turns Moor down, and he vows to wait.
Then Ottila herself shows up — wild and
beautiful and just visiting from Cuba — and
announces she's engaged to Warwick. Then
there is a series of misunderstandings that
causes Sylvia to think Warwick has married
someone else while she waited for him.
Rejected and bereft, she throws herself into
Moor's waiting arms.

The two are married, and on their wed-
ding trip they run into none other than Warwick, who has come at last to reclaim his
true love — Sylvia. He feels the same way
as she does — of course he does — but she
is married to the man they both love and
admire — the greathearted Geoffrey Moor.
There is lots of arguing, tearing of hair, and

gnashing of teeth before Warwick and Moor are both drowned in a dreadful shipwreck. Sylvia's decision is tragically no longer necessary. The reader almost breathes a sigh of relief.

How can the writer who created the powerful, moving portraits of dying men at the Union Hospital in *Hospital Sketches* and then, a few years later, the iconic feminine figures that still define our world in *Little Women,* have written a trite, labored melodrama like *Moods*? The book is certainly support for the old writing adage to write what you know. In *Hospital Sketches,* Alcott was writing from experience, an experience in which the intrinsic drama was so great that she was able to find power in appearing to tone it down. Men dying, wounded, men trying to reach their families before the end, bravery in the face of intense physical and psychological suffering, all animated Alcott's prose.

In *Little Women,* Alcott was also writing from experience, compressing years of difficult life into a few vividly remembered stories. The two books are suffused with real yearning, a yearning for a different kind of family, a yearning for a different kind of war, a fierce yearning for the extension of life itself. But the drama in *Moods* doesn't ring true, and too often it slips into a weaker version of Alcott's blood-and-thunder voice. Do writers know when they are writing well? In this case, the author herself loved the weakest book the best of the three.

At first, when *Moods* was finally published at Christmas in 1864, things seemed to go well. Loring ran out of the first printing of a hundred right away and had to bring out a second. In the meantime, Alcott's reputation had grown enough so that the editor James Elliott offered to give her $75 instead of $50 if she allowed him to put her real name on her latest blood-and-thunder story — "V.V.; or, Plots and Counterplots," a lurid tale of another gorgeous woman with a black heart and the men she lures to their doom. Alcott turned him down. Even an extra $25 in a year when her total earnings were less than $300 was not enough to allow Louisa May Alcott to emerge from the hiding place provided by A. M. Barnard.

As January and February unfolded, the response to *Moods* became less ebullient. For the first time in her writing career, Louisa May Alcott found her work under attack. People she didn't even know wrote her letters criticizing the book she loved so much. Sometimes she felt that readers had failed to understand her ideas because she had to shorten the book. "Moods is not what I meant to have it, for I followed bad advice & took out many things which explained my idea," she wrote another editor, Moncure Daniel Conway, in February. "I see my mistake now for I find myself accused of Spiritualism, Free Love & all sorts of horrors." Alcott was so upset and defensive at the reactions she got that by March she was even answering some of the critical letters from people she didn't know. "Half the misery of our time arises from unmated pairs trying to live their legal lie decorously to the end at any cost," she wrote one stranger, a Mr. Ayer. Later in the same letter, she switched defenses, asserting that the book is not about marriage at all but about "the effect of a moody person's moods upon their life."

Although the publication of *Moods* was painful, as her letter to Mr. Ayer shows, Alcott was swept away by what was happening in the world around her. In March 1865, President Abraham Lincoln was inaugurated for the second time, and in April the Civil War came to an end. Alcott's difficult spring was just one point of pain in perhaps the most painful months ever suffered by the United States of America. On March 4, as Alcott braced herself against criticisms of the book she loved the best, Washington, D.C., turned out for the inauguration.

If God is a storyteller and history is being written by a single intelligence, the events of March and April of 1865 suggest that He turned His computer over to Shakespeare for a while and went out to take a coffee break. The inaugural festivities started with bands and floats and the first companies of African-American Union troops.

Lincoln was not in his carriage; he was in the Senate Chamber preparing to give his second inaugural address, the speech of a lifetime. His words had to be powerful enough to reach both the victors in the war that had just claimed 600,000 lives and the bitterly defeated. For his new vice president, Lincoln had chosen a simple, eloquent speaker from Tennessee with a fervent devotion to the Union itself. A tailor by trade, and a former slaveholder, Andrew Johnson had not received the thorough investigation he might have at a moment when the president had less to do.

The pressures of an actual inauguration were apparently too much for this tailor from Tennessee. By the time he had entered the Senate Chamber to take the oath of office before a group that included the cabinet, the Senate, the Supreme Court justices, and Mrs. Lincoln, the fortifying whiskey he had probably been drinking all morning got the better of him. Standing before Chief Justice Salmon Chase to take the oath, Johnson instead launched into a drunken, obstreperous tirade. "Your President is a plebeian," he began, "I am a plebeian — glory in it." He berated the senators, who did not understand that they were only there because of the "little people." Johnson continued almost incoherently. His captive audience began to whisper in horror. "There is something wrong," said War Secretary Edwin Stanton. Attorney General James Speed closed his eyes. "Johnson is either drunk or crazy," he murmured. About halfway through Johnson's embarrassing display, President Lincoln entered the Senate Chamber holding his speech. As he left the chamber and walked out onto the Capitol steps to deliver his own address, Lincoln ordered those around him not to let Johnson outside.[12]

Lincoln's speech was short, brilliant, and one of the finest speeches ever made. Schoolchildren still learn it by heart. Its clear phrases ring absolutely true. If the country could have been healed with words, Lincoln's second inaugural might have done it. "With malice toward none; with charity for all; with firmness in the right, as God gives us to see the right, let us strive to finish the work we are in." Lincoln's voice rang out over the crowds now bathed in afternoon sunlight, the crowds of freed slaves and their former owners, the crowds of wounded soldiers and their widows and orphans, the crowds including the freed slave and leader Frederick Douglass, who had a premonition of murder that day, the crowds including John Wilkes Booth, who later boasted of being within shooting range.

The war wound down. "Richmond taken on the 2," Louisa May wrote in her journal at the beginning of April, "Hurrah!"[13] A week later, it was over; after four years of war, General Robert E. Lee officially surrendered to General Ulysses S. Grant at Appomattox Court House in Virginia. As Lincoln had forecast in his inaugural, the terms of the surrender were generous. The Confederate soldiers were free to go home with their horses, and officers were allowed to keep their guns. Six days later, President Lincoln went to Ford's Theater to see a comedy — *Our American Cousin* — and was mortally wounded by a shot fired at close range from southern patriot John Wilkes Booth. Concord and the rest of the nation were plunged into mourning. Six weeks after the inauguration, the eloquent, wise Lincoln was dead and Andrew Johnson was president.

Whatever went on in the world or in her own life, Alcott still nurtured an obsession with her first novel. The world may have had a mixed reaction to *Moods,* but she was not finished with it. In 1864 when it was first published, and in 1865 when reviews came in, she was in her early thirties, unworldly, a woman writing for the money to keep her family afloat. In 1882 her circumstances were entirely different. She was a middle-aged, wealthy, and well-respected writer, and she sat down and rewrote and restructured *Moods* yet again, trying to get it right once and for all. *Moods* was republished in 1882 in the new version. By that time, Alcott was a beloved mentor and writer for young girls, known for her cozy voice and stunning honesty. By that time, everything published under her name sold off the charts.

After the winter and spring of 1865, a dramatic time both for Louisa May Alcott and for the nation, one of Alcott's dearest wishes came true, although not in the way she had imagined it. As the nation careered toward disaster and impeachment, Reconstruction and its dreadful backlash, a wealthy Boston shipowner decided his invalid daughter, Anna, should travel to Germany to take the waters. Nineteenth-century health spas featured mineral baths and massage, and some of the most desirable of these were in Germany and Austria. William Fletcher Weld, who had his own Black Flag fleet of barks and brigs and steamships, had heard that Louisa May Alcott had nursing experience, and he asked Alcott if she would go to Europe as Anna's companion, embarking from Boston in July with Anna and her brother George, who would leave them at Liverpool.

Louisa had some doubts. She would be traveling as the paid servant of a pretty, wealthy, and querulous young girl — perhaps the nightmare of her service with the dreadful Richardson in New Hampshire flashed through her deciding mind. On the other hand, she was a thirty-two-year-old woman with wanderlust, who had never been outside of New England except for her memorable six weeks in Washington, D.C., during the war. The war was over now. Her career also seemed at a standstill. How could she resist a year of traveling abroad? So on July 18, she said her Concord good-byes and boarded the Fitchburg train for Boston. With passport stamped, she joined Anna Weld and her brother on board the steamship *China,* a packet of the Cunard line. On the morning of July 20 the *China* weighed anchor for the nine-day crossing to Liverpool, and Louisa watched as her world receded behind her, the hills of Boston fading in the distance.

At Liverpool the two women boarded a train for London at the Lime Street Station, and Louisa May Alcott began to believe that she was actually in another country, another world. Everything looked different. She was delighted by the neatness of the gardens and cottages of the English countryside. "Nothing was abrupt, nobody in a hurry, and nowhere did you see the desperately go ahead style of life that we have," she wrote her father from London. "The very cows in America look fast, and the hens seem to cackle fiercely over their rights like strong minded old ladies; but here the plump cattle stand up to their knees in clover, with a reposeful air that is very soothing, and the fowls cluck contentedly as if their well disciplined minds accepted the inevitable spit with calm resignation, and the very engine instead of a shrill devil-may care yell, like ours, did its duty in one gruff snort, like a beefy giant with a cold in his head."[14]

Writing is a craft like anything else. Much of it can be taught; practicing writing makes writing better. There are rules for good writing and ways of reading that foster good writing. At heart, though, there is a mystery to what brings sparkle and power to something as simple as a line of words on a page. Writers often write their best when they are feeling their worst. Sometimes subjects they would rather avoid elicit their finest prose. Writers rarely know what alchemy of time, place, and mood will find their truest voice. If they write every day, it's because they do not know which days are the ones that count. Louisa May Alcott was no exception.

The prose she cared about the most, whether it was her essay about six weeks of servitude in New Hampshire — an essay marred by her own unexplored feelings — or a novel about a love triangle, seemed to be the writing that had the least power, the least fluidity, the least leverage over her readers' hearts and minds. The writing she cared about the least, her letters home, is her best at this point in her life. Self-consciousness is one of the greatest enemies of good writing, and on this trip Alcott's awareness that she was writing with a capital *W* seemed to fade.

Suddenly, on the train to London, the

clunky, lurid prose of *Moods* fell away, and her words began to sizzle and snap with the exhilaration of what she was seeing and what she was feeling — a resurgence of her writing talent. Anna Weld, a young woman who despised books and spent her days playing backgammon, would turn out to be an annoying companion. Taking care of her required the patience of an angel, Alcott wrote. Traveling was uncomfortable. But from the beginning of her trip, Louisa May Alcott got her prose style back and her letters home — like the letters she wrote on her trip to Washington — are vivid, funny, and compelling.

During four rainy days in London, Alcott roamed the streets and squares of London, which were more real to her from her reading than they seemed to be now that she was finally there. She took a leaf of ivy for a book of pressed flowers she was collecting for her mother. The women crossed into France, and at Brest, Louisa wrote her mother that "Market women sit all about selling queer things, among which are snails: they buy them by the pint, pick them out with a pin like nuts and seem to relish them mightily."[15] Alcott loved Brussels, hated Cologne, and was enchanted by her journey up the Rhine.

It was comically disconcerting to be in a place where no one spoke English, and her rudimentary German didn't work. When she asked for a blanket, she was given an egg and when she thought she had ordered supper, a woman appeared with a pile of towels and an iron. At Schwalbach, the two women made their first planned stop, boarding in a family home, the house of Dr. Anton Genth, the author of *The Iron Waters of Schwalbach,* while Anna visited the local spa.

Spa life in the nineteenth century was a minuet in which the wealthy traveled as health tourists to take the mountain air of Germany and Switzerland and drink and bathe in water that was famous for its mineral content. Much discussion at Schwalbach centered on which mineral was predominant in the water and which was the most beneficial. While Anna Weld had massages and treatments, Alcott became increasingly bored. Louisa only had time to notice in her sharp way that visitors to the spa almost always followed the directives of a spa ditty which stuck in her head:

Arise betimes to pump repair,
First take the waters then the air,

Most moderate be in meat and drink,
and rarely, very rarely think.

August and September crawled by. Finally, after a long and anxious wait, there were letters from home. Anna seemed to feel better, and the duo were rejoined by Anna's brother George for the next leg of their trip — to the Pension Victoria at Vevey. It was lovely to be on the move again, stopping in Heidelberg and Baden-Baden, where Alcott was delighted by the cathedral. Her first look at the Alps came at the beginning of October. "Tall, white spectral looking shapes they were, towering above the green hills and the valleys that lay between," she wrote happily in her journal.[16] Freiburg was spectacular and romantic. Alcott was charmed and delighted by the town's many suspension bridges. Finally they reached Lausanne and Lake Léman (Lake Geneva) and then sailed across the lake to Vevey. There they checked into the Pension Victoria and George Weld once again left them for Paris.

"At the little town of Vevey, in Switzerland, there is a very comfortable hotel." So Louisa May Alcott's friend and critic Henry James begins *Daisy Miller,* his eponymous novel about a pretty, young American girl who will appear in the garden of the hotel named the Trois Couronnes and be befriended by an American named Winterbourne. Although Alcott and her pretty, young aristocratic American companion, Anna Minot Weld, checked into a different hotel in the small Swiss spa town on the eastern end of Lake Léman, the story of what happened there both to Anna and Louisa may have inspired Henry James ten years later. Here in Vevey, where James set his most romantic novel, Louisa May Alcott ran straight into the most romantic experience of her own life.

When Alcott and Weld checked into the Victoria, a well-run family house with comfortable rooms, the pension already housed a strange and fascinating group of guests. There was a Frenchwoman who offered Louisa discouraging lessons in the French language. Two Scottish ladies named Glennie who had met Sir Walter Scott delighted Alcott. There was a jolly Englishwoman and her daughter. A confederate Colonel Polk with his family was determinedly rude to the Yankee women. The Victoria sounds like any boardinghouse anywhere — and Louisa was used to boardinghouses — had, in fact, grown up in them in the Boston days before the Alcott family first moved to Concord.

But this particular boardinghouse in this particular Swiss village was about to be the scene of one of the most vivid experiences of Alcott's life. There is some disagreement among her biographers about the meaning of what happened next, but there is no disagreement about the fact that it happened in the person of a twenty-year-old Polish refugee who had fought in the Polish insurrection against Russia, whose lungs were deteriorating, leaving him with a brutal hacking cough, and who was a talented piano player. "I like boys and oysters raw," Alcott wrote, years later in a chapter of *Aunt Jo's Scrap Bag* titled "My Boys." "Though good manners are always pleasing, I don't mind the rough outside burr which repels most people, and perhaps that is the reason why the burrs open and let me see the soft lining and taste the sweet nut hidden inside."[17]

This particular sweet nut was named Ladislas Wisniewski — two hiccoughs and a sneeze will give you the name perfectly, Alcott joked. But she and Anna Weld called him Laddie. In an early encounter, Louisa asked Laddie to play the Polish national anthem, an anthem that had caused Cossack soldiers to massacre 500 Poles in Wisniewski's home village. As the villagers sang, Laddie told his sympathetic audience, the Cossacks attacked. Laddie was happy to oblige, but he told Alcott he would rather not play if it would offend a Russian guest. Alcott, infuriated on his behalf, told him to play it anyway, "I should rather enjoy that insult to your bitter enemy," she snapped. "Ah Mademoiselle it is true we are enemies," her new friend Laddie gently explained, "but we are also gentlemen." Laddie began by teaching Alcott a kind of manners that were as foreign to her as his language; both delighted her.

The thirty-three-year-old Yankee spinster and the sickly young Polish patriot took long walks around Vevey, enjoying the views of the Alps and the flat blue lake. They sailed on the lake and gave each other English and French lessons. The month of November passed in a lovely haze. "A little romance with L.W.," Alcott wrote in her journal. "L. very interesting and good."[18] Laddie brought his friend a flower at every dinner, tucked little affectionate notes under the door of her room, and asked her to call him by his family pet name Varho. The two of them spoke for hours after dinner.

"Lake Léman will never seem so lovely again as when Laddie and I roamed about its shores, floated on its bosom, or laid splendid plans for the future in the garden of the old château," Alcott wrote.[19] On December 6, Louisa and Anna said good-bye to Laddie and headed for Geneva, where they would meet George Weld again and head south to Nice as their itinerary dictated.[20] Alcott and Laddie said a sad good-bye, not realizing that they were to meet again soon.

During the four months Alcott spent in Nice, she worked on her French, saw the sights, and grew increasingly restless in her position of paid companion to a young woman who rarely even wanted to go out of doors. At first Alcott suffered from insomnia, and then she was driven stir-crazy by Anna, who was sick and fidgety and complained that nothing was right in heaven and earth. When it suited her, Anna would treat Louisa as a friend, but their underlying connection, based on money, seemed close to the surface when she got bored. Still, on her occasional days off Alcott visited an old Franciscan monastery, and the Villa Valrosa. At the local theater, she was able to see Adelaide Ristori in *Medea* and in *Elizabeth.* "Never saw such acting," wrote the former actress Alcott; "it was splendid and the changes from the young, violent, coquettish woman to the peevish old crone dying with her crown on, vain, ambitious & remorseful."[21]

By May, Alcott had had enough, although she had agreed to stay with Anna Weld for a full year. She quit, leaving Anna Weld to travel alone. On the first of the month, Alcott left for Paris alone, "feeling as happy as a freed bird," she wrote.[22] As her train from Nice approached Paris, Louisa May Alcott began to wish she might run into Laddie while she was there, but they had not communicated and she had no idea how that might happen. As she got off the train at the Gare du Nord feeling exhausted and homesick and bewildered after the twelve hours of sitting upright in a train car, she caught a flash of a blue and white cap waving wildly in the air. It was the irrepressible Laddie, who had found out where she was planning to stay and called the landlady every day until he figured out the day and train of her arrival. "Next day began the pleasantest fortnight in my year of travel," Alcott wrote.

Laddie escorted her to her lodgings at Madame Dyne's on the Rue de Rivoli, and the two friends spent the next days together seeing everything Paris had to offer and their evenings reading and writing and sharing a piano bench while Laddie played and Louisa listened. Louisa May Alcott's journals are detailed and voluble for the months she spends in Europe and traveling with Anna Weld. When they get to Paris, the journals stop and skip the seventeen days Louisa and Laddie spent together.

The difference in Laddie and Louisa's ages and the threat of death from his diseased and weak lungs made their romantic life an impossibility — they could not conceivably be courting — and this seemed to release both of them into an intimacy rare in Louisa May Alcott's life. Laddie encouraged her to call him *ma drogha* in Polish, saying that it was the word for "friend." Only when the two of them had an evening out with some of his French friends did she find that she had been calling him "my darling" all along.

He was her darling. The two of them went shopping for a hat for Louisa and settled on a becoming pearl-colored number with a simple crepe rose. They went to moonlight concerts in the Champs-Élysées, took trips out of the city, and, best of all, had long talks in Louisa's pleasant rooms with the gas turned low and the scenes of the Rue de Rivoli under her balcony. In "My Boys," Alcott tells of how Laddie confided his secret sorrow over a young woman he had loved but who had been forced to marry another man by her conventional parents. Who knows what she confided in him?

After their Paris interlude, they wrote letters to each other for a few years, and then his letters stopped, leading Louisa to conclude, sadly, that he had died. She used him, she admitted, as the model for Laurie, the lively next-door neighbor of the March girls in *Little Women* who falls in love with Jo, "as far as a pale pen and ink sketch could embody a living, loving boy."[23]

What really happened in Paris during those two weeks in the spring of 1866? It was a golden time in the world. In Paris, Degas was beginning to draw ballerinas, Monet was painting landscapes, and Courbet was painting a woman with a parrot. Baudelaire was writing poetry, and Émile Zola, essays and novels.

At home Reconstruction was proceeding full-tilt and hadn't yet met the local obstacles that would turn it into one of the most dreadful jokes of history. Over President Andrew Johnson's protests, Congress passed the Fourteenth Amendment, guaranteeing due process and the rights of former slaves. Two years later, President Johnson would be impeached by that same unruly

Congress. Did Louisa May Alcott and her Laddie become lovers? Did those long evenings lead to a physical intimacy to match the closeness of their hearts and minds? Probably not. Alcott's description of their good-bye, their last moments, in which they tenderly kissed and her heart was torn in two, does not sound as if they had done a lot of previous kissing.

Whether or not Louisa May Alcott ever had a lover at all is a matter of some debate. It's a measure of our narrow sexual standards in the modern world that many assume that, if she didn't have a male lover, she must have had longings for the same sex. A few years later, Alcott was visited by a young woman, Mabel Loomis, who was the embodiment of sexuality and who was studying at Boston's New England Conservatory of Music. As a curvaceous young nymphet, Loomis understood that her fortune lay in her looks, her slightly raised upper lip and young body, but she also wanted to be a writer. She was delighted to meet the by-then-famous writer Louisa May Alcott who, in a lighthearted aside, confessed to Loomis that she had never had a lover.[24] Loomis was mildly shocked.[25]

In speculating on Louisa May Alcott's sex life, we stumble over the ethics of context.

We can guess. Even Alcott's time with Laddie is so poorly documented that one biographer — Martha Saxton — writes that Laddie's affair was actually with Anna Weld and that the two lovers used Alcott as a foil for their romance. During the years when Alcott might have been dreaming about men, she was so worried about money and illness that her dreams were cut short. A need to survive can burn away a need for sexual intimacy. In fact, Alcott's two weeks in Paris were her first real vacation ever. The neediness of her family and the shadow of her father were far away, and although she missed them, their absence also seemed to liberate her.

Louisa had already written ahead to friends in England, and she was the kind of woman who kept to her schedule. She spent a pleasant ten days with one group of Alcott friends in their house near Wimbledon and another fortnight with a different family in their house in Notting Hill. At the Taylors', there were dinners and parties, and the American was introduced to anyone who was anyone in London. She met Theodore Parker's publisher and a friend of Elizabeth and Robert Browning, John Stuart Mill and the politicians William Gladstone and Benjamin Disraeli. With the Conways, she excitedly went to hear Dickens read and came away bitterly disappointed in the man and his performance. "Youth and comeliness were gone, but the foppishness remained, and the red-faced man, with false teeth and the voice of a worn-out actor had his scanty grey hair curled."[26]

While in London, Alcott also visited the publisher George Routledge, who agreed to publish *Moods* in England and pay the equivalent of $25. Then on the seventh of July she left London for Liverpool and boarded the ship *Africa* for a stormy, dull trip back across the North Atlantic during which she was often seasick. Her sister Anna's husband, John Pratt, was there to meet her when the ship finally docked in Boston Harbor at night. Her homecoming was satisfyingly dramatic. "Nan & babies at the gate, May flying wildly around the lawn & Marmee crying at the door." Everyone cried, and Louisa presented them with gifts. Books for her father on Raphael and Hegel and for her mother the bound volume of flowers and leaves pressed from everywhere she had traveled.

By the end of July, the old Concord problems had reasserted themselves along with the acerbic Yankee attitude. "Louisa has got back, didn't have a very good time, so confined that she had very little time to see until after she left her companion," John Pratt wrote to the family friend Alfred Whitman with classic New England black humor, "& then looking with all the eyes she had, & all the feet she had, & all the hands she had, & all the faculty she had till she contrived to see considerable for a lone woman, without funds, in a short space of time."[27]

In Louisa's absence, her mother had become sicker and bills had been left unpaid. Her sister Anna was living in Concord with her two sons and using an ear trumpet; her husband, John, visited his wife and family from his work in Boston on weekends. Her mother had borrowed money to extend Louisa's visit to England. First Louisa managed, with the help of John Pratt, to get William Weld to pay the remainder of the $300 owed her for her work as a companion to his daughter. Then referring to herself as "the money-maker," and grateful that she no longer had to teach or sew since writing had become her most reliable source of income, Louisa set to work writing twelve stories for almost as many editors during the remainder of the year. There were rejections. Her long tale and the first that shows the influence of her travels, titled "A Modern Mephistopheles," was turned down by

Elliott of Elliott, Thames & Talbot because he said it was too long and too sensational.

A book of fairy tales, which she had sent to Howard Ticknor in Boston, was, as he wrote her "lost in the hurly-burly." Later, Ticknor paid Alcott for the loss.[28] The moneymaker just ploughed through it all, writing about the men and women she had seen abroad churning out the more lucrative stories with titles like "Thrice Tempted," "Hope's Debut," "Taming a Tartar," "The Baron's Gloves," and "The Mysterious Key and What It Opened" for Frank Leslie.

By January, Louisa, obviously ill again, collapsed in exhaustion. The family debt oppressed her. She hated debts like the devil, she wrote in her journal. They seemed to be making her sick; they were certainly part of the cause of her exhaustion. Although she imagined that the mercury poison had been somehow reactivated in her system, this hardly seems likely. For five months, she had such severe headaches that she was unable to write and spent most of her time in bed. "Louisa Alcott has been alarmingly ill," Franklin Sanborn wrote to a friend. "Her head being overworked and taking revenge by neuralgia. She is now forbidden to either read or to write — which is to her a great deprivation."[29]

As always, the robust and reliable Louisa slowly got better. By April she was up and walking again and, of course, thinking of writing more stories for money to pay the bills. She relapsed and had to return to bed. It wasn't until May 2 that she finally was able to come downstairs.

The summer in Concord had its lovely healing effects. Summer had always been a good time for Louisa in the country, and the summer of 1867 was no exception. She had two interesting business offers, one from Thomas Niles, who had worked for James T. Fields and had been there on the day Fields turned down her essay about going out to service. Niles was now an editor at Roberts Brothers Publishing Company, and when she approached him about publishing her next novel, he suggested that she should try writing a book for young girls. She said she would try, but privately she rebelled. At the same time, she was offered the job of contributing editor at *Merry's Museum,* a children's magazine, for $500 a year.

Concord as a base of operations for her writing career seemed impossible to Louisa. It was hard to work in a place where there were always financial and physical emergencies. She moved to Boston and took the bold step of renting her own apartment, a room on the top floor of 6 Hayward Place in downtown Boston, a short walk from the *Merry's Museum* offices. With delight she christened her room Gamp's Garret after her erstwhile alter ego, Dickens's Sairy Gamp, and began writing and editing a magazine for children. In November her sister May joined her to give drawing classes, and Louisa wrote two mysteries and a story about four sisters named Nan, Lu, Beth, and May giving their breakfast to poor neighbors. Otherwise she did nothing at all about writing the book for young girls that Thomas Niles had suggested.

Her father, however, was not so forgetful. He and Abba both did better when Louisa was at home in Concord. Thomas Niles approached him, offering to publish his book *Tablets* — a manuscript consisting of excerpts from Bronson's diaries arranged by Zodiac signs — if his daughter wrote the book for young girls that Niles had mentioned to her. Under these pressures — her father, Niles, the debts, her parents' bad health and helplessness — Louisa May Alcott gave in.

# 8
## LITTLE WOMEN.
### 1868–1872

---

January 1868 found Louisa May Alcott back in Boston, happily ensconced in her attic. Alone at last with no one to answer to, in relatively good health, she was thrilled with her new arrangements, her few pieces of furniture and a pot of hyacinth bulbs in her sunny window. During the first week of the month, the first bulb to bloom, a white hyacinth, seemed a good omen and perfumed her rooms with its scent. After her return from Europe, Concord had seemed dumpy and remote. The small, cramped shops along the Milldam, once the bustling center of her little girl's world, seemed poky and dusty. The country store sold food for people and feed for horses as if there wasn't much difference. Asa Collier repaired watches and skates. Men with nothing better to do lounged along the walls above the Milldam.

On the other side of town, Orchard House

itself, the house that had so magnificently saved the family fortunes and become their first and only home, had peeling paint and a frayed roofline. Her father's famous zigzag split-rail fence looked as silly as people said — he had used twice as much lumber as he needed to create what he regarded as a thing of beauty. Her name for the house, Apple Slump, seemed more appropriate than ever. For the first time, she felt claustrophobic in the town where she had spent so much of her life. It was a great place to dream about, with its lazy rivers and rolling pastures, but she was relieved to get back to the city.

Boston wasn't London or Paris, but it had the rhythms and fashions of big-city life. The theater of the Boston streets was never boring. Alcott's luxury was a hyacinth blooming in January, but those with money found other, sillier things to delight them, and this delighted Alcott. Fashionable Boston women in the 1860s had embraced the bustle, a style that began with a corset laced as tightly as possible to create a tiny waist. Over that went a hoop skirt made of poplin, silk, or lawn, which was held out from the body with horsehair or metal hoops, and over *that* went an overskirt that was draped and tied as tightly as possible in the back. Necklines were low and trimmed with ribbon or lace. Although this fashion accentuated tiny waists and slender hips and long necks, it also made it impossible to walk normally, and chic women took helpless small steps in their dainty boots with front lacing and high heels and broad square toes. Louisa and her sister May, who had come to Boston in November to stay with Louisa and give drawing lessons, were fascinated and horrified by this spectacle of femininity literally bound and shackled in the fashionable clothes of the day.[1]

The city itself was in a time of tremendous growth. The Back Bay and the low-lying areas around the Public Gardens were being filled in to create more land, and the shape of the town — a narrow peninsula jutting out into the harbor — was filling in along the sides. Commonwealth Avenue had been laid out and landscaped, and sumptuous brownstones were going up along its broad sidewalks for the city's new merchant class. Louisa's mood reflected the mood of the time. "I am in my little room, spending busy, happy days, because I have quiet, freedom, work enough and strength to do it," Louisa wrote in her journal. "For many years we have not been so comfortable."[2]

This moment of solvency, created by Alcott's prodigious output the previous year, has an ironic sound to it now. The year ahead was to bring Alcott undreamed-of success and wealth, but she was thrilled to have much less than that. In January, Alcott wrote a sassy letter to a married man, Moses Coit Tyler, a University of Michigan professor, who had shown her around London. In her note, she suggested in a high-spirited way that they might return together. "I still cherish the dream of returning for another revel in dear, dirty delightful London. . . . Before sailing I'll drop you a line suggesting that you put your University in one pocket, your family in another, & come too."

Between writing stories and editing *Merry's Museum,* making a flannel bathrobe for her mother and a new bonnet for May, Alcott savored intellectual Boston. She heard Fanny Kemble read Shakespeare's *Merchant of Venice;* she went to dinner with Caroline Hall Parkman — the daunting Boston dowager who would be the mother of historian Francis Parkman; and she traded jokes with Oliver Wendell Holmes, Sr., who commented on her height. "How many of you children are there?" he asked, referring to the Alcott girls as he craned his neck to look up at Alcott's face.

On other evenings, she traveled to nearby Dorchester to appear at a benefit as Mrs.

Pontifex in Charles Dance's *Naval Engagements,* or she took the part of Lucretia Buzzard in John Maddison Morton's *The Two Buzzards.* On January 24, her second hyacinth bulb bloomed a pale blue. With her father she went to the annual meeting of the Anti-Slavery Society and heard Wendell Phillips give a lecture. "Glad I have lived in the time of this great movement," she wrote of abolition, "and known its heroes so well. War times suit me, as I am a fighting May."[3]

Although the Civil War had officially ended, the bitter disagreements between the North and the South had not. Eighteen sixty-eight was a time of struggle and desperation in much of the United States as President Andrew Johnson, a man who seemed to be in favor of flouting the intentions of Congress and the principles for which the war had been fought, approached impeachment.

So as circumstances seemed to get better for the Alcott family, the country sank into one of the ugliest and most disruptive times in history. In the North, people fervently believed that the war was fought over universal freedom for all men (women were still not mentioned), but many in the South insisted on believing that the war had been fought over the issue of secession. In the meantime, the population of 4 million African Americans, most of whom had no homes to return to or jobs or education, began to assimilate itself into the country as free men and women.

Into this miserable, violent mix came a small secret society that christened itself the Ku Klux Klan. Named for the Greek word *kuklos,* "circle," the Klan at first seemed nothing more than an expression of vigilante discontent. By 1868, however, the Klan's brutality and violent tactics were famous and had spread terror throughout the southern states.

On Friday, February 14, a week before Senator Thaddeus Stevens drafted a formal resolution of impeachment for President Johnson, Louisa May Alcott's third hyacinth bloomed a lovely, fragrant pink. Alcott wrote and did some sewing and then went out and bought a squash pie for dinner. It was a snowy cold day, and as she trudged back to her room, she dropped the pie box and watched helplessly as it fell end over end to the sidewalk. But things looked up as she got back to her building to find an editor, a Mr. Bonner of the *New York Ledger,*[4] who offered her a crisp $100 bill as an advance on a column she agreed to write about advice for young women. "So the pink hyacinth was a true prophet," Alcott wrote. "I planned my article while I ate my dilapidated pie."[5]

The job as editor of *Merry's Museum* paid $500 a year, and Alcott was able to supplement this with pieces for Frank Leslie, the *New York Ledger* column, and children's pieces for another magazine called *Youth's Companion.* In the wake of the Civil War, writing for children was enjoying a surge of popularity. Childhood, as Philippe Ariès has pointed out, is a relatively recent invention. Until the second half of the nineteenth century, children were thought of as small adults whose entire value was that, as adults, they would be able to work and take their place in society. Now, in the expansion of the Yankee consciousness, children were beginning to be perceived as something more, a species with their own special needs and desires.

Children's books like Oliver Optic's narratives and magazines for boys, and magazines like *Merry's Museum* and editors looking for advice for young women began to proliferate. Thomas Niles persisted in asking Alcott to write her book for young girls. From the Roberts Brothers offices at 143 Washington Street, he could see books by Oliver Optic being loaded from the booming publisher Lee & Shepard at 149 Washington Street. Mary Mapes Dodge's *Hans Brinker; or, the Silver Skates* was still selling well two years after publication. Surely, Niles reasoned, there must be a market for novels written for girls.

As Niles was well aware, his author Louisa May Alcott was swanning around Boston doing everything but writing a book for young girls. Again he approached Bronson Alcott, who had previously reassured him about his daughter's intentions.

In the meantime, in her pieces for *Merry's Museum,* Louisa was finding a rhythm of writing that seemed to work well for children's stories.

She would think about the stories for a while, let them grow in her mind, and then write them quite quickly with no revision or restructuring. Oddly she was finding that the material on which she spent the least time was the most successful. She still allowed herself to be sucked into a kind of writing vortex, but the process was much less agonizing, and when she had finished writing the story, she was done. She was beginning to feel her way into a fresher version of the style that had taken over when she wrote *Hospital Sketches.* Her prose simplified and gained power. She stopped

Writing and began to write.

Although Alcott's little room was precious to her, a sky parlor where she could spin yarns like a spider, the pull of her family's needs was stronger than the delights of independence. She was, in fact, married to her family and their needs as surely as if they had commemorated it with a ceremony and vows. Bronson Alcott came to Boston to consult with Thomas Niles about his book, *Tablets,* to once again promise Niles that Louisa was hard at work, and to remind Louisa that she had to write this book for girls. Bronson knew how to wield his paternal powers of persuasion. He summoned her back to Concord.

Reluctantly, but resigned to her own servitude at the hands of her parents, Alcott packed up the furniture and books in her beloved garret. "Packed for home as I am needed there," she wrote. "I am sorry to leave my quiet room, for I've enjoyed it very much." On February 28 after a few blissfully productive months — eight long tales, ten short ones, twelve stage appearances, and lots of editorial work — Louisa May Alcott quit her post as editor of *Merry's Museum* and headed home to Concord to write a book she didn't want to write in a place she didn't want to write it.

March is New England's mud season, and March of 1868 was unseasonably warm. The roads melted into icy slush, and the walking in Concord — especially for someone in long skirts — was plodding and unpleasant. New Englanders say that their weather year consists of nine months of winter and three months of "damn poor sledding." That March in Concord was damn poor sledding and not much of anything else good. For Louisa the chilly March sun and the endless errands of Concord made her days in Boston seem like a shimmering dream. In April she may even have regretted not getting in to see Dickens in his final American reading. Perhaps this time she would have seen beyond the crimped hair and false teeth to the writer whose work had meant the world to her.

As always, Dickens's readings were as carefully planned as his novels — he was part of London's theatrical community, the actress Ellen Terry was his longtime love, and he had tremendous respect for stage drama of all kinds. His readings always lasted exactly ninety minutes and used the same props — a maroon curtain behind him, a footrail next to the lectern, and a block to the side where he rested his hand or elbow during the performance. Dickens rehearsed his readings again and again, memorizing large sections of his own work and acting out different parts and voices under an arrangement of gaslights that made the scene even more dramatic. He knew the work so well that he could rewrite and improvise on the spot, depending on the mood of the audience. The book he appeared to be reading from was there as a prop.

Alcott had been disappointed by his age and artificiality when she saw the great man read in London. But in April in Boston, he was indeed an old man, nearing the end of his lecturing and his writing. The six-month tour of this country had left him exhausted, although it paid well, netting the amazing sum of $140,000. His final reading in Boston — he would be dead two years later — was a heartbreaker. He ended his reading after the applause with these words: "In this brief life of ours, it is sad to do almost anything for the last time. . . . Ladies and gentlemen, I beg most earnestly, most gratefully, and most affectionately, to bid you, each and all, farewell." He embarked for England just hours ahead of a federal agent who had been sent to collect taxes on his United States earnings.

By the time the elderly Dickens left Boston, Alcott, who still lived her life by memorized passages from *Martin Chuzzlewit* and *The Pickwick Papers,* was mired in the finally diminishing Concord mud. It wasn't until May, when the winter finally lifted and signs of new life were everywhere around her, that Alcott finally sat down to write her book for young girls.

There are two kinds of masterpieces: those that use great leaps of the imagination to bring extraordinary scenes and adventures onto the page, and those that reveal the ordinary. The latter show us in a fresh way the very things we have known all along. Until she sat down to write a book for children, Louisa May Alcott had been reaching for the extraordinary as she did in her blood-and-thunder tales and even in her serious novel. Now she relaxed.

Great writing will always be a mystery. Why now, after everything she had been through, reluctantly tackling a novel for young girls, did Louisa May Alcott get suddenly catapulted into greatness? There are two kinds of artists — those who seek and those who find.[6] The day she sat down to write during that May of 1868, Louisa seemed to shift from being an artist pushing toward meaning to being an artist able to relax and discover meaning — the way

Michelangelo purportedly said that he discovered his statues embedded in the marble he carved.

The muse often seems perverse. Brilliant men in book-lined studies with eager researchers somehow write wooden, muddy prose. Even writers with great ideas often subside into writing that makes those ideas incomprehensible. Instead, someone who has given up writing because he can't make a living at it, like Nathaniel Hawthorne, will sit down in the aftermath of his mother's death in a rented house and pour out an incredible, dazzling tale like *The Scarlet Letter.* Or a man intent on cutting down his drinking and spending by traveling to the south of France, like F. Scott Fitzgerald, will use the trip to write a masterpiece like *The Great Gatsby.* My own father wrote some of his best stories in a cheap tent, which he had pitched, on the lawn when the house was filled with his family and friends.

A lot has been written about the way great work happens. The poet Edward Hirsch supposes that it takes the ultimate pressure on the human soul to make this enchantment happen: artistic inspiration is "the presence of death," he wrote. Others, like Sigmund Freud and Arthur Koestler, liken the moment of creation to an accident or a joke. There's a feeling of lightness, of handing over the reins. The poet Jane Hirshfield has written: "You can think you're willing it, you can think the Muse mugs you, it's still a mystery. The kaleidoscope turns, the box is shaken and settles, and some new constellation appears, never seen before, which you either choose to take or you turn or shake again to see what else might come up."[7]

There is a parallel between the insights of great work and the insights of great invention that also often seem to happen by accident. Alexander Graham Bell, for instance, famously invented the telephone when he accidentally spilled battery acid on himself and called out for help from his assistant Tom Watson, who heard him through the wires in the next room. Although this particular accident is apocryphal, the two men did seem to discover that the sound was traveling through the wires one afternoon by accident. They were in separate rooms trying out a new system of batteries and solenoids when Bell heard a pinging through the wires, and when he spoke, Watson could hear him.[8] "Chance favors the prepared mind," as Louis Pasteur wrote.

If great works and great inventions hap-

345

pen by accident, careful research can also often show that the accident has been prepared for for years. It was Bell's understanding of sound, partly developed in his years of work with the deaf, that made him understand the pings he heard through the wire. Man's accidents are God's purposes, as Sophia Peabody might remind us. From the perspective of 1868, the writing of *Little Women* looked like an accident. Because of the accidental coming together of Alcott's need for a publisher, her concern for her parents, Thomas Niles's jealousy of other publishers' successes with children's books, Bronson Alcott's unpublished manuscript, and a dozen other things, in May of 1868, Louisa May Alcott after much stalling finally sat down and started writing *Little Women.*

Yet the accidents that caused the writing of *Little Women,* seen in hindsight, look more like destiny. Alcott had noticed the resurgence of children's literature, and she had grown up in a household where children were thought of as the incarnation of angelic good. She had just spent six months editing and writing for a children's magazine. She had already written at least three stories about a golden band of sisters, and her poem "In the Garret," just published in the

Boston weekly the *Flag of Our Union,* had begun to create the four characters of Nan, Lu, Bess, and May. In her novel, Anna's husband, John Pratt, would become a tutor and be named John Brooke because the Pratts had been at Brook Farm. Laurie, the boy next door, would give her a chance to verbally savor the deliciousness that was Polish Laddie in her memory, combined with another friend, Alf Whitman from Lawrence, Kansas. His father? Was that Emerson? The curmudgeon with the astonishing library and financial generosity and the heart of gold? A school she had seen at Vevey would become Laurie's background, the family post office begun by Abba at Fruitlands would be expanded, the family newspaper the *Olive Branch* became the *Spread Eagle,* and Alcott's Civil War illness, which cost her her luxuriant hair, became Jo's sacrifice of her hair for the Civil War cause.[9]

Alcott had come back to Concord partly to care for her aging mother, and the novel gave her a chance to pay homage to Abba in making her the irresistible Marmee. The sisters were easy. Anna would be beautiful Meg, Lizzie the quiet and perfect Beth, and May, headstrong May, became the obnoxious niminy piminy Amy. A little exaggeration, a little cleaning up of the rough edges, and she had a cast of characters.

The March family is clearly modeled on the Alcotts, but in writing this book Alcott allowed herself to create, instead of her real family, the family she had always dreamed of having. There would be a loving, loyal domestic — Hannah — to do much of the grunt work of washing, cleaning, and mending that had always been Alcott's job. Instead of the eccentric, difficult Alcott father, the March father would be heroic and far enough away not to intrude on this female idyll. Instead of Louisa May, the difficult child who was treated as if she belonged in a different family, the rebel who irritated her mother and her father equally until she started supporting them, Alcott created Jo, who shared her love of apples and cats and who, miraculously, was beloved even though she was a rebel.

As the month of May progressed, Alcott sank into the familiar creative vortex. Her journal entries stopped; she often forgot to eat or sleep. In June she sent Thomas Niles her first twelve chapters. She wasn't sure if the book could become a novel since its opening pages seemed to be a series of character sketches without a defining narrative. But chronology provided a narrative, and on July 15 she sent 402 pages to Niles at Roberts Brothers on Washington Street. Niles had thought the opening chapters dull when he received them, and Alcott was tempted to agree with him. The characters and the story seemed so ordinary. Alcott sent in her pages without much hope that the publisher would ask for a sequel.

Thomas Niles accepted the pages and Alcott took the train in to confer with him at his office, while her sister May got to work on illustrations for the book. In the small offices on Washington Street where Lewis A. Roberts created photograph albums out of leather and published books on the side, Alcott and the slender Niles went over her manuscript and began planning publication. Back in 1851, Alcott and Niles had been in a similar office on Washington Street when James T. Fields had told her to stick to her teaching.

Thomas Niles explained to Louisa that she could take payment one of two ways — either as a $300 fee with royalties of 6.66 percent on each copy sold,[10] or $1,000 to sell the manuscript outright. Niles recommended the royalty arrangement and in spite of what $1,000 would mean to her — her annual salary at *Merry's* had been $500 — she agreed. After all, the book had only taken two months to write.

On August 26, proofs of the book arrived in Concord along with the first positive words about the story. Niles had given the story to his visiting twelve-year-old niece, Lillie Almy, and she had devoured the book, both laughing and weeping as she read. Encouraged, Niles had given the proofs to a few other young girls, who all adored it. An old suitor and friend, George Bartlett from the Concord Amateur Dramatic Company, stopped by, and Louisa, as she discouraged his romantic fantasies, pressed him into service as a proofreader. By this time in her life, Alcott had clearly made up her mind that marriage was not for her. On September 30, just four months after she began writing it, for the price of $1.50 with three illustrations by May, Alcott's book was finally published with the title *Little Women: Meg, Jo, Beth and Amy. The Story of Their Lives. A Girl's Book.*[11]

Almost immediately, letters began to arrive. Thomas Wentworth Higginson wrote that he had loved *Little Women,* and Bronson mused in his diary that he worried his daughter did not take her genius seriously enough. There were good reviews in *The Nation* and the *Youth's Companion.* People were talking about the book — speculating on whether Laurie was Thoreau or perhaps Julian Hawthorne. Niles sold out the first printing and had orders for a few thousand more, as well as an order from a London publisher, so he asked Alcott to start writing her second volume.

Alcott was pleasantly surprised. "Much interest in my little women who seem to find friends by their truth to life,"[12] she wrote in her journal. Another kind of fan letter she found less pleasing. Dozens of young women wrote ecstatically to praise the book and to urge Alcott to allow Jo to marry Laurie at the end of the second part. To this Alcott responded with fury. "Girls write to ask who the little women marry, as if that was the only aim and end of a woman's life," she complained in her journal in November. "I *won't* marry Jo to Laurie to please anyone."

No, but she was prepared to marry Jo to a good-hearted professor with a strange accent. She had moved back to Boston, to a room on Brookline Street near Jamaica Plain, and she began the second part of the book with Meg's marriage to John Brooke, who took his happy bride to live in the Dovecote Cottage. Amy would win a trip to Europe and experience the trip on the Rhine that Louisa had made with Anna

Weld five years before. Louisa May Alcott's thirty-sixth birthday was spent alone in Boston; the November cold made her grateful she wasn't in the country. Her one gift was a copy of her father's *Tablets,* the book Niles had published at the same time that he had published *Little Women.*

In December, Alcott helped her parents shut down Orchard House for the winter. Her mother was going to live with Anna and John Pratt, and her father was off to western cities to give Conversations. "A cold, hard, dirty time, but was so glad to be off out of Concord that I worked like a beaver, and turned the key on Apple Slump with joy," Alcott wrote. She and May took a room in a new temperance hotel — an establishment that did not allow alcohol — on Beacon Street run by the fascinating, roly-poly Dr. Dio Lewis. Lewis was a medical man with ideas about health that ranged from the benefits of Turkish baths to homeopathy. Alcott was happy to be back on Beacon Street near the slow-flowing Charles, and the move was blessed by the receipt of $300 in royalties on the first part of *Little Women* from Thomas Niles. For the first time in her life, Alcott was able to pay the family's immediate debts and to give her rich Uncle Sam Sewall money to invest for her.

Although Alcott seemed to find her voice in writing the second part of *Lillle Women* — a combination of composites and fantasies laid delicately over the actual events of family life — she didn't think that it would be as successful as the first part, which had already sold 5,000 copies. Little did she know what was about to happen. The publication of *Little Women,* Part II, on April 14 created a firestorm of popularity. Four thousand copies had been ordered before publication, and by the end of the month letters flooded into Boston and another 13,000 copies were sold. Suddenly, Alcott was richer than she could have imagined, as her book flooded into every bookstore and home in New England.

Although it had been almost a year since she started writing the book, her success felt like some kind of overnight miracle. In her journal, she wrote, "I was very tired with my hard summer, with no rest for the brains that earn the money." But the brains that earned the Alcott money had suddenly broken through into fame and fortune. Although Alcott herself seemed slow to realize what had happened, in 1932 her Orchard House neighbor Julian Hawthorne told a different version of Alcott's experience.

According to the young Hawthorne, Alcott had traveled into Boston to the Roberts Brothers office to see Thomas Niles after she had turned in the second part of the book. Despondent, she hoped he might give her a word of encouragement or a small check, but she found her way to Niles's office blocked by a huge hubbub. The sidewalks were lined with packing cases of books and drays being loaded with more books. Clerks and stock boys crowded the doorway, making it hard for her to even get inside from Washington Street. Once indoors, she saw that there were many piles of books and impatient shopmen and porters; because of the chaos, Alcott feared the whole place was being seized to pay off back debts.

Timidly she made her way upstairs where Niles himself, "curved like a Capital G over his desk," sat writing checks and inventories without looking up. "Like the Duke of Marlborough, he was riding the whirlwind and directing the storm; something tremendous was evidently going on,"[13] as Hawthorne wrote remembering the story that Alcott had told her assembled neighbors when she got back to Concord later the same day. Approaching Niles's desk, Alcott cleared her throat and tried to get his attention. Without looking up, he waved her away impatiently. He was much too busy to be disturbed. She stood paralyzed.

When he finally angrily looked up from his desk and saw Alcott in her faded clothes standing there he jumped as if terrified. Louisa's impression was that he actually vaulted over the desk and landed at her feet, leaving his spectacles in midair and grasping her by both elbows. "My dear Miss Alcott," he sputtered, "you got my letter. Nothing to parallel it has occurred in my experience. All else put aside — street blocked — country aroused . . . a triumph of the century!" On the spot, he offered Alcott a check for any amount she might name. Her book had transformed his poky publishing house into a wildly successful business. All the fuss was about her. "Hard times for the Alcott family were forever over," Hawthorne wrote. "We that evening saw the first flowing of the liberating tide."[14] Alcott's success had many effects, not the least a newfound respect from her father who, after all, had been one of the people who urged her to write a book for young girls.

Noting that his daughter's book was one of few to focus on New England, Bronson wrote admiringly that "she takes her growing repute modestly, being unwilling to believe her books have all the merit ascribed to them by the public. Her health is by no means yet restored."[15] Always the optimist, Bronson Alcott seemed less surprised than his daughter when their life turned around. The man who called himself the Hoper had never stopped hoping. His journals reflect his conviction that her success is due to his wisdom in the way he conducted family life. She had the advantage, he congratulated himself not quite truthfully, of being raised by a man who knew enough not to send her to school. Thus, she was able to write from experience.

Bronson's attention was slightly distracted from the change in his fortunes by another one of his infatuations with a younger woman. Ellen Chandler, a teacher in Framingham, had sent him into a typical verbal spin. "In writing to my friend, whether man or woman, and to a maiden more especially, I may not express all I would, lest I shall be taken to imply more than I meant and offend the delicacy of the sentiment which I feel, as if it were no sentiment and were to be measured by the understanding solely," he wrote in characteristically incoherent explanation of his feelings.[16]

What happens when the financial pressures and disappointments of a lifetime vanish? Driven by adversity and stubbornness and endurance — prevailing against all kinds of discouragement and obstacles — Louisa May Alcott had finally, at the age of thirty-six, succeeded. Now she had nothing to fight for; she had won. "Paid up all the debts, thank the Lord! — every penny that money can pay — and now I feel as if I could die in peace," Alcott wrote in her journal.[17]

Personal prosperity for Alcott coincided with a burst of national prosperity that changed the character of the United States to what it is today. Just as Louisa May Alcott was being reluctantly transformed from a hardworking spinster who had devoted her difficult life to supporting her family, the expanding states went from being a scrappy survivalist nation of upstarts insistent on a bizarre democratic form of government to being the richest and most powerful nation in the world. First this primacy was territorial, as the Mexican War increased the size of the United States. With the driving of the golden spike in Promontory, Utah, that joined the western and eastern parts of the transcontinental railroad in 1869, the West and the Great Plains were open to massive expansion. Huge fortunes began to be made in mining, in land acquisition, and in investment in the railroads. The land tracts to be farmed were so gigantic that agriculture began to be mechanized, and this increased profits. Mechanical reapers raced down endless rows of grain, and this country began exporting so much wheat that it ultimately became the breadbasket of Europe. The business of America became business.

All this good fortune was not lost on those who heard about it in England and Europe. Immigration exploded, with 2.5 million people arriving in the 1850s to be added to a population that had grown from five million in 1800 to nearly 40 million in 1870. Left behind in this rush to prosperity, the southern states and their newly freed black populations went their own disastrous way. Former slaves now joined the disenfranchised Native American population as U.S. problems that somehow got left behind in the great rush to prosperity. "Poised on the brink of their most confident and successful era, Americans were not being hypocritical in forgetting the losers," writes historian J. M. Roberts.[18]

Looking back on Alcott's life in 1869 from our vantage point of almost 150 years, her story seems to reach a crescendo with the success of *Little Women.* Before the publication and its success, Alcott's life is one way; afterward, it is another way. Before, she is poor; afterward, she is rich. Before, she is unrecognized; afterward, she is famous and people come to Concord in order to catch a glimpse of the great writer. Before, she has a small audience; afterward, people stop her in the street wherever she goes. Before, she sells few copies of her books; afterward, everything she writes is immediately ordered in the tens of thousands.

This is how her life looks in our modern context, but in the context of her own experience the contrast seemed minimal. In 1868 she was a hardworking writer who was often ill, and in 1870 she was still a hardworking writer who was often ill. In the year her fortunes changed, she published even more stories than she had in previous years. Her account books for 1869 show dozens of stories written for *Merry's Museum,* *Youth's Companion,* and a magazine called *Hearth and Home.* "The Lace Makers"; "Foolish Fashions"; "Lafayette's Visits"; "Our Owl"; "Uncle Tom's Shipwreck"; "Playing Lady"; "Bunny's Revenge"; "Kitty's Cattle Show"; "In the Tower"; "Uncle Smiley's Boys"; "Betsey's Bandbox"; "Harriet Tubman"; "More People"; and "A Good Daughter" are some of the titles of essays and stories she wrote as *Little Women* sold off the charts. She couldn't stop.

Although her circumstances had changed, the pressure on her to write stories and novels never seemed to let up. Her last journal entry is about writing, and in her lifetime Alcott wrote more than a dozen novels under her own name including the beloved string of successors to *Little Women: Little Men, Eight Cousins, Rose in Bloom, Work, Under the Lilacs, Jack and Jill*, and *Jo's Boys*. Under her pseudonym A. M. Barnard, she produced an impressive group of thrillers and what she called "blood and thunder" novels and stories including "Pauline's Passion and Punishment," *Behind a Mask, A Modern Mephistopheles*, and *A Long Fatal Love Chase*, first published in 1995. In between novels she wrote more than three hundred stories.

In the summer months, she took a short vacation to visit some distant cousins in Canada at their home on the St. Lawrence River, and stopped with her sister May at Mount Desert Island in Maine for a visit. Then she came right back to Boston to work and make money for the family.

Illness had bothered Alcott in many forms ever since her nursing stint at the Union Hotel Hospital. She had suffered from extremely painful headaches as well as pains in her legs and other joints, which often kept her from sleeping or from moving. Toward the end of her life, this muscular and skeletal pain, sometimes kept at bay by the use of morphine, was joined by severe gastrointestinal pains and acid reflux, which Alcott called "brash." Her skin also regularly erupted in bumps and boils, and her feet became so swollen at times that she couldn't wear her shoes.

Then, in the winter of 1869, while boarding in pleasant rooms on Pinckney Street on Beacon Hill with May, Alcott lost her voice. This time, though, instead of homeopathic medication and hoping for the best, she had the money to afford a Dr. Bowditch who proceeded to do a series of painful cauterizations of her windpipe. Rheumatism also attacked again, causing pain in her feet and hands. Her head tormented her with pain and she was unable to sleep without drugs.

Her newfound fortune didn't seem to guarantee health, and her new admiration from her father came with certain obligations. Her next book, he decided in between his intense correspondence and visiting with Ellen Chandler, should be about him, about a philosopher who was always ahead of his time. It should be titled *The Cost of an Idea.* On his latest lecture trip west, Bronson had been hailed as the father of *Little Women,* experiencing more audience enthusiasm than he was used to. He quickly added a section about Louisa to his stock speech.

History has not been kind to Thomas Niles, the seemingly clueless editor who failed to see the greatness of *Little Women* until his own niece had to tell him what he had in hand. Yet a closer look reveals a more complicated man. *Little Women* was Niles's idea, and he had to bully the author into writing it. He also came up with the title *Little Women,* and, more important, he advised Alcott to go for a smaller advance with a royalty percentage instead of taking a flat fee. In her annotations to her journals in 1885, she made a note of the importance of this advice, complete with mangled fairy-tale references. "An honest publisher and a lucky author, for the copyright made her fortune, and the 'dull book' was the first golden egg of the ugly duckling."[19]

The second golden egg was *An Old-Fashioned Girl.* First a small story for *Merry's Museum* about Polly Milton, a simple country girl who goes for an extended visit to see her decadent cousins, Alcott expanded it into a novel that ran in *Merry's Museum* as a series and was then published by Niles at Roberts. Before publication, Alcott visited Niles to ask him to increase her royalty from 6.66 percent to 10 or even 12 percent. *Little Women* had already made him a fortune. He refused. His prediction was that *Little Women* had been a bubble, a once-in-a-lifetime book, and that Alcott's next book would not do as well.

But as Madeleine Stern has written, 1869 was Louisa May Alcott's *annus mirabilis.* The woman who had scraped together a living as a seamstress, governess, and teacher was now feted at teas and clubs as a literary lion. She hobnobbed with Julia Ward Howe and the Brahmin families of Boston, quietly remembering that she had taught their children. On a train, a sales boy tried to sell her a copy of her latest book. When she declined, the boy protested that it was a bestseller: "Bully book, ma'am, Sell a lot, better have it." Louisa was delighted by the boy's wide-eyed surprise when he found out who she was.[20]

*An Old-Fashioned Girl* reads as well as *Little Women,* and its narrative energy speeds it along. Alcott's growing public audience agreed, ordering 12,000 copies before publication and more than 24,000 afterward. It's written in simple, unaffected English, which was at the time a revolutionary way of writing that Alcott had really pioneered in *Little Women.* In the book, she apologizes for the simplicity of her language, noting that she hopes her readers will not be able to say "it's all very prim and proper, but it isn't a bit like us."[21] Instead, she hopes that the covers of her novel will be the dirtiest in the library.

In *An Old-Fashioned Girl,* Alcott writes with confidence and mastery, weaving her ferocious ideas about the effects of too much money and the unjust and cruel way society treats women, with a simple plot. The story revolves around the Shaw family with its two sisters, brother, money-earning father, and helpless shut-in mother. The heroine is their country cousin Polly, who brings to their attention all the characters she encounters in her impoverished city life — the saintly Mrs. Mills, who runs a boardinghouse for young women like Polly, the tragic girl Jane who tries to kill herself with a drug overdose because the effects of poverty have robbed her of hope, and a two-dimensional love interest, Arthur Sydney, who is captivated by Polly. She discourages him because, although his money would mean the world to her and her family, she does not truly love him.

Six generations later, Alcott's book is still on point. Young women without resources still marry for money, if only for the money to help their families. Money continues to corrupt and undermine the lives of children who have too much of it, especially when, as Alcott brilliantly depicts, the making of money has distracted their parents from the day-to-day contact that creates real families. Worst of all, women with money are still encouraged to make themselves into attractive ornaments rather than to develop any real skills. With the highest ambition for a woman often still marriage to a wealthy and powerful man — you don't think so? look around you! — women are still enslaved by society and all it entails. "I'm not a rampant women's rights reformer," says Mrs. Mills, "but I think women can do a great deal for each other, if they will only stop fearing what people think."[22]

Alcott's personal life seeps into the novel at many places. "All is fish that comes to the literary net," Alcott wrote in her journal.[23] There are a few pages describing the noble Revolutionary family that Polly claims as her own but which is actually the May family complete with Colonel May and his breeches and boots. In one scene, a woman who has come to see the Milton family's model children is met by shrieks and laughter and hoydenish tumbling out of a wheelbarrow just as Margaret Fuller was met on her visit to the Alcotts at Dovecote Cottage so many years before. Most of all, Alcott's outrage at the way women are treated by their families and by our culture lends an edge to the sweet story.

In Boston, which Alcott calls the most conceited city in the land, Polly Milton meets other young, independent, and talented women like herself, women who have broken away from the conventional ideals of womanhood to pursue their talents, or have just broken away because those ideals were too expensive financially or spiritually. "Purpose and principle are the two best teachers we can have," Alcott wrote, "and the want of them makes half the women of America what they are, restless, aimless, frivolous and sick."[24]

Alcott's heroine is pretty and poor and spirited and good, but the Shaw family is stuck in the corrupt toils of social acceptance. Then they lose most of their money. At that point, the elegant, idiotic Tom becomes a solid, loving son. The frivolous, fashion-obsessed Fan is transformed into a dutiful wife and daughter who learns to cook and clean and mend, and the bratty Maud morphs into a charming woman who ends up a happy spinster — an oxymoron in her previous world. The greatest transformation is that of the elder Shaw who, relieved of the obligation of supporting his family in the style to which they had become accustomed — but which was ruining them from the inside — stops being an absent father and becomes a guide and friend to his children. All ends well.

"Intimidated by the threats, denunciations, and complaints showered upon me in consequence of taking the liberty to end a certain story as I like," Alcott joked with her invisible readers about her refusal to marry Jo to Laurie at the end of her second popular novel, "I now yield to the amiable desire of giving satisfaction." Fan will marry Arthur Sydney, Polly her beloved Tom, and all will go on happily ever after.

By the time O.F.G., as Louisa May called the novel in her journals, was published, the author was getting ready to reap some of the benefits of her newfound fame and fortune. Anything with her name on it seemed to sell in the thousands. Even Redpath, who had brought out a new edition of

*Moods* to take advantage of Alcott's fame, found himself selling 10,000 copies, many more than had been sold on original publication. On the first of April, Louisa and her sister May left for New York on their way to France. The end of adversity had not made a dent in Louisa May Alcott's black humor. In her journals, she noted that April Fool's day was a fit day for her undertaking a trip.[25]

This time Alcott was going on the Grand Tour as a distinguished literary lion and a Boston lady, not as a paid nurse and servant. The going-away festivities included a huge party, a great cake that no one suggested that Louisa May should save for her guests, and a crowd at the Concord station to see them off. On April 2, Louisa, her sister, and their friend Alice Bartlett left New York on the French steamer *Lafayette* and arrived in Brest, France, twelve days later. At the same time, *An Old-Fashioned Girl* was being published in London to great sales and acclaim.

For May Alcott, whose career as a painter had paralleled her sister's career as a writer, living and working in Europe was essential both for her education as an artist and for her desire to be taken seriously. Europe was her Concord, and her sister's money gave her the ability to take advantage of European museums and masters. In France the sisters and their companion ran right into the declaration of the Franco-Prussian War. In July, France declared war on Germany as a result of anger that had been simmering for years. It came to a head after the deposition of Queen Isabella of Spain over the Prussian plan to replace her with a Hohenzollern. This would cede another part of Europe to the Germans.

But this was an old-fashioned war, and instead of being executed or hung by the neck until dead, Isabella decamped to luxurious exile in Switzerland, where the Alcott party ran into them taking the waters at Vevey with a crowd of sycophants and refugees. In September, as the war dragged on and the German armies seemed to win every battle, Alcott decided to head for Italy, partly because she had never been to Rome except in her imagination, and partly to feed May's hunger for the artistic stimulation of the Old Masters and the ruins of Roman art and architecture.

For New Englanders with their Yankee way of seeing things, Rome has always been an epiphany, an adventure in the opposite perspective. In Concord, houses and churches are built on a diminutive human scale. Ceilings are low and staircases are narrow. Climbing up the stairs to Louisa May Alcott's bedroom, many visitors have trouble with the narrow risers built to take up the least possible space. New England architecture is built to conserve heat in the brutal winters and protect against the weight of huge snowdrifts. The roofs are sharply peaked; the windows are high and small.

Roman architecture is the opposite, partly in response to a warmer, sunnier climate, but partly as a statement of the place of men and women in the universe. Roman ceilings are so high that the clouds and sky paintings that sometimes adorn them seem actually like a sky. In Rome, staircases are vast and ornate, with low marble risers that seem to have been built for the pleasure of the eye and the ease of the climbing.

In New England, prudishness reigned as a heritage from the dour Puritans. The female leg was never glimpsed, and many families even covered the shapely legs on their pianos, tables, and chairs. No one was even supposed to think about legs of any kind. Clothes hung out to dry were disguised in special cases lest a passerby be dreadfully tempted by the sight of a woman's undergarment blowing on the line. Rome is littered with statues of almost naked men and women. Everywhere you look, in frescos and sculpture, there are muscular male thighs and shapely female breasts.

Rome in the autumn, with its golden light and wild towers, its policemen dressed in feathers, gold braid, and spurs, and its street beggars, its feral dogs and solemn religious processions, its narrow alleys and grand squares, was a strange, magical place. Louisa, May, and Alice took an apartment in the Palazzo Barberini, in a vast Roman palace that seemed to have been built for a race of gods. The staircases had landings as big as Orchard House itself and the doors were so huge that smaller doors were cut into them for people to use. Their balcony overlooked the Piazza Barberini, with its fountain splashing around a statue of Triton, the God of the Sea, blowing his horn in their direction.

The women wandered among the ancient ruins where marble shards sat in piles and the ghosts of the vestal virgins who had lived in the Roman Forum seemed almost real. May haunted museums and took lessons with the young artist Frederic Crowninshield. Louisa, in her new capacity of literary lion, sat for her first oil portrait in George Healy's studio on the Via San Ni-

cola da Tolentino. Against a crimson background, Alcott posed only half believing that
she had earned the fortune and freedom
and distinction implied in what was happening as her portrait was painted. Instead
of talking about herself, she gave Shield/
Crowninshield advice about his daughter
Mary, who had written a novel, which, Louisa advised, should be sent to Roberts
Brothers in Boston.

At Roberts Brothers, the Alcott name was
synonymous with success; *Little Women* had
sold 60,000 copies and *An Old-Fashioned
Girl* almost 40,000. In Rome, Louisa also
spent more time with the sisters' companion
Alice Bartlett, a young Bostonian who
would later be the best friend and constant
companion of young Henry James during
his visits to Rome. It was Alice Bartlett who
told James the story on which he based
*Daisy Miller.* Alcott and Bartlett, although
thrown together as traveling companions,
got along well.

At the end of November, Alcott had a
quiet Roman birthday, little knowing that,
the day before, her brother-in-law John
Pratt had died after a short illness. When
the news reached the Alcott sisters, they
grieved for the man who had been such a
good husband to their sister and for the fact

that home, where they should be to mourn him, was so far away.

John Pratt had been a cause of great sorrow for Louisa when he married her older sister so soon after the death of her youngest sister. But the man had been loving and steady and won her over as a solid rock in a family that sometimes felt more like rushing rapids than the still water of the grassy Concord River. It was John who always met her boat or train in New York and John who became the reliable man of the family her father had never been.

Now, overwhelmed with emotion, Alcott did what she always did when feelings were too much for her — she wrote. For years she had expressed love by providing financial support, and she had provided through her writing. By this time, the link between her writing vortex and her love for her family was well established. She would begin another book and give the proceeds to Anna and her boys in case John had not left them enough to provide a good life. Sitting in the Palazzo Barberini with the sound of the fountain outside and the bells of Rome pealing the hour from the Piazza del Gesù, the pageantry of the city with its domes and towers outside her balcony window, Alcott channeled her longing back to Concord and

Boston. She remembered the thrilling days of her father's Temple School and the students who reveled in the freedom he gave them. She thought of the two beloved Pratt boys. "In writing and thinking of the little lads, to whom I must be a father now, I found comfort for my sorrow," she wrote in her journals.[26]

Alcott downplayed the writing of *Little Men* in her journals, but the boys of Plumfield came alive in her imagination as the three travelers settled in the eternal, windy city founded by Romulus and Remus, two impoverished orphan boys who had been rescued from certain death in the forest and raised by loving wolves in ancient times. Alcott wrote voluminously every day, escaping from her enchanted and strange surroundings into the world she longed for. Once again, yearning fueled her visions of what a school would be like run by Jo March; once again the real world receded as she wrote, and by the time the travelers left Rome, Alcott had sent her manuscript off to a delighted Thomas Niles.

Christmas in Rome permeates every corner of the city. The Piazza Navona with its fountains becomes a showplace of thousands of different versions of the crèche, its humble animals and tiny babe, its loving

Virgin, doting father, and silk- and jewel-bedecked magi. The center of Roman Catholicism, Rome boasts a church on every corner and in every square and each of them turns inside out at Christmas time. The streets are perfumed with incense; wreaths and crosses dot every surface. The deep sounds of organs and choral music bellow out onto the wide streets. Christmas in Concord is austere and simple; in Rome, Christmas is pageantry and excess. Just after Christmas, the travelers were treated to a Roman disaster when the Tiber flooded its banks.

Many churches were flooded although the Piazza Barberini stayed high and dry. The women's maid laid in supplies, and Alcott watched with amusement as Romans improvised new ways of life using rowboats and delivering food into the high windows of the great palazzos. In February the women enjoyed the pre-Lenten Carnival festivities, another great Roman celebration, which featured elaborate gowns and costumes and during which the streets become one big party. Money continued to flow in from Redpath and Niles, and even Loring in Boston. On the way home, the three women stopped in Albano, near Rome, then in Venice, and by the time the three of them reached London in May, *Little Men* had been finished and was being published.

In London, May studied with the painter Thomas Leeson Rowbotham, and Alice Bartlett left the two sisters for her trip home. Ten days later, Alcott embarked, typically writing "I am needed" in order to explain why she had to go. Her father and Thomas Niles met her boat in New York with a huge placard reading *Little Men* — the book had already sold 50,000 copies. By June she was back in Concord, catching up with paying the many debts her parents had incurred in her year away.

One debt in particular, paid back from Concord on July 3, 1871, after Alcott's return from Europe, provides a fitting end to the story of how Louisa May Alcott, against all odds and in spite of sharp criticism, became one of the world's most successful writers. In 1854 it was James Fields who had told Louisa that she should stick to her teaching. In January of 1862 when she was teaching, he had loaned her $40 to help establish a new kindergarten in Boston.

"Dear Mr. Fields," Louisa wrote. "Once upon a time you lent me forty dollars, kindly saying that I might return them when I had made 'a pot of gold.' As the miracle has been unexpectedly wrought I wish to fulfill my part of the bargain, & herewith repay my debt with many thanks. Very Truly Yours L. M. Alcott."

# 9

# SUCCESS.

## 1873–1880

*Little Men* was Alcott's sixth novel, the third to which she was willing to sign her name. It was begun in Rome where Alcott heard the sad news of the death of John Pratt, and it was finished, delivered, and published, and already a bestseller, by the time Alcott sailed back into Boston Harbor. She wrote the book for her sister Anna's sons Frederick and John, sometimes called Donny or Demi for Demi-John, and the two Pratt boys are the basis of two boys in the novel in the same way that the Alcott sisters were models for the March sisters. Alcott, always immensely practical, wrote the book to make the money to support her young nephews. It did this very well. But in many other ways, *Little Men* demonstrates less of Alcott's prodigious writing talent and more of her emotional exhaustion, physical illness, and a growing feeling that success would not bring her much of what she wanted.

*Little Men* tells the story of Jo March more than a decade after the happy ending of *Little Women* in which Jo and her odd but adoring true love — the bearish Professor Bhaer — walk off into the future together. In *Little Men,* Jo and Frederic (Fritz) Bhaer have started a school for young boys at Plumfield, an old house that Jo has somehow inherited from her cranky Aunt March. In writing *Little Men,* Alcott capitalized on her lifelong passion for young boys, whether they were romantic Polish refugees or her own nephews; the novel is a kind of hymn to the qualities of men before puberty. This novel also allowed her to memorialize her father's ideas about education. She wasn't going to write the book about him they had both planned — or she said she had planned. The novel that Louisa was supposed to write about her father titled *The Cost of an Idea,* in which a noble, brilliant, but misunderstood philosopher gave up financial and social success because of his high principles, was never even started. Nevertheless, she admired his educational philosophy.

The teaching at Plumfield is exactly like the teaching at the Temple School in Boston. The boys, and ultimately a few girls, are taught by example and by the discipline of their love and respect for Jo and her professor. They learn to read through enjoyment. They learn mathematics out of a desire to please. They learn to be good by following the unsullied direction of their own good hearts. Alcott, like her father, believed that children are born angelic.

At Plumfield there is no memorizing by rote. In one scene, when a boy needs to be punished, Professor Bhaer forces the boy to hit him with a ruler, just as Bronson Alcott sometimes asked his students to hit him, knowing that this would be much more frightening than the other way around. The ghost at Plumfield is less the shade of the benevolent John Pratt than the specter of the progressive Bronson Alcott at the dinner table pushing aside his own dinner and publicly going hungry in order to punish his children for some transgression of theirs.

Plumfield is the personification of Bronson Alcott's pedagogy, and it's a sweet, romantic book. Some of the boys are good, some bad, some talented, some almost — almost — beyond being civilized even by the loving comfort offered by their beloved Aunt Jo. But in making the character who is her stand-in older and wiser, Alcott expressed her own tiredness. While writing *Little Women,* she had been a daughter. In spite of everything she had been through, she was still a young, rebellious, and difficult girl forced to write something she didn't care for. By the time she wrote *Little Men* only a few years later, she was an old woman, a mother of her own family, shouldering the economic and emotional burdens of all of them.

The book is moving, with many vivid scenes, but it has none of the richness and surprise of *Little Women* or even of *Hospital Sketches.* The only real adversary in the novel is poverty. Years before she was to make a habit of visiting boys' homes and reform schools, Alcott had a vivid idea of what it was like to be an impoverished and abused child. She was one. Also, in watching her mother's various charitable organizations ebb and flow, she had seen her share of poverty and abuse in conditions far worse than what she and her sisters experienced.

The poverty and abuse of children obsessed Alcott, and this gave her the energy to write a book about them. In *Little Men,* the boys come to Plumfield with the suspicious natures and beaten-down souls and filthy starved bodies of children of the streets. Nat, a wide-eyed twelve-year-old, has been abandoned and abused. His late father and sleazy partner made him play the fiddle for pennies on street corners. At Plumfield it turns out that the loan of Professor Bhaer's violin is all it takes to transform him. Under the calluses and layers of grime is a talented musician. Boy after boy comes to Plumfield in trouble and is soothed by the loving and abundant routine of the place.

Once they get there, it is only a matter of time before the March magic turns them into adorable, loving versions of themselves. They reconnect with the clouds of glory they were trailing at birth. Longfellow rules! There is an occasional hard case. One boy, Dan, has to be sent away for a while to a harder country school before he can fit in at Plumfield.

Alcott is no innocent. She describes the boys as having deep scars of anger and inability to trust that come from their lives of adversity. Still, in this novel poverty and the scars of abuse are easy enemies to defeat. All it takes to reform the damaged boys is love and a few simple comforts. The complexity of *Little Women,* in which the real enemy is the glorious and dangerous perversity of the human soul — the desire of a sister to kill a sibling or the inability to love a man whom it would be convenient to love — is missing in *Little Men*. Alcott was no longer hungry, no longer yearning for the recognition she despaired of ever finding in her lifetime.

"I want something new; I feel restless, and anxious to be seeing, doing, and learning more than I am. I brood too much over my own small affairs, and need stirring up, so as I can be spared this winter I'd like to hop a little way and try my wings,"[1] Jo March confided in her mother soon after the pressures of realizing that Beth was sick again and that Laurie was in love with her. Life at Orchard House was becoming uncomfortable and the fictional Jo needed a break. The answer? New York City.

Most of the two sections of *Little Women* bear the same graceful, tenuous relationship to real life. Although Alcott often protested that all she did was write down what happened, this wasn't strictly true. She based the book on the lives of her sisters and her parents, but she shifted house and events and — most important — she made a happy story out of a story that had sometimes been grim and dreadful. She made herself popular when she was not. She made the Marches' poverty seem voluntary and high-minded, when the Alcotts' poverty was often desperate.

But in Part II of *Little Women,* in Chapters 33 and 34, "Jo's Journal" and "Friend," Alcott flung herself entirely into the world of the imagination. She had never been to New York City for more than a night on her way to Washington, D.C., and on her way to Europe. Yet she imagined that Jo, restless and discontent in Concord, might spend the winter in New York City at a friendly boardinghouse run by a friend of her mother's named Mrs. Kirke. This leap into the imaginary, fueled by the scraps of confidence Alcott was beginning to have as copies of the first part of *Little Women* continued to sell better than anyone had predicted, is her only real plot device.

What happens in New York neatly furthers the narrative and brings in the character of the forty-year-old professor Frederic Bhaer. The pressure on Alcott to marry off Jo was fierce as more and more young women wrote her fan letters that sounded as if the characters in *Little Women* were real and Alcott had the power to make them live or die, marry or stay single. Alcott refused to yield, but New York City and Professor Bhaer were her compromise.

In October of 1875, Alcott decided to attend the Women's Congress in Syracuse, New York. She had intended to observe and be company for her cousin Charlotte Wilkinson, her beloved Uncle Sam May's daughter, but instead she became a reluctant center of attention, a celebrity whose presence swept away the more serious concerns of the audience. "When the meeting was over, the stage filled in a minute . . . with beaming girls all armed with Albums and cards and begging to speak to Miss A.," she wrote in a letter to her father. One fan wanted a kiss, another lifted Alcott's veil to see her face. "I finally had to run for my life with more girls all along the way and Mas clawing me as I went," she wrote.[2] In her journal, she noted that she had been "kissed to death by blushing damsels." Alcott's ambivalence about her fans did not obscure her delight and gratitude about the money that continued to pour in.

Many writers will tell you that the imagination has strange powers and that scenes they have imagined sometimes strangely appear to come true. My father wrote a plane hijacking in a story of his, three years before the first plane hijacking, for instance. Alcott's imaginative powers seem even fiercer. Although Mrs. Kirke's boardinghouse did not exist, and Alcott had never been to New

York City for more than a night, on picturesque MacDougal Street there is a group of brownstones, one of which once bore a plaque saying that Louisa May Alcott lived there and that she wrote some of *Little Women* there. The pretty buildings, owned by New York University and used currently as Law School dormitories, are called the Alcott Houses, but the excellent NYU archivist Nancy Cricco has no idea where this name came from. She calls the story an "urban myth."[3]

Whoever named the buildings created a historical monster of inaccuracy. The so-called fact that Louisa May Alcott wrote *Little Women* while she was living on Mac-Dougal Street has spread like a virus to Wikipedia and many other Internet sites. Many sites add that the houses were owned by an Alcott uncle. This is also impossible, since the Alcott name was fabricated by Bronson Alcott, who began life as Amos Alcox and decided that A. Bronson Alcott was a name more fitting a man of his progressive and elegant ideas and appearance.

But this error is not restricted to the often-criticized Internet — it also appears in Frommer's guide to New York and many other print books. At least on Wikipedia, a search using different words uncovers the true story, which is, as you know, that Alcott wrote her book in her upstairs bedroom in Concord, Massachusetts. The Alcott Houses look very much like the sets of the four movies made of *Little Women* in which, as in the novel, the intrepid and fictional Jo March meets and, without knowing it, falls in love with the bearlike Professor Bhaer.

Much is made of the ways in which fact seeps into fiction — novels are sometimes read as if they were autobiography. But fiction also bleeds over into fact. The Alcott Houses are a nice example of this. Historically, their name is entirely inaccurate. Imaginatively they can be taken as the originals of Mrs. Kirke's imaginary boardinghouse.

By the time Louisa May Alcott visited New York City for more than the overnights required to sail to Europe, she was famous, exhausted, and often sick. "When I had the youth I had no money, now I have the money I have no time, and when I get the time, if I ever do, I shall have no health to enjoy life," she wrote.[4]

Everywhere she went, she was gawked at and admired. At a meeting of the Sorosis Club at Vassar College in Poughkeepsie, New York, the students had hoped that Alcott would make a speech. She declined.

Instead, they asked her to stand up and turn around slowly so that everyone could see her from every angle.

As Concord readied itself for a gala centennial to celebrate the shots heard round the world that had begun the Revolutionary War at the Old North Bridge, Alcott spent less and less time there. She hadn't liked Concord for a while and now that she was a local celebrity, she liked it even less. More than a hundred visitors a month made the pilgrimage to Concord and then out to Orchard House to speak with Alcott or to meet her or even just to see where she lived. "A whole school came without warning last week & Concord people bring all their company to see us," Alcott wrote a Mrs. Woods in July of 1875. "This may seem pleasant, but when kept up a whole season is a great affliction."[5]

So Alcott decided to go to a city where she would be one of many celebrities and planned her first real visit to New York in the winter of 1875, almost ten years after the writing of *Little Women,* and years after the writing of *Little Men, Shawl-Straps* and *Aunt Jo's Scrap-Bag* as well. Although Alcott was a spinster, a category of woman marginalized and often treated with contempt in nineteenth-century New England, she was also now a famous spinster, and this made it possible for her to travel and be welcomed in a way that was rare for a single, unmarried woman in her forties.

Alcott's position in society as a young woman and the decisions she had to make about the direction of her life are very much like the position of young women today. Yet in other ways, there has been tremendous progress in women's rights, progress that Alcott supported and monitored. Although women in their early forties who have never been married may be treated as if they have failed at some ineffable something, they have the freedom to travel and to make lives for themselves alone, and they are treated with respect — in fact, they are sometimes treated with more respect than accrues to a nonworking housewife living in her husband's financial and emotional shadow. The epitome of successful womanhood in the 1870s in this country — the obedient housewife of a middle-class husband — is now thought to be a shadow woman, a woman who hasn't bothered to develop her own identity.

In New York, Alcott moved into Dr. Eli Peck Miller's Bath Hotel at 39–41 West Twenty-sixth Street, a combination hotel, spa, and health club near Madison Square

Park where for $2.50 a day she got meals based on Mattie Jones's *Hygienic Cook-Book* — no coffee, spices, pickles, teas, or tobacco. Peck believed that disease could be avoided by living a healthy life, and health at his establishment was supplemented with dozens of special baths — hot air, vapor, Turkish — as well as Kidder's electromagnetic machine and a Swedish Movement Cure. Alcott could spend a day between the Frigidarium and the Suditorium, ending with a friction massage while reclining on a marble couch. Alcott wandered all over the city from Madison Square down to the Bowery, and as word of her presence spread, her social life in the most social city in the world began in earnest.

Dinner parties were given in her honor by hosts like Alcott's long-lost cousin Octavius Frothingham. At the Frothinghams' she chatted with Oliver Johnson, a prominent humanitarian who had known Harriet Tubman, and she talked with her new New York friend Mary Mapes Dodge. Dodge had also grown up in a family of four sisters and had written a children's book, which was, at the time, as much a sensation as *Little Women* — *Hans Brinker; or, the Silver Skates.*

The Concord country wren who had grown up in a genius cluster and had fame suddenly descend on her was perfectly comfortable chatting with politicians and other famous writers. She became friends with Anne and Vincenzo Botta. Anne Botta, whom Alcott found "lovely," was a poet who had married a handsome Italian Cavour scholar and whose home had become a center of intellectual New York.

Like Louisa's Boston friend Annie Fields, Anne Botta was lighthearted and generous and gathered individuals who interested her in her drawing room. The scholar D. G. Holland was typical of New York intellectuals eager to chat with Alcott about Walt Whitman, abolition, and writing. Holland's dinner party on Park Avenue was sandwiched between the theater — Alcott saw Edwin Booth acting at the new Fifth Avenue Theater — and ladies' lunches at the Lotos Club and the Sorosis professional women's club and winter drives in Central Park with another new New York friend also staying at Eli Peck Miller's hotel, Salley Holley.

Alcott had come to like parties, but her reformer soul was more interested in society than in Society with a capital *S*. Her fame gave her access to anything that aroused her curiosity. In between dinners and luncheons in her honor, she arranged visits to orphanages and prisons. All the money and celebrity in the world did not change what she cared about or dim the strength of her obsession with those who had less — with those who had very little. At Christmas, she joined friends in visiting Randall's Island, in the East River and owned by the City of New York, which held the House of Refuge for Delinquent Boys and Girls, an insane asylum, and an inebriates' home, the nineteenth-century equivalent of a rehab.

Bought by the City of New York in 1836, the island had been used since then for groups that required the quarantine provided by the rushing, swirling currents of the East River.[6] Accompanied by James and Abby Hopper Gibbons, who had often ministered to the waifs on Randall's Island, Alcott saw how low things could get for institutionalized children. "I've had a pretty good variety of Christmases in my day, but never one like this before," she wrote her family back in Concord. The children, after ecstatically receiving the bushels of candy and presents brought by the Gibbonses, performed pieces and songs for the visitors.

But it was the insane asylum for children, which she called the "idiot house," that Alcott thought she would be haunted by for a long time. There, abandoned children with serious mental illnesses — illnesses that were diagnosed only as "idiocy" — lived in sad conditions ministered to by pauper women and a devoted few. "The babies die like sheep, many being deserted so young nothing can be hoped or done for them," she wrote home. After food and presents were distributed and the ferry to Randall's Island took the visitors back to Manhattan, Alcott realized that she had missed out on Christmas dinner. "My Christmas day was without dinner or presents for the very first time since I can remember," she wrote home. "Yet it has been a very memorable day, and I feel as if I'd had a splendid feast seeing the poor babies wallow in turkey soup, and that every gift I put into their hands had come back to me in the dumb delight of their unchild-like faces trying to smile."[7]

In her intense New York visit, Alcott visited a New York City that few tourists ever see. At the Tombs, officially called the New York Halls of Justice and House of Detention, she was given a tour. The famously brutal city prison in an imposing neo-Egyptian building had been designed by John Haviland to suggest a huge, weighty Egyptian sarcophagus. Alcott was told that the prisoners in 148 double cells lived on black bread, tea, and coffee. The month of her visit, there were three executions at the Tombs.

Alcott was particularly interested in a home for indigent newsboys where for 5 cents a day a boy could live and sleep. Called the Newsboys' Lodging House, it was one of many institutions built to help the masses of indigent children who seemed to crowd the city streets. "One little chap, only six, was trotting round busy as a bee, locking up his small shoes and ragged jacket as if they were great treasures," Alcott wrote her young nephews Frederick and John about boys who were not as fortunate as they. "Six-year-old Peter was being supported by his nine-year-old brother who worked overtime to keep their family of two from being separated," wrote the boys' beloved Aunt Weedy. "Think of that Fred! How would it seem to be all alone in a big city, with no mamma to cuddle you, no two grandpas' houses to take you in, not a penny but what you earned and Donny to take care of?"[8]

Alcott was happy to support her nephews and anyone else in her family now that she had found a way to make money. She also longed for a level of appreciation that never seemed to materialize. Her sister Anna had often asked if Louisa might help her buy a house. Louisa thought it was better to have Anna and her boys at Orchard House. Finally, in 1877, Anna prevailed and her sister bought her the Thoreau house in the middle of Concord. Anna had her dream come true, courtesy of Louisa. Louisa was generous but still feeling overlooked. "Ought to be contented with knowing I help both my sisters by my brains," she wrote. "But I am selfish, and want to go away and rest in Europe. Never shall."[9] In spite of her huge success, Alcott felt lashed to the same old financial treadmill. Now instead of desperately struggling to pay the family bills, she was forced to struggle to keep up with the family dreams — perhaps a harder job in a family of professional dreamers.

While Louisa gallivanted in New York, Philadelphia, where she heard Henry Ward Beecher preach and was unimpressed, and Boston for the Centennial Ball, her mother became sicker and sicker during the winter back home in Concord. After a summer in Concord taking turns with May to care for their mother, Alcott dispatched May back to Europe to continue her studies in art. "The money I invest in her pays the sort of interest I like," she wrote in her journal. Through their travels in Europe and their cooperative care of the aging Abba, May and Louisa had become extremely close. Their bond seemed the strongest in either of their lives, a bond based on shared experience and mutual appreciation. All Louisa's anger at May's childhood fastidiousness had disappeared, and all of May's squeamishness at her sister's outspokenness had burned away in the fires of time. This time, though, the Alcott blessings were to lead May down a complicated path. While she studied in Paris, May met and fell in love with a Swiss businessman, Ernest Nieriker.

In the fall of 1877, Abba Alcott, surrounded by what was left of her family — Louisa, Anna, and Bronson — quietly sickened in the upstairs bedroom of her house in Concord, across from the portrait of her ancestor, the recanting witchcraft judge Samuel Sewall.

Nursing her panting, moaning mother was too much for Louisa and she collapsed, lying across the hall in her own bedroom for a week, seemingly near death herself. At this point in her life, as a forty-four-year-old woman with more than a decade to live, Alcott seems to have sickened again. For years the results of the mercury poisoning had been gone and she had led a relatively normal life. Now illness began to be her constant companion and preoccupation.

On the fourteenth of November both patients were carefully moved to Anna's new house in downtown Concord. There, Abba died quietly and happily with little pain. "O how beautiful it is to die, how happy I am,"[10] she told her gathered family. Abba was buried in Sleepy Hollow with a eulogy by the Reverend H. W. Foote, the minister of Boston's King's Chapel, where the lanky, reforming Abba Alcott had married the self-invented philosophical Bronson more than forty years earlier. Two days after the funeral, Louisa and her father quietly celebrated their forty-fifth and seventy-eighth birthdays.

Abba's death brought a new wave of exhaustion and despair for Louisa, who had realized her dream of financial stability but was often too sick or too tired to enjoy it. Anyone who dreams of wealth and fame might be warned by this story of a woman who struggled so hard to make money that by the time she reached her goal she could no longer appreciate its benefits. "My duty is done," she wrote after Abba's funeral, "and now I shall be glad to follow her."[11]

But the rich, contradictory life of Louisa May Alcott had a few acts left to go. This woman, who had grown up in the heart of

American Literature in a flowering New England where everything seemed possible for the minds and souls of men and even women, reached her forties having won a share of fortune and fame that few even dream of. She had moved so often that when she finally had a real family home — Orchard House — she felt claustrophobic and shut in between its narrow walls.

May was devastated with sorrow and guilt at not being home when her mother died. At the same time, she had fallen in love with the sensuous, visually ravishing way of life she had found in France. There, May had made a life for herself, and her work as a painter had been recognized. Back in Boston, she was known as the woman who had loaned tools to and encouraged the young sculptor Daniel Chester French. But in Paris, a still life of hers was chosen to hang in the same Paris salon that rejected two canvases by her friend Mary Cassatt. Her copies of Turner were hailed by no less a critic than John Ruskin. Her book *Studying Art Abroad and How to Do It Cheaply* also won her a reputation as an American writer.

In New England, her talents were eclipsed, first by those of her father and then by those of her sister. In France, where she and Ernest had settled near Paris in Meudon, she found an artistic home. She was also in love with France for many other reasons. The mouth-watering food, the heart-lifting landscapes, the French admiration for beauty in all its forms made her feel that she had at last found her place. In memory Concord seemed small, grim, and uncomfortable next to the delights of Paris and the French countryside. Ernest Nieriker, a twenty-two-year-old with a thriving French business, was fifteen years younger than May, but he seemed connected with the seriousness of art and the deliciousness of life in Europe. May married him in a quiet ceremony on March 22, less than six months after her mother's death, with none of her family in attendance.

Trapped in dreary old New England as she read May's sparkling letters, the sick Louisa let her jealousy show in her journals. "How different our lives are just now!" she wrote in reference to her erstwhile closest companion. "I so lonely, sad, and sick, she so happy, well, and blest. She always had the cream of things, and deserved it. My time is yet to come somewhere else, when I am ready for it."[12] Although May constantly urged her sister to visit, to come and live forever in the heaven-on-earth she had discovered, Louisa's illness intervened. Louisa planned to go in September, but Anna broke her leg. As always, her obligations to her family came first.

Time after time, Louisa planned to go back to Europe, and time after time, some crisis in the extended Alcott family made the trip impossible. If she had known what was going to happen, of course visiting May would have come first. But May seemed, as always, annoyingly happy in her new paradise. Perhaps it was hard to read her letters, with their condemnation of the very life Louisa was leading and had, in fact, devoted herself to leading. "America seems death to all aspirations of hope and work," May wrote thoughtlessly. "Nothing would ever induce me to live in Concord again." May gave a party in Meudon and lovingly described covering her table with "fine damask, my pretty silver and plenty of flowers and a green grape-leaf dish piled high with peaches, pears and grapes. . . . Salmon salad, Gervais cheese, cold tongue, nice cake and *paté douceurs* such as only the French can make, gave us a charming lunch, finished with wine." May wrote that if Louisa came to visit, "she will never want to live in Stupid America again."[13]

May's delight intrigued her sister but also disturbed her. The woman whom her father called "Duty's faithful Child" had always been less interested in her own comforts than in the comforts and opportunities of her family. May was very good at helping herself to what she needed; Louisa was very good at helping others get what they needed. Wrapped in her own moods, Alcott retreated to her bedroom, often refusing to come down and greet the many visitors her father entertained in his study. Her journals reflect her physical pain and psychic despair. "Life is not worth living this way,"[14] she wrote in April of 1879.

As always the coming of the warm weather lifted the spirits of everyone in Concord. Alcott bought herself a phaeton pulled by a little white horse to tool around in. Of course, Bronson used the little carriage as much as she did. The lilacs bloomed, the mud gave way to the earthy smells of moss and fern, and birdsong accompanied the sound of brooks. Alcott rented out Orchard House. Her father was off on another western tour, and she went back to Boston, where a new doctor, a Dr. Rhoda Ashley Joy Lawrence, who had studied at the Boston University School of Medicine and established a pleasant nursing home at Dunreath Place in Roxbury just south of Boston, told her that she was doing well. In the meantime, word came that May was pregnant.

Alcott still snapped out of her low mood to do the right thing as a reformer and concerned citizen. She visited the Concord prison one Sunday and spoke to the inmates, telling them a story and getting so carried away by their attentive faces that she spoke for longer than she intended. She was the first woman to register to vote in Concord school committee elections. She contributed essays on women's suffrage to the *Woman's Journal.*

In July her father's latest project, a School of Philosophy that drew 400 philosophers to Concord over the summer months, began in Bronson's study. His first lecture was on Plato. Later the school migrated to a frame structure behind Orchard House. Bronson's philosophers were fed and entertained and cleaned up after by Louisa and Anna. Both sisters found this a mixed blessing.

On November 8 in Paris, May Alcott Nieriker gave birth to a girl named Louisa May after Alcott. The baby was called Lulu. By the beginning of December, the news turned black. The baby was healthy, but May was not doing well. "The weight on my heart is not all imagination," Alcott wrote. "She was too happy to have it last."

Of course, Louisa blamed herself for not visiting and for not being there to help her sister in trouble. "Such a tugging at my heart to be by my poor May alone so far away."[15]

By all accounts, Ernest Nieriker was an exemplary husband, but apparently there was nothing he could do. On December 31, Louisa went downstairs to find her old friend and master Emerson in the parlor with tears in his eyes looking at the portrait of May hanging against the back wall. Nieriker, thinking this would make the blow easier, had sent Emerson a telegram saying that May was dead. The old man, bowed with yet another grief, had walked down the snowy incline of the Lexington Road and into town to bear his sad news. It actually seemed too much to bear. At least, Louisa wailed into the pages of her journals, Ernest would have the baby to comfort him.

Yet in a strange and generous last wish, May Alcott showed that for all her turning against America she had not lost the religion of her childhood and of her family — she was a devout Alcott first and everything else second. She had deeded her daughter Lulu to her sister, asking that the baby be sent to Concord as soon as possible to be raised by her maiden Aunt Louisa. There were delays.

The baby was sick. The baby couldn't travel. Perhaps Ernest Nieriker, having lost his wife, was not eager to give up his baby daughter.

Nevertheless, whatever their reluctance to part with the beautiful little girl, Nieriker and his sister Sophie decided to comply. Alcott sent a trusted nurse from Boston, a Mrs. Giles, to go to Switzerland and fetch her darling sister's baby. Thus a middle-aged New England spinster who had never lived with a man suddenly became the eager mother of a tiny, helpless ten-month-old baby. Just when Louisa was convinced her life was over and felt herself ready to die, her life began again.

# 10
## LULU.
### 1880–1888

The death of May was devastating. The two
sisters had become best friends in their
travels, and because of Louisa's financial
success, May had been able to build a
significant career as a painter out of a talent
that her family had found merely charming.
In this way, she was very much like Louisa
— she took her own art more seriously than
many who saw it. Then just as she had
found love and been starting her own family, the story was cut short in a way that was
unbearable for her family. "Of all the trials
in my life, I never felt any as keenly as this,"
Louisa wrote in her journal. "Tried to
write . . . to distract my mind, but the wave
of sorrow kept rolling over me & I could
only weep and wait till the tide ebbed
again."[1]

In the cold winter months after May's
death, Alcott received many letters from
Ernest Nieriker and his sister Sophie. A box

filled with May's possessions and clothes brought fresh grief. Soon, though, Alcott started making preparations for the arrival of her baby niece. May's last wish was eccentric; it would separate her baby from her only living parent. Did May realize that raising a child would be the only way to distract the Alcott family from their loss? During the summer, Alcott began to prepare. She made a will leaving her copyrights to John Pratt, who was to divide the profits from them between his brother, his mother, himself, and Lulu.

As the summer ended, Louisa spent evenings in the nursery she had created in the upstairs rooms, praying over the empty little white crib that she had prepared for her Lulu. On September 19, Alcott, frail and in ill health, took the train to Boston to wait on the wharf for the steamer that would bring her sister's baby to her new home. Each baby that came off the boat made her heart leap. Finally the boat's captain appeared holding "a little yellow haired thing in white, with its hat off as it looked about with lively blue eyes," Alcott wrote. She held out her arms for the baby, who seemed to sense that she was meeting her new mother. "Marmar," she said to Louisa, as if she had come home.

Alcott's journals, usually plain and graphic and filled with dry detail, allow some rhapsodizing about the amazing little Lulu. Her little body was perfectly formed, Louisa delighted, with a pug nose, yellow down on her head, and a tan from being at sea. "A happy thing laughing and waving her hands, confiding and bold, with a keen look in the eyes so like May who hated shams & saw through them at once," she wrote in her journal.

Orchard House had been rented out, so Alcott brought Lulu home to the new Alcott house on Main Street, the old Thoreau house that she had bought for Anna and her boys and which became the new center of the family. Abba moved to the new house in the last days of her life, but her death had blown the center out of the Alcott family. After decades in Orchard House, they returned to the kind of peripatetic life that had been characteristic of Louisa's early years. Then necessity had dictated many moves; now she chose to move. For the rest of her life, Louisa and everyone dependent on her would be perpetually moving from house to house.

In the winter of 1880, Bronson set off on another lecture tour — because of Louisa's success, his tours were suddenly mobbed with fans and unusually profitable — and Louisa rented her cousin Lizzie Wells's house on Beacon Hill in Boston. As it turned out, wealth did not insulate Alcott from domestic problems. The house was a nightmare, and Louisa spent a huge amount of time getting plumbers and handymen in to keep the place running. There, Lulu had her first birthday, which she thoroughly enjoyed. Dressed in new clothes, white boots, and a blue sash, and wearing a small green crown, "the little queen in her high chair sat & looked with delight at the tiny cake with one candle . . . rattle with bells, & some gay cards from her friends,"[2] Louisa wrote to Bronson, who had reached Syracuse. At 20 pounds, Lulu was a healthy baby, with typical picture books, flowers, a doll, a silver mug, and a growing vocabulary: Mama, Da, Up!, Bow-Wow, and Dranpa. Delighted by her picture books and with huge expressive blue eyes, the baby preoccupied and amazed her Aunt Weedy.

The old Thoreau house on Main Street had become a tourist attraction of sorts when Louisa was in residence. When Lulu was taken out for a walk, people would exclaim and try to reach into the carriage and kiss her. Even in Boston, Louisa had become a kind of national treasure in a way that usually offended her. It wasn't all bad. In the winter of 1880, she had a visit that pleased her from a young man who had heard her speak at the Concord prison and came to tell her that her story had changed his life. He was the best kind of fan — intelligent, grateful, and off to South America with a geological survey party.

In her fiftieth year, with a toddler to care for and an entire extended family — Anna and her two boys — dependent on her, Alcott kept writing, working on the third volume of what would become the March family trilogy, *Jo's Boys.* Her journals suffered. In April she went through her mother's diaries and destroyed them as her mother had wished. Alcott's journals record quite a lot of this kind of prophylactic destruction. Perhaps she was inspired by Charles Dickens, who in early September of 1860 had made a bonfire for all his papers and correspondence behind his house at Gad's Hill in London.

Louisa's old friend and idol Ralph Waldo Emerson had been increasingly ill as the years had passed. His memory faded in and out, and his daughter Ellen usually went out with him and traveled with him, often to remind him of basic things like the name of his wife or the town where he had lived his whole life. As this great man faded, many distinguished visitors arrived to say good-bye. Walt Whitman visited, but he and Louisa didn't talk about nursing.

Then in April, Emerson contracted pneumonia and died quietly in his sleep. Louisa felt that her world was slipping away. She was back in Boston, staying in rooms at a renovated Bellevue Hotel while Lulu stayed with Anna in Concord, when the news came from Concord that Bronson had suffered a paralytic stroke. Louisa rushed back to Concord, where the ecstatic greeting from Lulu was the only thing that cheered her. "I felt as if I could bear anything with this little sunbeam to light up the world for me," Louisa wrote.[3]

There was a lot to bear. Bronson, the anchor of Louisa's world, the man who had invented the religion of the Alcott family out of his own dreams, was inarticulate and felled like a great tree. "It is so pathetic to see my handsome, hale, active old father changed at one fell blow into this helpless wreck," she wrote her friend Maria S. Porter.[4] Although Bronson defied all predictions and recovered faster than the doctors had believed possible, he never wrote or traveled again.

Now Alcott had two babies to care for,

her aging father and the adorable Lulu. She needed help, and her attempts to find satisfactory child care sound familiar to anyone who has ever tried to get help with the complex, intimate task of raising a child. In May, Alcott complained that in Concord they could find no one to help dress, walk, and play with Lulu. Mrs. F., a nurse, turned out to be a drunk; she "got tipsey" and had to go. A pretty Dane was "too lofty" and knew nothing about children. Miss M. had "no idea of government" and she was "sick and sad." "The ladies are incapable or proud, the girls vulgar or rough, so my poor baby has a bad time with her little tempers & active mind and body," Louisa wrote.[5]

When one of the babysitters, a Miss Cassall, who was "cold & tired & careless" came upon the great American authoress on the floor with her hair down, roaring and romping with her niece, she was horrified by the lack of dignity in her distinguished employer. When Lulu went to kindergarten, Louisa was distressed to see that the teachers were almost as bad as the babysitters. Lulu's teacher was good at teaching from books, Louisa noted, but she had no ideas about amusing children, and her heart was not in her work. Most of the time, Louisa took care of Lulu, dashing away to care for her father when she had time.

Lulu's teething was a huge crisis, and the child was sometimes fretful. Yet her courage and exuberance never failed to thrill her fragile, aging aunt. In the ocean at Nonquit, the three-year-old plunged into the sea and started walking toward Europe. Alcott was very close to her two nephews, John and Fred, but taking care of a child of her own was quite different than visiting children who were well taken care of by their mother. Anna and her boys often took Lulu for days at a time, days that later would become weeks and months, but the pressures of actually raising a child both invigorated and exhausted Alcott, who continued to write and to share in the care of her father. To make matters more interesting, Lulu had a questioning, ferocious personality that was uncannily like that of her namesake, her beloved Aunt Weedy.

Alcott seemed obsessed with Lulu's health and gave her homeopathic remedies for everything. Lulu had a variety of health problems. Louisa had been raised to think that the aim of life was the "regular movement of the bowels," and, like an old-fashioned governess, she monitored Lulu's digestion and even considered dosing the little girl with her own opium, which she had relied on for years.[6] She was as frustrated as any parent at Lulu's misbehavior — the little girl could not seem to do things on time, and she was always asking questions instead of expressing polite obedience.

Although Louisa tried to apply her father's loving educational methods, and although she truly believed, along with Coleridge, Wordsworth, and the great Bronson Alcott, that children were wise and innocent and closer to God than adults, she found Lulu's lack of obedience trying. In the year 1884, when Lulu turned four and began to have the kind of temper tantrums that are typical of a four-year-old, Alcott's journals went from thirty years of voluble entries detailing her day-to-day life to terse one-line comments.

On New Year's Day of 1884, in an incident that must have painfully evoked her own childhood, Lulu was so naughty that Louisa decided she needed an official spanking. Urged on by the heartless Miss Cassall, Louisa explained to her Lulu that she was going to be forced to spank her because of Lulu's bad behavior. Lulu was beside herself with guilt and fear. She wanted to get it over with as fast as possible. "Do it, do it," she urged her reluctant aunt. It's hard to imagine that the frail, ill Alcott could administer much of a spanking, but the effect was disastrous at any rate. Lulu is "heart broken at the idea of Aunt Wee's giving her pain," Alcott wrote in her journal. "Her bewilderment was pathetic, & the effect as I expected a failure. Love is better but also endless patience."

In June of 1884, Alcott finally sold Orchard House to educator William Torrey Harris and his family for $3,500. The place was filled with memories, the small rooms haunted by Alcott's life as a young woman in her twenties and by the characters she had created and set in those rooms in *Little Women.* The scene of Bronson's final successes at the Concord School of Philosophy in the arched wooden structure behind the house gave another dimension to what Alcott was leaving behind. "Places have not much hold on me when the persons who made them dear are gone," Alcott wrote.[7]

With the money from the sale of Orchard House, the always frugal Alcott bought a cottage on Buzzards Bay at Nonquit, a lovely small seaside town where Alcott could enjoy the seascapes, so different from the gloomy Concord woods. In Nonquit, Lulu ran wild with pleasure. In the fall, the family moved back to Boston, first to the Bellevue Hotel and then to rented rooms in

Chestnut Street. Eventually, Alcott would lease a townhouse in the heart of Beacon Hill at 10 Louisburg Square, trying to create an urban center for the family that would be more convenient than Orchard House had been.

As she played with Lulu and tried to keep the feisty young girl in line, and as she took care of her sick father and moved back and forth from house to house, Alcott's own illness took up more and more of her time. Her delight in being Lulu's parent faded as the pain in her body grew worse and worse. She suffered from tremendous aches in her legs, severe digestive problems, and lungs that seemed to have some kind of blockage.

The world around Alcott was changing and she struggled to change with it. An extraordinarily open-minded woman even as she sickened and lost her energy, she often signed herself in her letters "yours for reforms of all kinds." She wasn't kidding. Historically it was becoming clear, as President Grant gave way to President Hayes and the country again suffered the trauma of an assassinated president when James Garfield was murdered in 1881 and succeeded by President Chester Arthur, that reform was in the air. Alcott was in favor of women's suffrage; she deplored what was happening in the southern states; she watched as Henry James took her ideas and characters and made his own brilliant career. In 1886 he published *The Bostonians,* a novel that comments on the communities in which she had grown up.

Over in England, Sir Arthur Conan Doyle published the first Sherlock Holmes story, *A Study in Scarlet,* which Alcott was too sick to read. Robert Louis Stevenson published *Dr. Jekyll and Mr. Hyde,* and in France the pointillist painters broke up the unified surfaces of representation, and Georges Seurat showed his fabulous *Un dimanche après-midi à l'Île de la Grande Jatte* to horrified viewers.

In medicine, however, advances were few and far between. It was the age of invention, the age of electricity, and the soon-to-be-invented telephone, but it wasn't until 1890 that the knowledge of the way bacteria are spread finally filtered down to the practice of surgery and the surgeons at Johns Hopkins donned rubber gloves to perform. When it came to helping her health, Alcott was as willing to try new things as she was in every other area of her life. Alcott was happy to have a go at everything available, including in 1884 the fashionable mind cure practiced by Anna B.

Newman, a follower of Mary Baker Eddy, whose Christian Science movement was already gathering followers and properties. Mrs. Newman, like Eddy and others, believed that if the mind were cleansed, the body would follow suit. She urged her famous patient to clear her brain of thoughts and imagine blue sky and sunshine.

Although Alcott persisted in trying Mrs. Newman's mind cure, she was deeply skeptical of psychological cures for her physical ailments. First, Mrs. Newman told her to be passive; she complained, and then Mrs. Newman told her she wasn't positive enough. "God & nature can't be hustled about every ten minutes," she wrote in her journal. "Too much money made and too much delusion all around."

In her rejection of the mind cure and the theories of Mary Baker Eddy, Alcott was also rejecting her father, who was a fan and disciple of Mrs. Eddy. Born in Bow, New Hampshire, the daughter of strict Congregationalists, Eddy was a slender girl with serious health problems. She suffered from fits in which she shook and fell on the ground — what we call grand mal seizures. These fits alternated with what seemed to be acute paranormal powers. She married George Washington Glover, a building contractor, when she was twenty-two.

One day after a fall on the ice, Mrs. Glover felt that she was able, by calling on her inner spirit, to heal herself. This event led to the founding of Christian Science, whose bible was Mrs. Eddy's book *Science and Health*. In her early days of practice, Mrs. Eddy's patients were limited to local people, including the millworkers in and around Lynn, Massachusetts, where she had moved in 1864. Her first visitor from the world of the intellect, the Boston world, was none other than Bronson Alcott, who was drawn by what now may seem like old-fashioned faith healing but which at the time seemed a rational alternative to nineteenth-century medicine.

Of course, Alcott was always a believer, and after reading Mrs. Eddy's book, he called on her at her house in Lynn, where he was to pay many visits. Bronson was favorably impressed by Mrs. Eddy. He wrote in his journal that he found her one of the "fair saints." He was moved by her accounts of "metaphysical healing — curing by sympathy with spiritual power over the mind. .... Drugs are wholly unused and her cures have been many."[8]

Mrs. Eddy was building an empire, and although Bronson was not an empire builder

— he almost entirely lacked worldly ambition — he was impressed. He wasn't alone. The most popular minister in Boston, the Reverend Edward Everett Hale, wrote of Mrs. Eddy that "she has taught me more truth in twenty minutes than I have learned in twenty years." My own family, which in the nineteenth century clustered on Boston's South Shore, were avid followers of Mrs. Eddy. My grandmother believed that doctors made everything worse and that the only cures were available through the spiritual world — not as eccentric a belief then as it would be now. When my father had tuberculosis as a child, she probably saved his life by avoiding medical treatment in a hospital where he might have been exposed to bacteria carried on every doctor's dirty hands. (He was born in 1918, but modern medicine came slowly to the Boston suburbs.) When she broke her leg, she set the bone herself in unimaginable pain. She limped for the rest of her life.

But when Bronson brought the happy news of this new healing method to Concord and described it to the gathering of intellectuals and neighbors in Emerson's library, he felt a distinct chill. There was something about Mrs. Eddy that grated. Perhaps it was her dreadful use of the

English language, a problem for which Mark Twain unmercifully attacked her in his book about Christian Science. A fan of Emerson's, Eddy nevertheless wrote more like Alcott — not a good thing. "Emerson says, 'hitch your wagon to a star,' " she wrote. "I say Be allied to the deific power, and all that is good will aid your journey, as the stars in their courses fought against Sisera."[9]

Perhaps it was her ambition — as Mrs. Eddy's movement grew, it became a huge business with its own real estate, its own newspaper, and a significant endowment. Twain pointed out that Mrs. Eddy was doing with the human spirit what Jay Gould and Andrew Carnegie were doing with the country's natural resources. She was a robber baron of the soul. "A marvelous woman; with a hunger for power such as has never been seen in the world before," Twain wrote of Eddy. "No thing, little or big, that contains any seed or suggestion of power escapes her avaricious eye."[10]

Bronson continued to be a fan and even took his failing daughter Louisa to see his new enthusiasm. Louisa was unimpressed but desperate. Hence when her illnesses got worse, she turned to a similar idea of mind cure with Mrs. Newman. Unlike her father,

Alcott had become infinitely practical. Even as he had scrupulously avoided accepting the way the world works and the ability of men and women to sink to depths of greed and manipulation, his daughter had been forced to learn the truth about human nature the hard way. If her father was the Hoper, she was the Realist. While Bronson and Mrs. Eddy exchanged flowery complimentary letters, Louisa turned her attention to a different kind of healing — massage. She found massage helped as much as mental or spiritual manipulations.

As Alcott's illnesses moved to the center stage of her life, her time was taken up more and more by fainting spells, dizzy collapses, vertigo, fatigue, rheumatism, rebellious stomach, and fright, as she wrote in her journal.[11] She almost never felt well enough to work anymore, and her human interactions were pushed away as she focused on getting through each day and the long, often-sleepless nights. Her beloved Lulu spent more and more time with Anna and her boys. Even as the burden of raising a child was lifted more and more from the ailing Alcott, the intense joys of raising a child were also diminished.

In August of 1885 during a relatively pain-free summer with Lulu at Nonquit, Louisa sorted through letters and journals and again burned many of them in a ritual that she carried out more and more frequently as she became more famous and her feelings of being besieged and intruded on became sharper. "Not wise to keep for curious eyes to read & gossip lovers to print by & by," she wrote in her journal.[12] Although the Alcott version of privacy had always included total access by the family to each other's private journals and letters, as Elizabeth Peabody found out to her horror, the family ethic also was to protect the family from talk in the outside world. In a note on her journals in 1878, Alcott had written, "These journals are kept only for my own reference, & I particularly desire that if I die before I destroy them they may all be burnt unread."

On the other hand, Alcott took the time to annotate her own journals, and on the same day that she was sorting and burning, she seemed to have a desire to leave some of them behind. "Experiences go deep with me," she wrote. "I begin to think it might be well to keep some record of my life if it will help others to read it while I'm gone."

Intermittently, Alcott kept on working. Her work had become the center of her world — the activity that kept her feeling worthwhile and alive. Under the care of Dr. Conrad Wesselhoeft, she persuaded him that she should be allowed to work thirty minutes a day. In July of 1886, she finally finished *Jo's Boys,* the third novel in the trilogy that included *Little Women* and *Little Men,* which were still selling in the thousands of copies every month. Thomas Niles ordered 50,000 copies as a first printing of *Jo's Boys,* and the orders poured in for it before the press even started to roll.

As Alcott's energy faded and her illnesses caught up with her, her work became more autobiographical. The energy of fiction fueled by yearning seemed to fade away, and she no longer had the fire or the passion to transform her life into art. *Jo's Boys* is a sad, subdued novel in which Jo writes about trying and failing to accept fame and being happy that she has been able to provide for her beloved Marmee. Jo considers herself "a literary nursery-maid who provides moral pap for the very young."

After finishing her last book, Alcott took her father to what would be his final session at the Concord summer school. The old man had recovered amazingly from his stroke, but he was fading again and used his ailing daughter, as always, as his maid, nurse, and financial support. The two fragile old people heard Julia Ward Howe talk about the women of Plato's republic and chatted with Elizabeth Peabody and savored the deliciousness of the Concord summer days. "Very hot," Alcott wrote in the abbreviated notation that had become the language of her journal. "Queer people. Glad it's done."

Back in Boston, Alcott, desperate for a way to stay healthy enough to function at all, was helped once again by Dr. Rhoda Lawrence, who ran the convalescent home in Roxbury. In an effort to improve her health, she was ready to cut herself off from her family and from Lulu, probably the sources of whatever good health she had. A young woman named Hatty Haskell had finally solved Alcott's child-care problems. With the exception of occasional arguments that wearied Alcott more than she could express, Haskell would become Lulu's babysitter for her remaining years with her failing Aunt Weedy.

In January of 1887, feeling very sad and lonely about it, Alcott moved into Dr. Lawrence's home on Dunreath Place and away from her family, who now rotated between the Thoreau house in Concord, the house at 10 Louisburg Square, and the house in Nonquit. "Away from home &

worn out with the long struggle for health," she wrote. "Have had many hard days but few harder than this."[13] At last she would have all the rest she needed.

Whatever Alcott's illness might have been, by this time it required much more than Dr. Lawrence had to offer. Even relieved of the cares of family and work, Alcott got worse. She had nightmares and delusions like the ones that had dogged her after the Civil War when her body suffered mercury poisoning. She thought she saw dead people; she thought Lulu had been killed. She was unable to digest solid food, and lumps appeared on her neck and legs. She was "so tired of such a life!" she wrote. She began to predict her own death. Her journals become a soulless recounting of every day's illnesses, doses of homeopathic remedies, narcotics, and other substances, as if she had gone to dutifully recording changes in her health from actually writing a journal that reflected her life. Lulu visited often, and on good days Alcott was driven to see her family in Boston and Concord, but she never again was at the center of family life in the way that had both nurtured her and driven her crazy for all of her fifty-five years.

Even in the last months of her life, there were moments of hope when the symptoms eased and Louisa felt physically well enough to enjoy whatever there was to enjoy at Dr. Lawrence's Roxbury home. Her doctors promised her that after another year of rest she could look forward to twenty years of life; a fine example of the delusions of nineteenth-century medicine.

On the first of January, she wrote that although still alone "and absent from home I am on the road to health at last."[14] But she was not on the road to health at last. Whether Louisa May Alcott was suffering from an immune disorder like lupus, or whether a combination of exhaustion, lousy nutrition, and the damage done by the mercury that poisoned her system twenty-five years earlier, she was slowly losing the battle with death. She was also less needed than she had been for years. Anna seemed to do well at running the household that now consisted of Lulu and her governess, Anna's two boys, and the ailing Bronson.

In the final months of her life, Alcott seemed shut down but content. Her journals show short visits to Concord, exhilaration over Fred's glorious marriage, and concern over her father's health.

Bronson, who had never completely recovered from his stroke, was now fading fast and, as always, with an inappropriate amount of hope and great expectation. "Most people buy religion, I have it," he announced to his daughter, now his beloved Weedy, on one of his clearer days. Still, in February, Louisa was sad to see her father's skinny, dying, diminished form. She had, as always, a clear view of reality that escaped him in all circumstances. "A mere wreck of a beautiful old man," she wrote. "Sorry he did not slip away sooner."[15] Even in the last month of her own life, Louisa took care of her family. She sent money to Anna to run the household. She wrote as much as she could of a new story titled "Sylvester" and a collection of children's tales she was writing for a fictional Chinese version of her Lulu titled "Lu Sing."

A lot has been written about Louisa's final visit to her father on his deathbed in the house on Louisburg Square. In Madeleine Stern's account of the events of March 1, 1888, which she based on letters, journals, and news accounts of that day, and specifically on a letter written by Anna Alcott Pratt to Alf Whitman, Louisa walked past his two nurses, undid her shawl, and leaned over the beloved old man. She brought flowers. Her sister Anna stood on the other side of the bed.

"Father, here is your Louy," Alcott said

gently. "What are you thinking of as you lie there so happily?" With his final feeble gestures, Bronson took Louisa's hand and said, "I am going up. *Come with me.*"

Her answer? "Oh I wish I could." Her father kissed her. "Come soon," he said. Distracted, and perhaps already embarked on that journey to which her father had just invited her, Louisa forgot her wrap as she stepped out into the cold March air on Louisburg Square.

In Louisa's journals, the final visit is less dramatic. Her father is sweet and feeble and asks her to "Come soon." But as her journal shows, Louisa had a lot on her mind even at her father's deathbed. Later that day, she made out the bills and receipts for the month of February: the rent, Dr. Lawrence's bill, and the bill for cab rides. Three days later, around eleven in the morning of March 4, Bronson took his final breaths. His daughter, south of the city of Boston on Dunreath Place, went on about her business. No one told her the news. She wrote letters. She paid a few remaining bills. She hoped her health would continue to improve.

The next morning, still not knowing that her father had died the day before, Alcott wrote a note to her sister complaining of a headache that felt like a weight pressing down on her. She sent for the doctor; he wasn't sure what was wrong and prescribed rest. Although she didn't know it consciously, Alcott had passed into a strange country where the people she had lived for had all left this ephemeral life of ours. Only one sister remained — Anna — and Louisa's money provided well for her. Lulu was no longer a baby.

Both Louisa's parents, those goads and educators, those needy, loving, critical, and supportive people, were gone. Although she had millions of readers, she had lost her first and truest audience. Alone and in a strange place, Louisa May Alcott obediently settled down in bed and closed her eyes. Before anyone had been able to tell her that her father was dead, less than forty hours after his death, she had passed into a coma. At three-thirty on the morning of March 6, just five days after accepting her father's invitation to join him in heaven, Louisa May Alcott died, as her father lay in his coffin at Louisburg Square awaiting burial. Did she decide to accept his mysterious invitation? Death is a mystery, but life is filled with light and clarity. We can't know what happened to Louisa May Alcott after March 6, 1888, but we have her last journals, which show the generous, talented Alcott taking care of business as she always did. Her final journal entry is a snapshot of the concerns of the last chapter of her life: "Write letters. Pay Ropes $30, Notman 4. Sew. Write a little. L to come."

# EPILOGUE:

## 2009

On the sixth of March, as his daughter passed from this world to the next, Bronson was buried in Sleepy Hollow cemetery on a ridge above Concord, a short walk from Orchard House. Two days later, when the earth over his grave was still fresh, Louisa was buried next to him. Father and daughter were forever together in the little town that had been so often the center of their real and imaginative lives. Only Anna remained alive.

Lulu, who had lost her second mother in her first ten years of life, was the focus of Anna's concern. Sophie had already gone home. Lulu's father visited Concord and a year later sent a relative to fetch his daughter. Anna traveled with them to be sure that Lulu was well settled. Lulu eventually married an Austrian, Emil Rasim, moved to Switzerland, and lived to be ninety-six. The Alcotts were rarely spoken about in her household. She learned most of the story of her own family from reading Martha Saxton's biography of Louisa May Alcott when it was published in 1977. Anna Alcott Pratt survived her father and sister by only five years. Her sons and their families remained in Concord.

"Tell me she had a happy life!" the woman next to me at dinner pleads when she finds out that I am writing a biography of Louisa May Alcott. I have just been chatting about her final years, and I know that I need to change the subject. "I always wanted to be Jo!" the woman says. "Yes, she had a happy life," I say. Privately, I wonder, what is a happy life, exactly?

Earlier in the evening, I had tried to start a conversation with a famous artist. He announced to me that he had a happy life: a long marriage to a woman now standing across the room, great professional recognition, money, many successful and loving children. That's many men's version of a happy life. Women are more complicated. When I mention that my children are also extraordinary, he loses patience with me. "Everyone says that," he informs me, "but my children are truly extraordinary."

What I think but don't say to my dinner partner is that Louisa May Alcott had a happy life but that she had something even more important — a life and a body of work that are still fresh and enlightening today. What if you could choose a pleasant, so-called happy life or a real immortality through your work? The problems Alcott encountered as a young woman, and the choices she made are still the problems and choices that most women have today. Do we want to be appreciated for our beauty — our sexual currency? Or do we want to be respected for what we do?

Alcott's life was what she made it, what she chose. From the beginning, she hoped to support her family; she did. From the beginning, she aimed to have a voice in the world; she did. And from the beginning, she wanted a life that would allow her to keep the freedom to travel, to set her own course, to say what she pleased. She did. Perhaps this isn't our version of happiness, which is often still mired in fairy-tale ideals of romantic marriages and adorable children — but it was her happiness.

It is this, I think, this expanded vision of what is possible for women, a vision evident in Alcott's life and in her art, that makes *Little Women* such a powerful book today. This is why Henry James took on its theme and its heroine and wrote about them in novel after novel. This is why we still love reading it and why we still imagine we are Jo March. Even Louisa May Alcott wanted to be Jo. She didn't quite get her wish, but she got something better.

# ACKNOWLEDGMENTS

During the ten years I have been writing about Louisa May Alcott, I have been buoyed up by an outpouring of energy from hundreds of people including inspired archivists, passing tourists, my beloved children, and many men and women who have listened to me rant about Louisa May Alcott and the choices women make. I am also deeply indebted to the writers and scholars who have gone before me; dozens of wonderful books and editions of Alcott's letters and journals were indispensable to my writing. There is only one author's name on the cover of this book, but in fact the book is a community effort.

The list of my collaborators begins with my brilliant agent Gail Hochman and editor Sydny Miner who both believed fervently in this book. I like to read aloud at least once everything I write, and I am forever in the debt of the writers who have

435

accommodated this time-consuming habit — my brother Ben Cheever and my friend Jane Hitchcock, both extraordinary writers as well as inspired listeners. Warren and Sarah, my beloved and astonishing children — both writers themselves — have also been part of the development of this book from its beginning. Warren's research has been invaluable. Other friends who have been immeasurably patient and helpful include Adam Bock, Tina Brown, Ken Burrows and Erica Jong, Molly Jong-Fast, Amy Belding Brown, Marcelle Clements, Ned Cabot, Judy Collins, June Iseman, Ron Gallen, Eliza Griswold, Jeannette Watson Sanger who surprised me with the idea for this book ten years ago, Mary-Beth Hughes, Muriel Lloyd, Nancy Tilghman, Ruthie Rogers, and Maggie Scarf. My colleagues at Bennington continue to inspire me, reminding me of the seriousness of this enterprise. My students at Bennington and the New School teach me as much as I could ever teach them.

My deepest thanks go to Leslie Wilson, scholar and archivist at the Concord Free Public Library, to the staff of the Houghton Library at Harvard, and the staff of the New York Society Library. Researchers Kelsey Ford and Richard Smith were invaluable.

Jan Turnquist at Orchard House was immensely helpful and always good humored. The work of Robert Richardson, Dan Shealey, Joel Myerson, Ednah Cheney, Madelon Bedell, Madeleine Stern, Martha Saxton, John Matteson and many other Alcott scholars has been the foundation of everything I have written.

At Simon & Schuster I have had much needed help from Michelle Rorke and Michele Bové, Sarah Hochman who gracefully and enthusiastically took over the editing of this book at the last minute, Gypsy da Silva, Fred Wiemer, Victoria Meyer, the incomparable Brian Ulicky, and of course David Rosenthal, whose support has been generous and unstinting.

Without my time at Yaddo, that magical place where the air seems to sparkle with words, I would not have been able to write this book.

# NOTES

The bulk of my research was done in the archives at the Concord Free Library in Concord and at the Houghton Library at Harvard University. I also worked in the New York Public Library and at the incomparable New York Society Library.

Louisa May Alcott has been a subject of great interest since the first biography of her, written by Ednah Dow Cheney a decade after Alcott's death. As a result I have been the beneficiary of a century and a half of publication of Alcott materials, including Louisa May Alcott's journals and correspondence as well as Bronson Alcott's journals and letters, and many other journals and reminiscences from people who knew the Alcotts first hand. In 2005 Louisa May Alcott joined the prestigious group of literary writers collected in a Library of America volume edited by Elaine Showalter.

In writing this book, I have tried to write

in Alcott's personal voice — culled from her letters and journals — as often as possible. She destroyed many, many records for fear of gossip and publicity, but her tart, elegant voice is still apparent in almost everything she wrote, especially after 1863.

**Preface: A Trip to Concord**

1. L. M. Alcott, *Little Women* (2000), p. 9.
2. L. M. Alcott, *The Journals of Louisa May Alcott,* p. 197. 3. Ibid., p. 167.

**1: Trailing Clouds of Glory. 1832–1839**

1. *Journals of Louisa May Alcott,* p. 165.
2. Ibid., p. 158.
3. *Little Women,* p. 87.
4. *Journals of Louisa May Alcott,* p. 166. "May prove interesting, though I doubt it" — in a later notation in these journals after *Little Women* became successful, Louisa May Alcott said of her denigration of the book "(good joke)."
5. *Little Women,* p. 259.
6. The State of Massachusetts, 1835 meteorological report.
7. Elizabeth Peabody, *Record of a School,* p. 55.
8. William Wordsworth, *Intimations of Immortality.*
9. B. Alcott, "Researches on Childhood," as

quoted in Charles Strickland's essay: "A Transcendentalist Father," in *Perspectives in American History,* Vol. III, 1969, p. 49.

10. Penelope Leach, *Spanking: A Shortcut to Nowhere,* 1999. http://nospank.org.

11. Louisa May Alcott, "Recollections of My Childhood," an essay in *Louisa May Alcott: An Intimate Anthology,* p. 5.

12. Shepard, *Pedlar's Progress,* p. 12.

13. Alex V. G. Allen, *Jonathan Edwards* (Cambridge, Mass.: The Riverside Press, 1899), p. 191.

14. Journals of Abigail May Alcott at Houghton Library, Harvard.

15. Shepard, *Pedlar's Progress,* p. 120.

16. *Journals of Bronson Alcott,* ed. Odell Shepard, Sept. 2, 1828.

17. Megan Marshall in her introduction to Elizabeth Peabody's *Record of a School,* p. x. The Summerhill School was started in 1921, but it was headmaster A. S. Neill's 1960 account of the school, *Summerhill,* which brought it popular attention in the United States' alternative-education community.

18. *Little Women,* p. 76.

19. Mary Peabody letter to Elizabeth Peabody, in Marshall, *The Peabody Sisters,* p. 323.

20. *Journals of Louisa May Alcott.*

21. L. M. Alcott, *Louisa May Alcott: Her Life, Letters, and Journals,* ed. Ednah D. Cheney, p. 27.

22. Strickland, "A Transcendentalist Father," p. 69.

23. Ibid., p. 164.

24. L. M. Alcott, "Recollections of My Childhood," in *Louisa May Alcott: An Intimate Anthology,* p. 4.

25. This story is told many places, most notably in Alcott's "Recollections of My Childhood," a memoir piece written in 1888 and printed in the *Women's Journal* long after she became famous. Alcott omits being tied up by her mother, which is cited in Saxton, *Louisa May Alcott,* p. 100.

26. Bronson Alcott, *How Like an Angel Came I Down. Conversations with Children on the Gospels,* p. 121.

27. Peabody, *Record of a School,* 2nd ed., p. vii.

28. *Letters of Elizabeth Peabody,* April 1836, p. 157.

29. Ibid., p. 160.

30. Ibid., p. 162.

31. Lord Harold Acton in a letter to Bishop Mandell Creighton, 1887.

32. L. M. Alcott, "Recollections of My Childhood," p. 4.

33. Matteson, *Eden's Outcast,* p. 80.

34. Emerson, *Letters of Ralph Waldo Emerson.* March 24, 1837 (New York: Columbia Univ. Press, 1939), p. 61.

35. B. Alcott, *How Like an Angel Came I Down. Conversations with Children on the Gospels.*

36. V. W. Brooks, *The Flowering of New England,* p. 232.

37. Journals of Abigail May Alcott, Houghton Library.

38. Journals of Bronson Alcott, January 24, 1828.

39. Ibid., p. 121. (In a footnote, Shepard defines "mettle" as sperm.)

40. James Russell Lowell, *Fable for Critics.*

41. B. Alcott, *How Like an Angel Came I Down. Conversations with Children on the Gospels,* p. 73.

42. Ibid., p. 307.

**2: Concord. Louisa in Exile. 1840–1843**

1. *Little Women,* p. 234.

2. B. Alcott, *The Letters of A. Bronson Alcott,* December 28, 1839.

3. Robert Richardson, *Emerson: The Mind on Fire.* This visit was a turning point for Emerson. In his journal, he wrote: "I visited Ellen's tomb and opened the coffin."

4. Madelon Bedell, *Alcotts,* p. 150, cited in Matteson, p. 91.

5. B. Alcott to Sam May, April 1840, *Letters of A. Bronson Alcott.*

6. Thoreau, *The Journals of Henry David Thoreau,* 1840.

7. Lydia Hosmer Wood, *Beth Alcott's Playmate, a Glimpse of Concord Town in the Days of* Little Women. *Alcott in Her Own Time,* p. 165.

8. *Letters of A. Bronson Alcott.* April 16, 1840, to Sam May, "Dear Brother . . ."

9. L. M. Alcott, "Recollections of My Childhood," p. 4.

10. B. Alcott to L. M. Alcott, June 21, 1840, *Letters of A. Bronson Alcott.*

11. Colonel May, Last Will and Testament, in Sarah Elbert, *A Hunger for Home: Louisa May Alcott and* Little Women (Philadelphia: Temple Univ. Press, 1984), p. 43.

12. L. M. Alcott, "Recollections of My Childhood," p. 6.

13. Ibid., p. 8.

14. L. M. Alcott, *Moods,* p. 36.

15. *Selections from Ralph Waldo Emerson* ed. Stephen E. Whicher (Boston: Houghton Mifflin, 1957), p. 127.

16. O. Shepard, *Pedlar's Progress,* p. 241.

17. *Selections from Ralph Waldo Emerson,* p. 126.

18. *Selected Letters of Ralph Waldo Emerson,* January 1842 (New York: Columbia University Press, 1999), p. 262.

19. Bronson Alcott to his wife, *Letters of A. Bronson Alcott,* May 7, 1842.

20. Ibid., June 12, 1842.

21. Ibid.

22. Journals of Abigail May Alcott, Houghton Library. November 29, 1842.

**3: Fruitlands. Family in Crisis. 1843–1848**

1. L. M. Alcott, *Transcendental Wild Oats,* p. 24.

2. Ibid., p. 47.

3. Ibid., p. 48.

4. Ibid.

5. B. De Voto, *The Year of Decision,* p. 32.

6. Sanford Salyer, *Marmee,* p. 100.

7. *Journals of Louisa May Alcott,* p. 47.

8. Letters from Fruitlands to Sam and Charles, November 11, 1843, Abigail May Alcott Family Letters.

9. Bedell, *The Alcotts,* p. 228.

10. Saxton, *Louisa May Alcott,* p. 149.

11. Matteson, *Eden's Outcast,* p. 158.

12. L. M. Alcott, *Transcendental Wild Oats,* p. 59.

13. Ibid., p. 55.

14. *Selections from Ralph Waldo Emerson,* p. 130.

15. Abigail May Alcott to her brother, Sam May.

16. Bronson Alcott to Abigail May Alcott from Oriskany Falls, N.Y., where he is traveling with Anna Alcott, July 19, 1844, *Letters of A. Bronson Alcott.*

17. B. Alcott to his brother Junius, June 15, 1844.

18. Henry David Thoreau, *Walden* (New York: Barnes and Noble Books, 1993), p. 112.

19. P. Brooks, *The People of Concord,* p. 112.

20. *A. Bronson Alcott Journals,* ed. Shepard, p. 172.

21. Bedell, *The Alcotts,* p. 236.

22. Cornelia Meigs, *Louisa May Alcott: Invincible Louisa* (New York: Scholastic, 1965), p. 39.

23. *Journals of Louisa May Alcott,* p. 59.

24. Dr. Berry Brazelton, *Cultural Context of Infancy* (New York: Ablex, 1991).

25. L. M. Alcott to Sophia Gardner, *Selected Letters of Louisa May Alcott,* September 23, 1845, p. 4.

26. *Journals of Bronson Alcott,* pp. 188, 190.

27. H. D. Thoreau, *Walden,* p. 126.

28. *Journals of Louisa May Alcott.*

29. R. W. Emerson, *Poems* (Cambridge,

Mass.: Houghton Mifflin, 1904), p. 90.

30. Edward W. Emerson, *Alcott in Her Own Time* (Iowa City: University of Iowa Press, 2005), p. 91.

31. Thoreau, *Walden,* p. 126.

32. Ibid., p. 223.

33. Ibid., p. 270.

34. L. M. Alcott, "Recollections of My Childhood," p. 9.

35. Ibid., p. 10.

## 4: Boston. "Stick to Your Teaching." 1848–1858

1. Declaration of Sentiments. *The Dial,* July 1848.

2. *Journals of Louisa May Alcott,* May 1850, in a section of the Journal titled "The Sentimental Period," p. 62.

3. Matteson, *Eden's Outcast,* p. 202.

4. L. M. Alcott, "Recollections of My Childhood," p. 9.

5. *Journals of Louisa May Alcott,* April 8, 1851. This meeting of fervent abolitionists that Louisa attended with her father also appears in Bronson's journal, p. 65.

6. Alcott loved cats. In an essay, "Seven Black Cats," she describes her favorites — the Czar, Blot, Imp, and Cuddle Bunch.

7. *Journals of Louisa May Alcott.*

8. Ibid.

447

9. Bronson Alcott. In the unpublished diaries of Bronson Alcott archived at the Houghton Library as quoted by Bedell in *The Alcotts,* p. 305.

10. L. M. Alcott, "When I Went Out to Service," in *Louisa May Alcott: An Intimate Anthology,* p. 12.

11. Ibid., p. 14.

12. Ibid., p. 17.

13. Ibid., p. 21.

14. N. Hawthorne. *Selected Letters of Nathaniel Hawthorne* (Columbus: Ohio State University Press, 2002), p. 160.

15. Rose Hawthorne Lathrop, *Memories of Hawthorne* (Boston: Houghton Mifflin, 1897).

16. Journals of Abigail May Alcott, Houghton Library.

17. L. M. Alcott to Alf Whitman, June 22, 1862, *Letters of Louisa May Alcott,* p. 79.

18. The late Madeleine Stern, who wrote a Louisa May Alcott biography in the 1970s, and her partner Leona Rostenberg, are responsible for discovering this new dimension of Louisa May Alcott. Through determined sleuthing in the Alcott papers at the Houghton Library at Harvard, Rostenberg unearthed a large cache of hidden material — the potboilers that Alcott had written early in her career under the

pseudonym A. M. Barnard. These stories, first published in 1975, are important for two reasons. With their melodramatic tone and extravagant plots, which Alcott adopted in writing for magazines that paid for such stories, they seem to reflect Alcott's inner yearnings and conflicts. They are also solid evidence of the work she had to do — work she was ashamed of — in order to help support her family.

19. L. M. Alcott, "How I Went Out to Service," p. 21.
20. *Journals of Louisa May Alcott,* 1854, p. 71.
21. Saxton, *Louisa May Alcott,* p. 196.
22. *Journals of Louisa May Alcott,* p. 109. The way this is phrased in the journal entry of May 1862 suggests that it happened in the past: "School finished or me. . . . I went back to my own writing which pays much better, though Mr. F did say, 'Stick to your teaching, you can't write.' "

**5: Orchard House. 1858–1862**

1. *Journals of Bronson Alcott,* September 18, 1858, p. 308.
2. N. Hawthorne to Charles Ticknor, *Letters of Nathaniel Hawthorne,* Vol. 15 (Columbus: Ohio State University Press,

1987), p. 127.

3. *Journals of Louisa May Alcott,* p. 98.

4. Scarlet fever begins with the exotoxins of the bacterium *Streptococcus pyogenes,* spread from human to human through contact or sneezing and coughing. The swine and filth at the house where the Halls lived did not cause scarlet fever. Nowadays the first signs of strep throat, caused by the same type of bacteria as scarlet fever, send us to a doctor who does a strep test or culture and treats our children with antibiotics; we have forgotten the problem within a week. The Alcott sisters only slowly recovered, May completely and Lizzie enough to think that perhaps she was all right.

Social epidemiologists who study the way disease moves through populations have written a lot about the rise of Streptococcus A scarlet fever in the 1840s and '50s and its mysterious disappearance at the end of the century. By the 1900s, scarlet fever was almost as rare as it is today. Where did it go? In many ways, the original epidemic was a result of progress, the same forces that brought the railroad to Concord and established the industrial mills downriver and made it possible for the Alcotts to live more comfortable and cosmopolitan lives. The huge immigrations of the 1840s, with their crowding, slums, and poor nutrition, created perfect conditions for communicable disease.

Slowly, toward the end of the nineteenth century, with what epidemiologists call the "hygiene revolution," the disease lost its hold. Sanitation and public health measures were taken in cities. One of the Alcotts' circle, Dr. Oliver Wendell Holmes, wrote in 1844 that doctors should wash their hands before an operation, an idea that was roundly mocked. "Doctors are gentlemen and gentlemen have clean hands," wrote one critic. The diseases caused by Group A Streptococcus can become rheumatic fever, a disease that attacks the heart and leads to carditis, an inflammation of the heart, and congestive heart failure over a period of months and years.

5. Salyer, *Marmee*, p. 161.
6. *Journals of Bronson Alcott*, March 13, 1858, p. 306.
7. Ibid., March 14, 1858, p. 307.
8. *Journals of Louisa May Alcott*, 1858, p. 89.
9. Ibid., April 1858. The Alcotts first rented rooms on Bedford Street and later rented their old house from the Hawthornes while Orchard House renovations were

being done and the Hawthornes were in Liverpool.

10. *Journals of Bronson Alcott,* p. 308.

11. Ibid., April 7, p. 308.

12. *Journals of Louisa May Alcott,* 1858, p. 89.

13. Ibid., and annotations twenty years later.

14. Ibid., August, p. 90.

15. Ibid., October, p. 90.

16. Ibid.

17. Ibid.

18. Robert Penn Warren, *John Brown: The Making of a Martyr* (Nashville: J. S. Sanders, 1993), p. 245.

19. L. M. Alcott to Alf Whitman, *Selected Letters of Louisa May Alcott,* Nov. 8, 1859, p. 49.

20. Louisa May Alcott poem to John Brown and journal annotations made later, *Journals of Louisa May Alcott,* p. 89.

21. Anne Brown Adams, "Louisa May Alcott in the Early 1860's," included in *Alcott in Her Own Time,* p. 8.

22. *Journals of Louisa May Alcott,* 1859, p. 94.

23. Ibid., May 1860, p. 99.

24. Ibid.

25. Ibid., May 1861, p. 105. "Felt very martial and Joan-of-Arcy."

26. Bruce Catton, *The Centennial History of the Civil War: The Coming Fury* (New York: Doubleday, 1965), p. 460.

27. Ibid., p. 130.

**6: Fredericksburg. At the Union Hospital. 1863–1865**

1. Drew Gilpin Faust, *Republic of Suffering.* p. 3.

2. *Memoirs of WTS* (New York: D. Appleton, 1904), p. 196.

3. L. M. Alcott, "Pauline's Passion and Punishment," p. 3.

4. L. M. Alcott, *Moods,* p. 79.

5. *Journals of Louisa May Alcott,* February 1861, p. 103.

6. Ibid., p. 109.

7. *Journals of Louisa May Alcott,* p. 105.

8. This is actually a quote from James Boswell, who wrote that Samuel Johnson used to quote a saying of Richardson's that "the virtues of Fielding's heroes were the vices of a truly good man."

9. *Journals of Louisa May Alcott,* p. 104.

10. Nathaniel Hawthorne, "Chiefly About War Matters," *Atlantic Monthly,* July 1862.

11. *Journals of Louisa May Alcott,* p. 106.

12. J. Hawthorne, *Memories of the Alcott Family. Alcott in Her Own Time,* p. 205.

13. Ibid., p. 189.

14. L. M. Alcott, *Hospital Sketches,* p. 52.
15. There are many accounts of the sack of Fredericksburg. One that was the basis of this description is Gary Gallagher, ed., *The Fredericksburg Campaign: Decision on the Rappahannock* (Chapel Hill: University of North Carolina Press, 2008).
16. L. M. Alcott, *Hospital Sketches,* p. 67.
17. Bruce Catton, *This Hallowed Ground* (Chatham, G.B.: Wordsworth Military Library), p. 188.
18. Ibid., p. 189.
19. Faust, *Republic of Suffering,* p. 209.
20. Alice Rains Trulock, *In the Hands of Providence: Joshua L. Chamberlain and the American Civil War* (Chapel Hill: University of North Carolina Press, 1992), p. 100.
21. Robert Stiles, *Four Years Under Marse* (Fredericksburg: Va.: Neale Publishing Co., 1904), p. 173.
22. Brenda Wineapple, *White Heat* (New York: Knopf, 2008), p. 113.
23. Robert Roper, *Now the Drum of War* (New York: Walker & Co., 2008), p. 113.
24. Faust, *Republic of Suffering,* p. 124.
25. L. M. Alcott, *Hospital Sketches,* p. 59.
26. *Civil War Nurse: The Diary and Letters of Hannah Ropes,* John R. Brumgardt, ed. (Knoxville: University of Tennessee Press,

1980), p. 112.

27. L. M. Alcott, *Hospital Sketches,* p. 70.

28. Ibid., p. 71.

29. Ibid., p. 60.

30. Ibid., p. 64.

31. *Journals of Louisa May Alcott,* p. 115.

32. Ibid., p. 114.

33. Ibid.

34. L. M. Alcott, *Hospital Sketches,* p. 82.

35. Ibid., p. 76.

36. Ibid., p. 87.

37. Ibid., p. 82.

38. *Journals of Louisa May Alcott,* p. 115.

39. L. M. Alcott, *Hospital Sketches,* p. 106.

40. *Letters of A. Bronson Alcott,* p. 333.

41. L. M. Alcott, *Hospital Sketches,* p. 107.

42. *Journals of Louisa May Alcott,* pp. 116, 117.

43. Ibid., p. 117.

44. Ibid.

45. Saxton, *Louisa May Alcott,* pp. 257–58.

46. Roper, *Now the Drum of War,* p. 101.

**7: The Writer. 1861–1867**

1. *Journals of Louisa May Alcott,* p. 128.

2. Ibid., pp. 129, 135n.

3. Ibid., p. 131.

4. Helen R. Deese, "Louisa May Alcott's 'Moods': A New Archival Discovery," *The New England Quarterly* 76, No. 3, Septem-

ber 2003, pp. 439–55. org/stable/4289157, found by Helen Deese, Prof. Emeritus, Tennessee Tech.

5. *Journals of Louisa May Alcott,* p. 132.

6. *Little Women,* pp. 262–63.

7. Review of *Moods* in L. M. Alcott, *Moods,* p. 219.

8. Alfred Habegger, "Precocious Incest: First Novels by Louisa May Alcott and Henry James," *The Massachusetts Review* 26, No. 2/3 New England (Summer–Autumn 1985), pp. 233–62.

9. Introduction to L. M. Alcott, *Moods,* xxxix. Sarah Elbert is a professor of history at SUNY Binghamton and the author of *Hunger for Home: Louisa May Alcott's Place in American Culture* (New Brunswick, N.J.: Rutgers University Press, 1987).

10. Matteson, *Eden's Outcast,* p. 304.

11. Charles Lamb, "The Sanity of True Genius," *Essays of Elia* (Boston: William Veazie, 1860), p. 312.

12. This account of Andrew Johnson comes from David O. Stewart, *Impeached: The Trial of Andrew Johnson and the Fight for Lincoln's Legacy* (New York: Simon & Schuster, 2009), and Garry Wills, "Lincoln's Greatest Speech?" *Atlantic Monthly* 284, no. 3 (1999): pp. 60–70.

13. *Journals of Louisa May Alcott,* p. 140.
14. *Letters of Louisa May Alcott,* p. 111.
15. Ibid., p. 130.
16. *Journals of Louisa May Alcott,* p. 143.
17. L. M. Alcott, *Aunt Jo's Scrap-Bag* (Charleston, S.C.: BiblioLife copy of 1871 edition), p. 2.
18. *Journals of Louisa May Alcott,* p. 145.
19. L. M. Alcott, *Aunt Jo's Scrap-Bag,* p. 28.
20. Martha Saxton in her biography of Alcott interprets this note differently — "sad times for A. and L.," the note reads, and she assumes that the romance was between Anna and Laddie, who would have been closer in age and more suitable to such a romance. This seems unlikely, however, both because Alcott's journals explicitly detail the romance between Alcott and Laddie, and because a few years later Alcott wrote a long essay about Laddie for the magazine *Youth's Companion,* the essay that was later used again in the "My Boys" section of *Aunt Jo's Scrap-Bag.*
21. *Journals of Louisa May Alcott,* p. 151.
22. Ibid.
23. L. M. Alcott, *Aunt Jo's Scrap-Bag,* p. 44.
24. I am indebted for this story — as for many other things — to the writer Lyndall Gordon, whom it is my privilege to have as a colleague at the Bennington Col-

lege writing seminars.

25. Later, Mabel Loomis Todd and her husband David Todd moved to Amherst, Massachusetts, so that he could be a professor of astronomy at Amherst College. They became friends with the Dickinson family — Emily the poet, her brother Austin, and his wife Susan. Austin Dickinson and Mabel Todd fell deeply in love, causing all kinds of passionate anger and bitterness in the family that lasted for generations. As a result of her connection to Austin, Mabel Loomis Todd was the publisher of Emily's first book, which might never have been published otherwise. The resentment of Austin's rejected wife and children resulted in a scandalous lawsuit and in many of the Dickinson poems and papers being locked up for years.

26. *Journals of Louisa May Alcott,* p. 155, n. 9.

27. Ibid., p. 155.

28. Ibid., p. 156.

29. Ibid., p. 160.

**8: *Little Women*. 1868–1872**

1. Martha Saxton's biography *Louisa May Alcott* is rich in the physical and historical details of the time. Saxton's eye for cloth-

ing and seemingly extraneous information is the source of the shimmering texture of her book. Alcott wrote about the way fashionable women dressed in many of her stories.

2. *Journals of Louisa May Alcott,* p. 162.

3. Ibid., p. 164.

4. Stern, *Louisa May Alcott,* p. 168.

5. *Journals of Louisa May Alcott,* p. 165.

6. Malcolm Gladwell in conversation. Picasso also said, "I do not seek, I find."

7. E-mail message to me from Jane Hirschfield, October 19, 2008.

8. Watson was my great-grandfather, and the story of the battery-acid accident first appears in his brilliant memoir *Exploring Life,* written almost fifty years after the wires came alive that afternoon.

9. For this analysis of the sources of *Little Women,* I am indebted to Madeleine Stern, whose biography *Louisa May Alcott* is extraordinarily thoughtful and detailed on this subject.

10. For comparison, today's writers usually receive a royalty of 12 to 15 percent on sales.

11. Roberts Brothers' first printing of *Little Women.*

12. *Journals of Louisa May Alcott,* p. 167.

13. *Alcott in Her Own Time,* pp. 200–201.

14. Ibid., p. 201.
15. *Journals of A. Bronson Alcott,* p. 396.
16. Ibid., p. 399.
17. *Journals of Louisa May Alcott,* p. 171.
18. J. M. Roberts, *The Penguin History of the World* (London: Penguin, 1992), pp. 752–53.
19. *Journals of Louisa May Alcott,* p. 166.
20. Ibid., p. 174.
21. Stern, *Louisa May Alcott,* p. 191.
22. L. M. Alcott, *An Old-Fashioned Girl,* p. 167.
23. *Journals of Louisa May Alcott,* p. 182.
24. Ibid., p. 179.
25. Ibid., p. 174.
26. Ibid., p. 177.

**9: Success. 1873–1880**
1. *Little Women,* p. 319.
2. *Letters of Louisa May Alcott,* p. 198.
3. Even the *amazing* NYU archivists have only been able to find references to the fact that Alcott wrote *Little Women* on MacDougal Street, nothing about how that fact came to be manufactured.
4. *Journals of Louisa May Alcott,* 1874, p. 191.
5. *Selected Letters of Louisa May Alcott,* July 20, 1875, p. 193.
6. Currently, Randall's Island contains a

sports complex and the vast Carl Icahn Stadium, where summer rock concerts blast away so loudly that they can be heard for miles.

7. *Letters of Louisa May Alcott,* p. 212.
8. Ibid., p. 204.
9. Saxton, *Louisa May Alcott,* p. 341.
10. Ibid., p. 344.
11. *Journals of Louisa May Alcott,* p. 206.
12. Ibid., p. 209.
13. May Alcott to L. M. Alcott, Houghton Library correspondence of May Alcott, as quoted in Saxton, *Louisa May Alcott,* p. 348.
14. *Journals of Louisa May Alcott,* p. 214.
15. Ibid., p. 218.

## 10: Lulu. 1880–1888

1. *Journals of Louisa May Alcott,* p. 223.
2. *The Selected Letters of Louisa May Alcott,* ed. Myerson, Shealy, Stern. Letter to Bronson, November 10, 1880, p. 250.
3. *Journals of Louisa May Alcott,* p. 235.
4. Ibid., p. 237nn.
5. Ibid., p. 237.
6. Saxton, *Louisa May Alcott,* p. 368.
7. *Journals of Louisa May Alcott,* p. 244.
8. Robert Peel, *Christian Science: Its Encounter with American Culture* (New York: Holt, 1958), p. 52.

9. Ibid., p. 101.

10. Mark Twain, *Christian Science* (New York: Oxford University Press, 1996), p. 211.

11. Saxton, *Louisa May Alcott,* p. 370.

12. *Journals of Louisa May Alcott,* p. 262.

13. Ibid., p. 287.

14. Ibid., p. 327.

15. Ibid., p. 333.

# BIBLIOGRAPHY

Alcott, A. Bronson. *Concord Days.* Ann Arbor: Scholarly Publishing Office, University of Michigan Library, 2007 (orig. 1872).

————. *How Like an Angel Came I Down: Conversations with Children on the Gospels.* Hudson, N.Y.: Lindisfarne Press, 1991.

————. *The Journals of Bronson Alcott.* Edited by Odell Shepard. Boston: Little, Brown, 1938.

————. *The Letters of A. Bronson Alcott.* Edited by Richard L. Herrnstadt. Ames: Iowa State University Press, 1969.

————. *Tablets.* Boston: Roberts Brothers, 1868.

Alcott, Louisa May. *An Old-Fashioned Girl.* Mineola, N.Y.: Dover Publications, 2007.

————. *Behind a Mask: The Unknown Thrillers of Louisa May Alcott.* Edited by Madeleine Stern. New York: Morrow, 1995.

————. *Hospital Sketches.* Boston: Bedford/

St. Martin's, 2004.

———. *The Inheritance.* Edited by Joel Myerson and Daniel Shealy. New York: Penguin Putnam, 1997.

———. *The Journals of Louisa May Alcott.* Edited by Joel Myerson and Daniel Shealy. Athens: University of Georgia Press, 1997.

———. *Little Women.* Boston: Little, Brown, 1968.

———. *Little Women.* New York: Random House, 2000.

———. *Little Women.* With an Introduction by Susan Cheever. Modern Library Paperback. New York: Random House, 2000.

———. *Little Women, Little Men and Jo's Boys.* Edited by Elaine Showalter. New York: Library of America, 2005.

———. *Louisa May Alcott: Her Life, Letters, and Journals.* Edited by Ednah D. Cheney. Boston: Roberts Brothers, 1889.

———. *Louisa May Alcott, An Intimate Anthology.* New York: Doubleday, 1997.

———. *Moods.* New Brunswick, N.J: Rutgers University Press, 1999. American Women Writers Series.

———. *Selected Letters of Louisa May Alcott.* Edited by Joel Myerson, Daniel Shealy, and Madeleine Stern. Boston: Little, Brown, 1987.

————. *Transcendental Wild Oats and Excerpts from the Fruitlands Diary*. Boston: Harvard Common Press, 1981.

Allen, Gay Wilson. *Melville and His World*. New York: Viking, 1981.

Andrews, Joseph L., Jr., et al. *Revolutionary Boston, Lexington, and Concord*. 3rd ed. Beverly, Mass.: Concord Guides Press, 2002.

Applegate, Debby. *The Most Famous Man in America: The Biography of Henry Ward Beecher*. New York: Doubleday, 2006.

Bedell, Madelon. *The Alcotts: Biography of a Family*. New York: Clarkson N. Potter, 1980.

Blanchard, Paula. *Margaret Fuller: From Transcendentalism to Revolution*. Reading, Mass.: Addison-Wesley, 1987.

Bonfanti, Leo. *Biographies and Legends of the New England Indians*. Vols. I and II. Burlington, Mass.: Pride Publications, 1970.

Bosco, Ronald A., and Joel Myerson, eds. *Ralph Waldo Emerson: A Bicentennial Exhibition at Houghton Library of the Harvard College Library* (Exhibit Catalog). March 26–June 7, 2003.

Brogan, Hugh. *The Penguin History of the United States of America*. New York: Penguin, 1992.

Brooks, Geraldine. *March: A Novel.* New York: Viking, 2005.

Brooks, Paul. *The People of Concord: One Year in the Flowering of New England.* Chester, Conn.: Globe Pequot Press, 1990.

Brooks, Van Wyck. *The Flowering of New England, 1815–1865.* New York: Dutton, 1936.

Buell, Lawrence. *Emerson.* Cambridge: Belknap Press of Harvard University Press, 2003.

————. *The Environmental Imagination: Thoreau, Nature Writing, and the Formation of American Culture.* Cambridge: Belknap Press of Harvard University Press, 1995.

————. *Literary Transcendentalism: Style and Vision in the American Renaissance.* Ithaca: Cornell University Press, 1973.

————. *New England Literary Culture from the Revolution to the Renaissance.* Cambridge: Cambridge University Press, 1986.

Buell, Lawrence, ed. *The American Transcendentalists: Essential Writings.* New York: Random House, 2006.

Bunyan, John. *The Pilgrim's Progress.* Mineola, N.Y.: Dover Publications, 2003.

Catton, Bruce. *The Coming Fury.* New York:

Doubleday, 1961.

Chapin, Sarah. *Concord, Massachusetts.* Images of America Series, Charleston, S.C.: Arcadia Publishing, 1997.

Chapin, Sarah, with Claiborne Dawes and Alice Moulton. *Then and Now: Concord.* Charleston, S.C.: Arcadia Publishing, 2001.

Chevigny, Bell Gale. *The Woman and the Myth. Margaret Fuller's Life and Writings.* Boston: Northeastern University Press, 1994.

Dapper, Julie, ed. *The Concord School of Philosophy: A Short History.* Concord, Mass.: Louisa May Alcott Memorial Association, 1991.

Dee, James. *Colonial Concord: A Study in Pen and Ink.* Concord, Mass.: James Dee, 1951.

DeGraaf, Richard M., and Mariko Yamasaki. *New England Wildlife: Habitat, Natural History, and Distribution.* Hanover, N.H.: University Press of New England, 2001.

Delano, Sterling. *Brook Farm: the Dark Side of Utopia.* Cambridge: Belknap Press of Harvard University Press, 2004.

Delbanco, Andrew. *Melville: His World and Work.* New York: Knopf, 2005.

De Voto, Bernard. *The Year of Decision 1846.* Boston: Little, Brown, 1943.

Drake, Nelson Manfred. *A Short History of American Life.* New York: McGraw-Hill, 1952.

Duvergier de Hauranne, Ernest. *A Frenchman in Lincoln's America — Huit Mois en Amerique: Lettres et Notes de Voyage, 1864–1865.* Translated and edited by Ralph H. Bowen. 2 vols. Chicago: R. R. Donnelley & Sons, 1975.

Emerson, Ralph Waldo. *First We Read. Then We Write.* Ed. Robert D. Richardson. Iowa City: University of Iowa Press, 2009.

———. *Representative Men — Seven Lectures.* New York: Random House, 2004.

———. *The Selected Letters of Ralph Waldo Emerson.* New York: Columbia University Press, 1998.

———. *Self-Reliance and Other Essays.* New York: Barnes & Noble, 1995.

Faust, Drew Gilpin. *This Republic of Suffering: Death and the American Civil War.* New York: Vintage/Random House, 2008.

Felton, R. Todd. *A Journey into the Transcendentalists' New England.* Berkeley, Calif.: Roaring Forties Press, 2006.

Fleming, Donald, and Bernard Bailyn. *Perspectives in American History.* Vol III.

Cambridge: Harvard University Press, 1969.

Frothingham, Octavius Brooks. *Transcendentalism in New England, a History.* New York: Harper, 1959.

Fuller, Margaret. *Women in the Nineteenth Century.* Mineola, N.Y.: Dover Publications, 1999.

————. *"My Heart Is a Large Kingdom": Selected Letters of Margaret Fuller.* Edited by Robert Hudspeth. Ithaca: Cornell University Press, 2001.

Grant, Ulysses S. *Personal Memoirs of U. S. Grant.* New York: Charles L. Webster & Co., 1894.

Gura, Philip F. *American Transcendentalism.* New York: Hill & Wang, 2007.

Harding, Walter. *The Days of Henry Thoreau: A Biography.* New York: Dover Publications, 1962.

Harris, Seymour. *John Maynard Keynes: Economist and Policy Maker.* New York: Scribner, 1955.

Hawthorne, Nathaniel. *The House of the Seven Gables.* New York: Penguin Books, 1981.

————. *Letters of Nathaniel Hawthorne.* Edited by Joel Myerson. Columbus: Ohio State University Press, 2002.

———. *Mosses from an Old Manse.* New York: Modern Library, 2003.

———. *The Scarlet Letter.* New York: Barnes & Noble, 2001.

———. *Twenty Days with Julian and Little Bunny by Papa.* New York: New York Review of Books, 2003.

Howe, M. A. DeWolfe. *Memories of a Hostess: A Chronicle of Eminent Friendships.* Boston: Atlantic Monthly Press, 1922.

James, Henry. *Hawthorne.* Ithaca: Cornell University Press, 1997.

James, William. *The Varieties of Religious Experience: A Study in Human Nature.* New York: Adamant Media/Elibron Classics, 2005.

King, B. A. *Snow Season* (photographs). New London, N.H.: Safe Harbor Books, 2005.

Kornfeld, Eve. *Margaret Fuller: A Brief Biography with Documents.* Boston: Bedford Books, 1997.

Leech, Margaret. *Reveille in Washington, 1860–1865.* New York: Time, Inc., 1962.

Longsworth, Polly. *Austin and Mabel: The Amherst Affair and Love Letters of Austin Dickinson and Mabel Loomis Todd.* New York: Farrar, Straus & Giroux, 1984.

Marshall, Megan. *The Peabody Sisters.*

Boston: Houghton Mifflin, 2005.

Matteson, John. *Eden's Outcasts: The Story of Louisa May Alcott and Her Father.* New York: Norton, 2007.

Matthiesen, F. O. *American Renaissance: Art and Expression in the Age of Emerson and Whitman.* New York: Oxford University Press, 1968.

McAdow, Ron. *The Concord, Sudbury, and Assabet Rivers.* Marlborough, Mass.: Bliss Publishing, 1990.

McCuskey, Dorothy. *Bronson Alcott, Teacher.* New York: Macmillan, 1940.

McFarland, Philip. *Loves of Harriet Beecher Stowe.* New York: Grove Press, 2007.

McMurry, Andrew. *Environmental Renaissance: Emerson, Thoreau, and the Systems of Nature.* Athens: University of Georgia Press, 2003.

Meltzer, Milton, and Walter Harding, *A Thoreau Profile, Drawn Largely in His Own Words with 250 Pictures.* New York: Thomas Y. Crowell and Co., 1962.

Miller, Perry, ed. *The American Puritans, Their Prose and Poetry.* New York: Columbia University Press, 1982.

————. *The American Transcendentalists: Their Prose and Poetry.* Garden City, N.Y.: Doubleday/Anchor Books, 1957.

————. *Consciousness in Concord — The Text of Thoreau's Hitherto Lost Journal, 1840–1841.* Boston: Houghton Mifflin, 1958.

————. *The Transcendentalists: An Anthology.* Cambridge: Harvard University Press, 1950.

Mitchell, John Hanson. *Walking Towards Walden: A Pilgrimage in Search of Place.* Reading, Mass.: Addison-Wesley, 1995.

Novak, Barbara. *The Ape and the Whale: An Interplay Between Darwin and Melville in Their Own Words.* Moose, Wyo.: Homestead Publishing, 1995.

Peabody, Elizabeth. *Letters of Elizabeth Peabody, American Renaissance Woman.* Edited by Bruce Ronda. Middletown, Conn.: Wesleyan University Press, 1984.

————. *Record of a School.* Bedford, Mass.: Applewood Books, 2005 (1845 ed.).

Perry, Bliss, ed. *The Heart of Emerson's Journals.* Boston: Houghton Mifflin, 1926.

Petrulionis, Sandra Harbert. *To Set This World Right: The Antislavery Movement in Thoreau's Concord.* Ithaca: Cornell University Press, 2006.

Richardson, Robert. "We Too Must Write Bibles: Emerson on Creative Reading and Writing." Unpublished Manuscript. Iowa

City: University of Iowa, 2008.

Richardson, Robert D., Jr. *Emerson: The Mind on Fire.* Berkeley: University of California Press, 1995.

————. *Henry Thoreau: A Life of the Mind.* Berkeley: University of California Press, 1986.

Roberts, J. M. *History of the World.* New York: Penguin Books, 1995.

Roper, Robert. *Now the Drum of War: Walt Whitman and His Brothers in the Civil War.* New York: Walker & Co., 2008.

Salt, Henry S. *The Life of Henry David Thoreau.* Urbana: University of Illinois Press, 2000.

Salyer, Sandford. *Marmee, the Mother of Little Women.* Norman: University of Oklahoma Press, 1949.

Saxton, Martha. *Louisa May Alcott: A Modern Biography.* New York: Farrar, Straus & Giroux, 1995.

Schlesinger, Arthur M. *The Almanac of American History.* New York: Putnam, 1983.

Schreiner, Samuel A., Jr. *The Concord Quartet: Alcott, Emerson, Hawthorne, Thoreau, and the Friendship that Freed the American Mind.* Hoboken, N.J.: Wiley, 2006.

Scudder, Townsend. *Concord: American Town.* Boston: Little, Brown, 1947.

Sears, Clara Endicott, comp. *Bronson Alcott's Fruitlands.* Harvard, Mass.: Fruitlands Museum and Applewood Press, 2004.

Sewall, Richard B. *The Life of Emily Dickinson.* Cambridge: Harvard University Press, 1990.

Shealey, Daniel, ed. *Alcott in Her Own Time: A Biographical Chronicle of Her Life Drawn from Recollections, Interviews, and Memoirs by Family, Friends, and Associates.* Iowa City: University of Iowa Press, 2005.

Shenk, David. *The Forgetting: Alzheimer's, Portrait of an Epidemic.* New York: Doubleday, 2001.

Shepard, Odell. *Pedlar's Progress: The Life of Bronson Alcott.* Boston: Little, Brown, 1937.

Smith, Harmon. *My Friend, My Friend: The Story of Thoreau's Relationship with Emerson.* Amherst: University of Massachusetts Press, 1999.

Stearns. Frank Preston. *Sketches from Concord and Appledore.* New York: Putnam, 1895.

Stern, Madeleine B. *Louisa May Alcott: A Biography.* Boston: Northeastern University Press, 1996.

Stewart, Randall. *Nathaniel Hawthorne: A Biography.* New Haven: Yale University Press, 1948.

Stowe, Harriet Beecher. *Uncle Tom's Cabin.* New York: Hart Publishing Co., 1976.

Stowe, Harriet Beecher, and Catherine Beecher. *American Woman's Home.* Hartford: Stowe-Day Foundation, 1998.

Strickland, Charles. "A Transcendentalist Father: The Child-Rearing Practices of Bronson Alcott." *Perspectives in American History* 3 (1969): 5–73.

Tharp, Louise Hall. *The Peabody Sisters of Salem.* Boston: Little, Brown, 1951.

Thoreau, Henry David. *Cape Cod.* Princeton: Princeton University Press, 2004.

————. *The Journals of Henry David Thoreau: Volume 1, 1837–1846.* Edited by Bradford Torrey and Francis H. Allen. Salt Lake City: Peregrine Smith Books, 1984.

————. *The Portable Thoreau.* Edited by Carl Bode. New York: Penguin Books, 1947.

————. *Thoreau on Birds: Notes on New England Birds from the Journals of Henry David Thoreau.* Edited by Francis Allen; illustrated by Louis Agassiz Fuertes. Boston: Beacon Press, 1993.

———. *Walden: An Annotated Edition.* Edited by Walter Harding. Boston: Houghton Mifflin, 1995.

———. *Walden and Other Writings.* New York: Barnes & Noble, 1993.

———. *Walking: A Little Book of Wisdom.* New York: HarperCollins, 1994.

———. *A Week on the Concord and Merrimack Rivers.* With an introduction by John McPhee. Princeton: Princeton University Press, 1980.

———. *Wild Apples.* Chester, Conn.: Applewood Books, 1992.

Trefousse, Hans L. *Impeachment of a President: Andrew Johnson, the Blacks, and Reconstruction.* New York: Fordham University Press, 1999.

Warren, Robert Penn. *John Brown: The Making of a Martyr.* Nashville, Tenn.: J. S. Sanders, 2002.

Weber, Katharine. *The Little Women.* New York: Farrar, Straus & Giroux, 2003.

Wheeler, Ruth R. *Concord: Climate for Freedom.* Yarmouth Port, Mass.: Concord Museum, 1967.

Wilkins, William Glyde. *Charles Dickens in America.* New York: Scribner, 1911.

Wilson, Leslie Perrin. *In History's Embrace: Past and Present in Concord, Massachu-*

*setts.* Hollis, N.H.: Hollis Publishing, 2007.

Wineapple, Brenda. *White Heat: The Friendship of Emily Dickinson and Thomas Wentworth Higginson.* New York: Knopf, 2008.

# ABOUT THE AUTHOR

**Susan Cheever** is the bestselling author of thirteen previous books, including *American Bloomsbury,* the memoirs *Note Found in a Bottle* and *Home Before Dark* (about her father John Cheever), and five novels. She has written for many publications, including the *New Yorker* and the *New York Times;* her work has been nominated for the National Book Critics Circle Award; and she has been awarded a Guggenheim Fellowship, a Boston Globe Winship Medal, and an Associated Press Award. She is on the faculty of the Bennington College MFA Program, has taught at Yale University and at the New School, serves as a director of the Yaddo Corporation, and is a member of the Authors Guild Council. Cheever lives in New York City with her family. To learn more, visit www.susancheever.com.